Primality
and
Cryptography

Wiley–Teubner Series in Computer Science

Kemp: Fundamentals of the Average Case Analysis of Particular Algorithms
Loeckx, Sieber, Stansifer: The Foundations of Program Verification
Kranakis: Primality and Cryptography

Primality
and
Cryptography

Evangelos Kranakis
Universiteit van Amsterdam
Fakultaire Vakgroep Informatica
Amsterdam, Netherlands

AND

Yale University
Department of Computer Science
New Haven, USA

B. G. TEUBNER
Stuttgart

JOHN WILEY & SONS
Chichester · New York · Brisbane · Toronto · Singapore

Library of Congress Cataloging in Publication Data:

Kranakis, Evangelos
    Primality and cryptography.
    (Wiley–Teubner series in computer science)
    Includes index.
    1. Telecommunication—Security measures.   2. Numbers,
Prime.   3. Cryptography.   I. Title.   II. Series.
TK5102.5.K66 1986   005.8′2   85–29485

ISBN 0 471 90934 3

British Library Cataloguing in Publication Data:

Kranakis, Evangelos
    Primality and cryptography.—(Wiley–Teubner series in
    computer science)
    1. Computers—Access control   2. Cryptography
    I. Title
    001.6   QA76.9.A25

ISBN 0 471 90934 3

CIP-Kurztitelufnahme der Deutschen Bibliothek:

Kranakis, Evangelos:
Primality and cryptography/Evangelos Kranakis.—Stuttgart:
Teubner; Chichester; New York; Brisbane; Toronto; Singapore:
Wiley, 1986.
    (Wiley Teubner series in computer science)
    ISBN 3 519 02104 8 (Teubner)
    ISBN 0 471 90934 3 (Wiley)

Printed and bound in Great Britain

Dedicated to Eda,
my best friend and lifelong companion.

*C'est en forgeant
que l'on devient forgeron.*
(Medieval Latin Proverb)

PROLOGUE

The art of ciphering, hath for relative an art of deciphering,
by supposition unprofitable, but as things are, of great use.
(Francis Bacon)

Ciphering has been widely used throughout history in military and diplomatic communication in order to make the meaning of transmitted messages incomprehensible to unauthorized users. According to Francis Bacon[1] the following must be among the preferred virtues of cipher systems:

- that they be not laborious to write and read,
- that they be impossible to decipher, and,
- in some cases, that they be without suspicion.

The three principles of Bacon listed above are still valid today. But, to quote Diffie and Hellman:

> the development of computer controlled communication networks promises effortless and inexpensive contact between people or computers on opposite sides of the world, replacing most mail and many excursions with telecommunications. For many applications these contacts must be made secure against both eavesdropping and the injection of illegitimate messages. At present, however, the solution of security problems lags well behind other areas of communication technology. Contemporary cryptography is unable to meet the requirements, in that its use would impose such severe inconveniences on the system users, as to eliminate many of the benefits of teleprocessing.[2]

This need for secure transmission of information among many users via electronic media, has made inevitable the departure of cryptography from the old notion of absolute security to embrace the new notion of relative

---

[1] *The Advancement of Learning*, Basil Montague, ed., Vol II, London: William Pickering, 1825, page 200.

[2] W. Diffie and M. Hellman, *New Directions in Cryptography*, IEEE Transactions on Information Theory, IT 22, pp. 644 - 654, 1976.

security. Thus, in the first case the designer bases the security of the cryptosystem on absolute criteria (e.g. Shannon's information theory), while in the second case one proves that the system designed is secure assuming that a certain problem (usually in number theory) is difficult to solve. This new idea has made it possible to construct what are termed public key cryptosystems, in which, according to Diffie and Hellman[3]:

> two parties communicating solely over a public channel and using only publicly known techniques can create a secure connection.

The purpose of the present book, which is an outgrowth of a series of lectures given at Yale University in the Spring of 1984, is to isolate and explain the most important mathematical notions arising from the recent literature on primality tests, pseudorandom generators and public key cryptosystems. In doing this, I have made every effort to make the book as self-contained as possible.

Section 1 develops the techniques of computational number theory which are necessary to understand the recent literature on pseudorandom generators and public key cryptosystems. In addition to basic number theory concepts, the following notions and algorithms are presented: *threshold schemes, modular exponentiation by repeated squarings and multiplications, the Adleman, Manders, Miller algorithm on computing square roots and the Pohlig, Hellman algorithm on computing indices.*

Section 2 presents some of the most important primality tests known today. For completeness it starts with the *sieve of Eratosthenes.* Following Williams,[4] primality tests can be classified into three categories: *tests using special functions (e.g. Lucas - Lehmer test), unproved hypothesis tests (i.e. tests whose efficiency depends on the Extended Riemann Hypothesis) and Monte Carlo tests (e.g. Solovay - Strassen, Rabin).* In addition, *Pratt's test* is given; this can be used to determine the complexity of the set of binary representations of prime numbers. The section concludes with the very fast *Rumely - Adleman test.*

Section 3 is an introduction to those basic notions of probability theory needed in the development of *pseudorandom generators* and *public key cryptosystems.* Highlights include the *weak law* as well as *Bernshtein's law of large numbers.*

---

[3]Ibid.

[4]H. C. Williams, *Primality Testing on a Computer*, Ars Combinatoria, 5, (1978), pp. 127 - 185.

Neither **Section 4** nor **Section 5** is meant to give an exhaustive study of all the existing *pseudorandom generators* and *public key cryptosystems* available in the literature. The intention is to present only some basic generators and cryptosystems to make clear the connection between number theory and modern public key cryptography. In addition, the subject of *nonpublic key cryptography* is totally omitted. But the reader can find material to his heart's content in: David Shulman's, *An Annotated Bibliography of Cryptography*,[5] as well as in the literature quoted in the present book.

Finally, **Section 6** outlines the general theory of *pseudorandom generators* and *public key cryptosystems*. Material presented includes: the equivalence of the *next bit test* and *Yao's statistical test, pseudorandom functions* as well as the *XOR theorem*, on which the construction of *unapproximable predicates* and *one way functions* are based.

The reader will probably notice the absence of factoring algorithms in the present book. This subject is beautifully treated in the articles *Factorization Algorithms of Exponential Order*, by M. Voorhoeve,[6] and *Analysis and Comparison of Some Integer Factoring Algorithms*, by C. Pomerance.[7]

An effort has been made to present the material in the most direct and straightforward manner, with mathematical rigor. For as David Hilbert[8] once said:

> ... it is an error to believe that rigor in the proof is the enemy of simplicity. On the contrary we find it confirmed by numerous examples that the rigorous method is at the same time the simpler and the more easily comprehended. The very effort for rigor forces us to find out simpler methods of proof. It also frequently leads the way to methods which are more capable of development than the old methods of less rigor.

A guide to the bibliography is presented in the *Bibliographical Remarks* at the end of each section. The reader should be aware of the many different viewpoints given in the papers cited in the bibliography, naturally not all of which could be included in the present study. In addition, topics omitted

---

[5] Garland Publ., Inc., 1976.

[6] *Computational Methods in Number Theory*, H. W. Lenstra and R. Tijdeman eds., Mathematical Centre Tracts, 154, Vol. 1, Mathematisch Centrum Amsterdam, 1982.

[7] Ibid.

[8] *Mathematical Problems*, address presented at the 1900 International Congress of Mathematics in Paris, Bulletin AMS, 8, 1901 - 2, pp. 437 - 479.

include: *Information Theory, Data Encryption Standard, Digital Signatures, Voting Schemes and Authentication techniques.* It is expected that one will turn to the references if a more thorough picture of the subject is desired.

The results of the book presuppose the mathematical maturity of a beginning graduate student in theoretical computer science or mathematics. Some knowledge of the basic notions of algebra (e.g. group, ring, homomorphism) will be useful.[9] Since readers' backgrounds can be so diverse, is hard to say what the proper order of reading this book should be. However, the diagrams of figure 1 can give an idea of section dependencies. Thus, sections

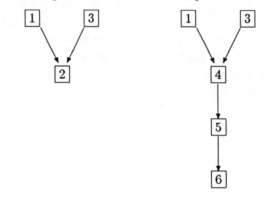

Figure 1: Section Dependencies

1 and 2 can be read together independently of the remaining text; section 3 is used only in subsection 2.16 (probabilistic primality tests) as well as in sections 4, 5 and 6. In addition, the reader already familiar with the basic material on pseudorandom generators and public key cryptosystems can proceed directly to the study of section 6.

The exercises given at the end of most subsections are of three types: those that give a different proof of a result proved in the main text, those that give additional results, and those which remind the reader that he must complete the details of a proof given in the main text. In any case, the exercises will test and deepen the reader's understanding of the material and should all be attempted.

The concept of *efficient algorithm*, which is used extensively in the book, should be considered identical to *probabilistic polynomial time algorithm*.

---

[9]See Van der Waerden, *Algebra*, Vol. 1, Ungar, New York, 1970.

I have made every possible effort to attribute the results presented in the text to their original inventors. If sometimes I failed to do so it is due to ignorance rather than intent. At the same time I accept full responsibility for whatever flaws or errors the book may contain, and I would be grateful to receive any comments and suggestions that will improve the presentation.

I would like to acknowledge my indebteness to the many colleagues, who offered their criticisms and corrections on earlier versions of the book. In addition, I am particularly thankful to the insightful comments of the seminar participants during the original lectures. These included: Dana Angluin, Josh Cohen, Mike Fischer, Dan Gusfield, Neil Immerman, Ming Kao, Philip Laird, Susan Landau, Jerry Leichter, Jingke Li, Angus Macintyre, Lenny Pitt, Philip Scowcroft, David Wittenberg and Carol Wood. Special thanks go to Dan Gusfield who motivated me to study primality tests, and to Silvio Micali who suggested numerous improvements in the organization and commentary of the last three sections. I would also like to express my deepest appreciation to Mike Fischer for his undiminishing support and encouragement as well as for the numerous penetrating discussions that helped me improve the presentation of section 6.

The typesetting was done by the author at the Yale Computer Science Department using LaTeX,[10] a version of TeX.

Evangelos Kranakis[11]
Yale University,
August 1985

---

[10]L. Lamport, *The LaTeX Document Preparation System*, 1983, LaTeX *Update*, Version 2.08, May 13, 1985.

[11]Preparation of the book was supported in part by NSF under grant number MCS - 8305382 and NSA under grant number MDA904 - 84 - H - 0004.

PROLOGUE vii

TABLE OF CONTENTS xiii

1 NUMBER THEORY 1
  1.1 Introduction 1
  1.2 The Homomorphism Theorem 2
  1.3 Fibonacci Numbers 3
  1.4 Congruences 4
  1.5 The Chinese Remainder Theorem 7
  1.6 Modular Exponentiation 10
  1.7 Primitive Roots 11
  1.8 Artin's Conjecture 14
  1.9 The Carmichael Function 15
  1.10 The Legendre Symbol 16
  1.11 The Legendre-Jacobi Symbol 17
  1.12 Computing Square Roots 21
  1.13 Indices 24
  1.14 Computing Indices 25
  1.15 The Prime Number Theorem 28
  1.16 Continued Fractions 31
  1.17 Bibliographical Remarks 37

2 PRIMALITY TESTS 39
  2.1 Introduction 39
  2.2 The Sieve of Eratosthenes 40
  2.3 Wilson's Test 41
  2.4 Lucas's Test 42
  2.5 Sum of Two Squares Test 43
  2.6 Pratt's Test 46
  2.7 Proth's Test 49
  2.8 Pepin's Test 51
  2.9 Lucas-Lehmer Test 51
  2.10 Extended Riemann Hypothesis 55
  2.11 Solovay-Strassen Deterministic Test 56
  2.12 A Variant of the Solovay-Strassen Test 58
  2.13 Miller's Deterministic Test 59
  2.14 An Improvement of Miller's Test 62
  2.15 Selfridge-Weinberger Test 63

2.16 Probabilistic (Monte Carlo) Primality Tests 65
2.17 Solovay-Strassen Test 66
2.18 Rabin's Test 68
2.19 Rumeley-Adleman Test 73
2.20 Bibliographical Remarks 78

3 **PROBABILITY THEORY**   **80**
3.1 Introduction 80
3.2 Basic Notions 80
3.3 Random Variables 82
3.4 The Binomial Distribution 88
3.5 Chebyshev's Law of Large Numbers 90
3.6 Bernshtein's Law of Large Numbers 91
3.7 The Monte Carlo Method 94
3.8 Bibliographical Remarks 96

4 **PSEUDORANDOM GENERATORS**   **98**
4.1 Introduction 98
4.2 The Linear Congruence Generator 99
4.3 The $(1/p)$ - Generator 104
4.4 Quadratic Residues in Cryptography 108
4.5 Factoring and Quadratic Residues 110
4.6 Periodicity of Quadratic Residues 111
4.7 The Circuit as a Model of Computation 114
4.8 The Quadratic Residue Generator 117
4.9 The Quadratic Residuosity Assumption 124
4.10 The Index Generator 127
4.11 The Discrete Logarithm Assumption 135
4.12 Bibliographical Remarks 136

5 **PUBLIC KEY CRYPTOSYSTEMS**   **138**
5.1 Introduction 138
5.2 The Setup of a Nonpublic Key Cryptosystem 139
5.3 The Setup of a Public Key Cryptosystem 140
5.4 The RSA System 142
5.5 RSA Bits 145
5.6 The Rabin System 151
5.7 Rabin Bits 153
5.8 The Merkle - Hellman System 155

5.9 Security of the Merkle - Hellman System (Outline) 157

5.10 The Quadratic Residue System 160

5.11 Bibliographical Remarks 168

6 TOWARDS A GENERAL THEORY   **170**

6.1 Introduction 170

6.2 Security Tests 171

6.3 Pseudorandom Functions 178

6.4 Xoring 180

6.5 Proof of the XOR Lemma 186

6.6 Two Applications of the XOR Lemma 199

6.7 (One to One) One Way Functions 201

6.8 Random Polynomial and Deterministic Time 206

6.9 Bibliographical Remarks 208

REFERENCES   **210**

FREQUENTLY USED NOTATION   **223**

INDEX   **228**

1 NUMBER THEORY

... an inexhaustible storehouse of interesting truths.
(C. F. Gauss)

... a building of rare beauty and harmony.
(D. Hilbert)

1.1 Introduction

The present section is intended, first, to introduce the reader to the basic concepts of number theory. Second, it is intended to give some efficient procedures arising from the study of certain problems in number theory. The concepts and results thus introduced will be essential to the discussion of primality tests, pseudorandom generators and public key cryptosystems.

The concepts introduced in this section include: Fibonacci numbers, the Euler function, primitive roots, the Carmichael function, Legendre-Jacobi symbol, indices and continued fractions. In addition, complete proofs of the following theorems are given: Gauss's theorem on the characterization of those m for which the multiplicative group Z_m^* is cyclic, in theorem 1.9, the law of quadratic reciprocity, in theorem 1.13, Chebyshev's proof of a weaker version of the prime number theorem, in theorem 1.20, and a theorem on Diophantine approximations, in theorem 1.24. Theorem 1.7 provides an application of the Chinese remainder theorem to threshold schemes.

The algorithms described include: the method of exponentiation by repeated squarings and multiplications, in theorem 1.8, the method of Adleman, Manders and Miller for computing square roots modulo a prime, in theorem 1.15, and the method of Pohlig and Hellman for computing indices, in theorem 1.18.

It is true, that the details of some of the proofs given in this section (e.g. theorems 1.9, 1.13 and 1.20) are not necessary to understand the concepts included in the sections on pseudorandom generators and public key cryptosystems. However, a thorough study of the proofs and the exercises that follow the individual subsections will undoubtedly enhance the reader's proficiency with the number theory concepts involved.

1.2   The Homomorphism Theorem

Let G, H be two abelian groups such that H is a subgroup of G. For $a \in G$ consider the **coset** $H + a = \{h + a : h \in H\}$, where $+$ is the group operation on G. G/H is the **quotient** group of G modulo H. It consists of all cosets $H + a$, where a ranges over G. The group operation $\oplus$ on G/H is defined by $(H + a) \oplus (H + b) = H + (a + b)$. It is not hard to show that G/H with this operation is also an abelian group. It is clear that the family $\{H + a : a \in G\}$ of cosets is a partition of G into sets each of which has size exactly $|H|$. It follows that $|H|$ divides $|G|$.

Let f be an **epimorphism** (i.e. a group homomorphism which is onto) from G onto another group H. The **kernel** $K = Ker(f)$ of f, is the set of all elements $a \in G$ such that $f(a) = $ the identity element of H. It is not hard to show that the group G/K is an abelian group which is isomorphic to H. The required isomorphism is given by the mapping $F(K + a) = f(a)$. Hence the proof of the following theorem has been outlined:

Theorem 1.1 *(Lagrange)*

   (i) If H is a subgroup of G then $|H|$ divides $|G|$.

   (ii) If f is an epimorphism of the abelian group G onto the abelian group H and K is the kernel of f then the group G/K is isomorphic to the group H. Moreover, $|G| = |H| \cdot |K|$.

   (iii) For all $a \in G$, $f^{-1}\{a\}$ is a coset in G/K and $|f^{-1}\{a\}| = |K|$ •

EXERCISES

1: Let G be a finite abelian group. Show that all equations of the form $x^2 = a$, where $a \in G$, have exactly the same number of solutions in G. **Hint:** Consider the abelian group $H = \{a^2 : a \in G\}$ and let f be the epimorphism $f(x) = x^2$. Then use theorem 1.1.

2: Extend exercise 1 to equations of the form $x^n = a$, where $a \in G, n \geq 1$.

3: Show that the definition of the operation $\oplus$ is independent of the coset representation.

In the next two exercises H is a subgroup of the abelian group G. Complete the details of the proof of theorem 1.1 by showing that:

   4: for all $a \in G$, $|H + a| = |H|$.

   5: $\{H + a : a \in G\}$ forms a partition of G.

1.3   Fibonacci Numbers

The sequence $f_0, f_1, \ldots, f_n, \ldots$ of **Fibonacci numbers** is defined by induction on $n \geq 0$ as follows:

$$f_n = \begin{cases} 0 & \text{if } n = 0 \\ 1 & \text{if } n = 1 \\ f_{n-1} + f_{n-2} & \text{if } n \geq 2 \end{cases}$$

It will be useful to know the order of magnitude of the n-th Fibonacci number. This is easily determined as follows. The quadratic equation $x^2 = x + 1$ has the two square roots $(1 + \sqrt{5})/2$ and $(1 - \sqrt{5})/2$. The positive square root $(1 + \sqrt{5})/2$ is called the **golden ratio**, and is abbreviated as R. It is now easy to check by induction on n, that for all $n > 1$, $f_n \geq R^{n-2}$. Indeed, assume that $f_m \geq R^{m-2}$, for all $m \leq n$. Then, $f_{n+1} = f_n + f_{n-1} \geq R^{n-2} + R^{n-3} = R^{n-3}(R+1) = R^{n-3}R^2 = R^{n-1}$.

The Fibonacci numbers arise very naturally in the study of the number of steps needed to evaluate the greatest common divisor of two integers via the Euclidean algorithm. Indeed, assume that $a > b > 0$ are two given integers. Use the Euclidean algorithm to define sequences

$$0 < r_n < r_{n-1} < \ldots < r_1 < r_0 = b < r_{-1} = a, \ d_1, d_2, \ldots, d_n, d_{n+1}$$

such that $r_{i-2} = d_i r_{i-1} + r_i$, $i = 1, \ldots, n$, and $r_{n-1} = d_{n+1} r_n$. It is clear that $r_n = \gcd(a, b)$ (see exercise 1 below). It follows by reverse induction on $i = n, n-1, \ldots, 0, -1$ that $r_i \geq f_{n+1-i}$. In particular, $a \geq f_{n+2}$ and $b \geq f_{n+1}$. However, it is clear that the number of division steps needed to compute $\gcd(f_{n+2}, f_{n+1})$ via the Euclidean algorithm is exactly $n+2$, which is also the number of division steps needed to compute $\gcd(a, b)$. Since $a \geq f_{n+2} \geq R^n$, it follows that $\log_R a \geq n$. Therefore the following theorem has been proved:

Theorem 1.2 *(G. Lamé) If N is an integer > 0, then for any pair a, b of positive integers $\leq N$, the number of division steps required to compute $\gcd(a, b)$ via the Euclidean algorithm is at most $-2 + \lfloor \log_R N \rfloor$* •

EXERCISES

1: Use the notation above to show that $r_n = \gcd(a, b)$.

2: Show that the Euclidean algorithm leads to an efficient algorithm which given any integers a, b will compute integers α, β such that $\gcd(a, b) = \alpha a + \beta b$. Generalize this to the greatest common divisor of n integers.

3: Prove a theorem similar to theorem 1.2 for the greatest common divisor of n integers.

4: Prove a similar theorem for the least common multiple of n integers. **Hint:** Use the identity $\operatorname{lcm}(a_1, \ldots, a_n) = (a_1 \cdots a_n) / \gcd(a_1, \ldots, a_n)$.

5: Show that the length of the side of the canonical decagon inscribed in the unit circle is equal to R, where R is the golden mean.

1.4   Congruences

Let a, b be integers. The symbol $a | b$ means that a divides b i.e. $b = ka$, for some integer k. The integers a, b are called **congruent** modulo the integer m, and this will be abbreviated $a \equiv b \bmod m$, if $m | (a - b)$, otherwise a and b will be called **incongruent** modulo m, and this will be abbreviated by $a \not\equiv b \bmod m$. It is clear that for each fixed m, the relation $\equiv \bmod m$ is **reflexive, symmetric**, and **transitive**, and hence it is an **equivalence** relation on the set Z of all integers. For each integer a let $\mathbf{a}$ denote the equivalence class of a, i.e. the set of all integers x such that $x \equiv a \bmod m$. For each m there exist exactly m equivalence classes modulo m, namely $\mathbf{0, 1, \cdots, m-1}$. $Z_m = \{\mathbf{0, 1, \cdots, m-1}\}$ is the set of all equivalence classes modulo m, and $Z_m^* = \{\mathbf{a} \in Z_m : \gcd(a, m) = 1\}$.

One can define two operations, addition (denoted by $+$) and multiplication (denoted by $\cdot$) on the set Z_m as follows: $\mathbf{a} + \mathbf{b}$ (respectively $\mathbf{a} \cdot \mathbf{b}$) $=$ the equivalence class of $a + b$ (respectively $a \cdot b$). The set Z_m endowed with these two operations forms a commutative ring with unit, but is not necessarily a field because it can have zero divisors. However, both $< Z_m, + >$ and $< Z_m^*, \cdot >$ are abelian groups.

Example 1.1 *Figure 1 gives the multiplication table of Z_{11}^*.*

If $\gcd(a, m) = 1$ then there exist integers b, c such that $ab + cm = 1$. Hence, $\mathbf{a} \cdot \mathbf{b} = \mathbf{1}$, i.e. $\mathbf{a}$ is invertible in Z_m^*. The order of the group Z_m^* is denoted by $\varphi(m)$, and φ is called the **Euler totient function** or simply the **Euler function**.

An important corollary of the considerations above is the following:

Theorem 1.3 *(Euler-Fermat)* For all $a \in Z_m^*$, $a^{\varphi(m)} \equiv 1 \bmod m$.

. || 1	2	3	4	5	6	7	8	9	10
1	1	2	3	4	5	6	7	8	9	10
2	2	4	6	8	10	1	3	5	7	9
3	3	6	9	1	4	7	10	2	5	8
4	4	8	1	5	9	2	6	10	3	7
5	5	10	4	9	3	8	2	7	1	6
6	6	1	7	2	8	3	9	4	10	5
7	7	3	10	6	2	9	5	1	8	4
8	8	5	2	10	7	4	1	9	6	3
9	9	7	5	3	1	10	8	6	4	2
10	10	9	8	7	6	5	4	3	2	1

Figure 1: Multiplication table of Z_{11}^*

Proof: Let a be as above, and let $\mathbf{u}_1, \ldots, \mathbf{u}_{\varphi(m)}$ be an enumeration of all the elements of Z_m^*. It is clear that $\mathbf{a} \cdot \mathbf{u}_1, \ldots, \mathbf{a} \cdot \mathbf{u}_{\varphi(m)}$ is also an enumeration of all the elements of Z_m^*. Consequently, $\mathbf{a} \cdot \mathbf{u}_1 \cdots \mathbf{a} \cdot \mathbf{u}_{\varphi(m)} = \mathbf{u}_1 \cdots \mathbf{u}_{\varphi(m)}$ and hence $\mathbf{a}^{\varphi(m)} \cdot \mathbf{u}_1 \cdots \mathbf{u}_{\varphi(m)} = \mathbf{u}_1 \cdots \mathbf{u}_{\varphi(m)}$. But it follows from the observations above that the element $\mathbf{u}_1 \cdots \mathbf{u}_{\varphi(m)}$ is invertible in Z_m. Consequently, $a^{\varphi(m)} \equiv 1 \bmod m$ •

In order to avoid unnecessary notational complications, from now on and for the rest of the book the same symbol will be used for an integer a and for its equivalence class a (modulo an integer m). This should cause no confusion because it will always be clear from the context which of the two notions is meant.

Theorem 1.4 *(Euler)* $\sum_{d|m} \varphi(d) = m$.

Proof: Let $\varphi_d(m) = |\{x \in Z_m : \gcd(x, m) = d\}|$. It is then clear that $\sum_{d|m} \varphi_d(m) = m$. However, $\varphi_d(m) = \varphi(m/d)$, provided that d divides m. It follows that

$$m = \sum_{d|m} \varphi_d(m) = \sum_{d|m} \varphi(d/m) = \sum_{d|m} \varphi(d),$$

which completes the proof of the theorem •

Any congruence of the form $f(x) \equiv 0 \bmod m$, where $f(x)$ is a polynomial expression in the variable x with coefficients in Z_m is called **polynomial**

congruence modulo m. Such a congruence is called **solvable** if there is an $x \in Z_m$ such that $f(x) \equiv 0 \bmod m$; the set of all $x \in Z_m$ which satisfy this congruence is called the set of **solutions** of that congruence. One of the most important questions in number theory is to develop methods to solve congruences of the form $f(x) \equiv 0 \bmod m$, where $f(x)$ is a polynomial expression in the variable x with coefficients in Z_m. For linear congruences with one unknown this question is answered in the theorem below.

Theorem 1.5 *The linear congruence $ax \equiv b \bmod m$ is solvable if and only if $g = \gcd(a, m)$ divides b. In fact, if x_0 is any solution of $ax \equiv b \bmod m$, then the list*

$$x_i = x_0 + \frac{im}{g}, \text{ where } i = 0, \dots, g - 1,$$

forms the complete set of its distinct solutions modulo m.

Proof: If the congruence $ax \equiv b \bmod m$ is solvable then m must divide $ax - b$. Since $g|m$ and $g|a$ it is clear that $g|b$. Conversely, assume that $g|b$. It follows that $b = kg$, for some integer k. It is well known, however, using basic properties of the greatest common divisor, that there exist integers λ, μ such that

$$g = \lambda a + \mu m.$$

It follows that

$$b = kg = k\lambda a + k\mu m = (k\lambda)a + (k\mu)m,$$

and hence $k\lambda$ is a solution of the congruence $ax \equiv b \bmod m$.

It is not hard to see that if x_0 is any solution of the congruence above, then so are any of the x_i's defined in the statement of the theorem. Moreover, the solutions x_i are distinct modulo m. It remains to show that any arbitrary solution c of $ax \equiv b \bmod m$, is equal to some x_i. Indeed, since $ac \equiv ax_0 \equiv b \bmod m$, it follows that $m|a(c-x_0)$. But $g = \gcd(a, m)$, and hence $(m/g)|(c-x_0)$, which completes the proof of the theorem $\bullet$

<u>**EXERCISES**</u>

1: Show that for all $n > 1$, n is prime $\Leftrightarrow \varphi(n) = n - 1$.

2: Show that for all $t \geq 1$ and all prime p, $\varphi(p^t) = (p-1)p^{t-1}$. Use this to compute $\varphi(n)$ for all integers $n > 0$.

1.5   The Chinese Remainder Theorem

Systems of linear congruences do not necessarily have solutions even if each congruence of the system does.

Example 1.2 *Both congruences:*

$$x \equiv 0 \bmod 3, \quad and \quad x \equiv 1 \bmod 6$$

have solutions, but the system does not.

However, if the moduli are pairwise relatively prime, the system will always have a solution.

Example 1.3 *23 is a solution of the following system of congruences:*

$$x \equiv 2 \bmod 3, \quad x \equiv 3 \bmod 5, \quad and \quad x \equiv 2 \bmod 7.$$

The following theorem provides the general framework for solving systems of linear congruences.

Theorem 1.6 *(Chinese Remainder Theorem)*
 The system $a_i x \equiv b_i \bmod m_i$, $i = 1, \ldots, k$ has exactly one solution modulo $m = m_1 \cdots m_k$, provided that $m_1, \ldots, m_k$ are pairwise relatively prime and $\gcd(a_1, m_1) = \cdots = \gcd(a_k, m_k) = 1$.

Proof: The uniqueness of the solution follows easily from the hypothesis of the theorem. To prove the existence, find integers c_i such that $a_i c_i \equiv 1 \bmod m_i$, where $i = 1, \ldots, k$. If $m = m_1 \cdots m_k$ and $n_i = m/m_i$ then it is clear that $\gcd(n_1, \ldots, n_k) = 1$. Hence, it follows from the basic properties of the greatest common divisor, that there exist integers $t_1, \ldots, t_k$ such that

$$t_1 n_1 + \cdots + t_k n_k = 1.$$

Put $e_i = t_i n_i$. Then one can easily verify that

$$e_i \equiv \delta_{i,j} \bmod m_j,$$

where $\delta_{i,j} = 1$, if $i = j$, and $\delta_{i,j} = 0$, if $i \neq j$. Now, choose

$$c = e_1 c_1 b_1 + \cdots + e_k c_k b_k.$$

It remains to show that c is a solution of the foregoing system of congruences. Indeed, for each i,

$$a_i c \equiv a_i b_1 e_1 c_1 + \cdots + a_i b_k e_k c_k \equiv a_i b_i e_i c_i \equiv b_i \bmod m_i,$$

and the proof is complete •

A further generalization of the Chinese remainder theorem, which does not assume that the moduli are pairwise relatively prime can be found in theorem $3 - 12$ of [L13] (see also exercise 2).

An interesting application of the Chinese remainder theorem, which also relates to the security of message transmission, concerns the construction of (k, n) threshold schemes. A (k, n) **threshold scheme** consists of n people $P_1, \ldots, P_n$ sharing a secret S in such a way that the following properties hold:

(1) $k \leq n$.

(2) Each P_i has some information I_i.

(3) Knowledge of any k of the $\{I_1, \ldots, I_n\}$ enables one to find S easily.

(4) Knowledge of less than k of the $\{I_1, \ldots, I_n\}$ does not enable one to find S easily.

Theorem 1.7 *For all $2 \leq k \leq n$ there exists a (k, n) threshold scheme.*

Proof: The construction of (k, n) threshold schemes is based on the construction of (k, n) threshold sequences, which were defined by Mignotte as follows: a (k, n) **threshold sequence** is an increasing sequence $m_1 < \cdots < m_n$ of pairwise relatively prime positive integers such that

$$m_1 \cdot m_2 \cdots m_k > m_n \cdot m_{n-1} \cdots m_{n-k+2}. \qquad (1)$$

Assume that a threshold sequence $m_1 < \cdots < m_n$ has been constructed and let $M = m_1 \cdot m_2 \cdots m_k$, $N = m_n \cdot m_{n-1} \cdots m_{n-k+2}$. Let the secret S be any integer such that $N \leq S \leq M$ and let the information I_i be defined by

$$I_i \equiv S \bmod m_i, \ i = 1, \ldots, n.$$

Next it will be shown that secret S and informations $\{I_1, \ldots, I_n\}$ defined above form a (k, n) threshold scheme. Indeed, let $\{I_{i_1}, \ldots, I_{i_k}\}$ be given. By the Chinese remainder theorem, the system

$$x \equiv I_i \bmod m_i, \ i \in \{i_1, \ldots, i_k\},$$

has exactly one solution. The proof of theorem 1.6 shows that this solution is S and is given by

$$S \equiv e_{i_1} \cdot I_{i_1} + \cdots + e_{i_k} \cdot I_{i_k} \bmod (m_{i_1} \cdots m_{i_k}),$$

where $e_i \equiv \delta_{i,j} \bmod m_j$. It follows from (1) that $S \le m_{i_1} \cdots m_{i_k}$ and hence it is true that

$$S = e_{i_1} \cdot I_{i_1} + \cdots + e_{i_k} \cdot I_{i_k}.$$

On the other hand if only $\{I_{i_1}, \ldots, I_{i_{k-1}}\}$ are given, then it follows again from the Chinese remainder theorem that

$$S \equiv e_{i_1} \cdot I_{i_1} + \cdots + e_{i_{k-1}} \cdot I_{i_{k-1}} \bmod (m_{i_1} \cdots m_{i_{k-1}}). \qquad (2)$$

Clearly, (2) is the only congruence available in order to compute the value of S. It follows that one will need to search among at least $\frac{M-N}{N}$ possible values in order to find the secret S satisfying (2).

To conclude the proof of the theorem it remains to construct (k, n) threshold sequences such that the quantity $\frac{M-N}{N}$ is big. This will make it difficult to compute S if less than k of the $\{I_1, \ldots, I_n\}$ are known. This is done using the main inequality in exercise 3 of subsection 1.15. Indeed, find t such that the previously mentioned inequality holds. It follows that there exist at least n distinct primes in the interval $(p_t^{(k^2-1)/k^2}, p_t]$. Let $m_1, \ldots, m_n$ be the last n primes in this interval, i.e. $m_i = p_{t-n+i}$, where $i = 1, \ldots, n$. It remains to show that this is a (k, n) threshold sequence. Indeed,

$$M = m_1 \cdot m_2 \cdots m_k \ge p_t^{\frac{k^2-1}{k}} > p_t^{k-1} \ge m_n \cdot m_{n-1} \cdots m_{n-k+2} = N.$$

This completes the proof of the theorem, since

$$\frac{M - N}{N} \ge (p_t^{(k^2-1)/k} - p_t^{k-1})/p_t^{k-1} = p_t^{(k-1)/k} - 1 \bullet$$

EXERCISES

1: If r is the number of distinct prime factors of $m > 1$, then $x^2 \equiv x \bmod m$ has exactly 2^r distinct modulo m solutions. **Hint:** Use the Chinese remainder theorem.

2: The following generalization of the Chinese remainder theorem does not presuppose that the moduli are pairwise relatively prime. To be more precise show that the following statements are equivalent:

(i) The system $x \equiv b_i \bmod m_i$, $i = 1, \ldots, n$, has a solution.

(ii) For any pair of indices $1 \leq i, j \leq n$,

$$b_i \equiv b_j \bmod(\gcd(m_i, m_j)).$$

Moreover the solution, if it exists, is unique modulo $\operatorname{lcm}(m_1, \ldots, m_n)$.

1.6   Modular Exponentiation

Given a fixed modulus m and an exponent e, the problem arises to compute $x^e \bmod m$, for any given x. The method described below, which solves this problem, is called the method of **exponentiation by repeated squarings and multiplications**.

Theorem 1.8 *There exists an efficient algorithm A such that given as inputs m, e, x it will output $A(m, e, x) = x^e \bmod m$. The algorithm A requires at most $\lfloor \log_2 e \rfloor$ squarings, $\lfloor \log_2 e \rfloor$ multiplications, and $\lfloor \log_2 e \rfloor$ divisions.*

Proof: Let e, m, x be integers as above. Consider e's representation in the binary system, i.e. $e = 2^n e_n + 2^{n-1} e_{n-1} + \cdots + 2 e_1 + e_0$, where $n = \lfloor \log_2 e \rfloor$. Then $x^e \equiv x^{2^n e_n + \ldots + 2 e_1 + e_0} \bmod m$. Define the sequences $x_0, \ldots, x_n$ and $y_1, \ldots, y_n$ by reverse induction as follows: $x_n = x^{e_n}$, $y_n \equiv x_n^2 \bmod m$ and for $i \geq 1$, $x_{n-i} \equiv y_{n-i+1} x^{e_{n-i}} \bmod m$, $y_{n-i} \equiv x_{n-i}^2 \bmod m$. It follows easily that $x_0 \equiv x^e \bmod m$.

The foregoing recursive construction is also exhibited in the algorithm below:

Input: e, m, x.

Step 1: Compute n, and bits $e_0, e_1, \ldots, e_n$ such that

$$e = 2^n e_n + 2^{n-1} e_{n-1} + \cdots + 2^1 e_1 + e_0, \text{ where } e_n \neq 0.$$

Step 2: Set $y = 1$.

Step 3: For $i = n, n-1, \ldots, 0$ **repeat**

$$\text{set}: \quad y \equiv y^2 x^{e_i} \bmod m.$$

Output: $y \bullet$

Example 1.4 *Using the preceding algorithm, the table in Example 1.1, and the fact that $13 = 2^3 \cdot 1 + 2^2 \cdot 1 + 2^1 \cdot 0 + 2^0 \cdot 1$, the table in figure 2 will show that $7^{13} \equiv 3 \bmod 11$.*

| EXERCISES |

1: Find a similar algorithm for modular multiplication.

i	e_i	$y \equiv y^2 \cdot 7^{e_i} \bmod 11$	$Output$
3	1	$1^2 \cdot 7^{e_3}$	7
2	1	$7^2 \cdot 7^{e_2}$	2
1	0	$2^2 \cdot 7^{e_1}$	4
0	1	$4^2 \cdot 7^{e_0}$	2

Figure 2: Computation of $7^{13} \bmod 11$.

1.7 Primitive Roots

Call an integer $g \in Z_m^*$ a **primitive root** modulo m if g generates the multiplicative group Z_m^* i.e. $Z_m^* = \{g, g^2 \bmod m, \ldots, g^{\varphi(m)} \bmod m\}$. If there is a primitive root modulo m, then the group Z_m^* is cyclic, and vice versa. In the sequel, it will be useful to know for which m the group Z_m^* is cyclic. The following theorem gives the complete answer:

Theorem 1.9 (Gauss) *For all m, Z_m^* is cyclic if and only if m is equal to one of $1, 2, 4, p^k, 2p^k$, where p is an odd prime and k is a positive integer.*

Proof: ($\Leftarrow$)

If m is equal to either of 1, 2, 4, it is easy to see that Z_m^* is cyclic (see exercise 2). Next it will be shown that for each of the possible values of m the group Z_m^* is cyclic. Let p be an odd prime.

Z_p^* **is cyclic:**

The **order** of an element $x \in Z_p - \{0\}$ is the least exponent e such that $x^e \equiv 1 \bmod p$. For each divisor d of $p - 1$, let $S_d = \{x \in Z_p$: the order of x is $d\}$. However, for each $x \in S_d$ and each $c < d, x^c \in S_d \Leftrightarrow \gcd(c, d) = 1$. (Indeed, on the one hand, ($\Leftarrow$) if $x^{ci} \equiv 1 \bmod p$ then $d|ci$, and hence $d|i$. Thus, the order of $x^c \bmod p$ is d, and on the other hand ($\Rightarrow$) if $k = \gcd(c, d)$ then $(x^c)^{d/k} \equiv (x^{c/k})^d \equiv 1 \bmod p$ which implies that $k = \gcd(c, d) = 1$.) Let a be an arbitrary element of S_d. Then it is clear that $a^d \equiv 1 \bmod p$. Since Z_p is a finite field, the equation $x^d \equiv 1 \bmod p$ can have at most d solutions, namely $a, a^2, \ldots, a^d$ (see exercise 6). Therefore, $S_d \subseteq \{a, a^2, \ldots, a^d\}$. It follows from the above characterization of S_d that if S_d is nonempty then $|S_d| = \varphi(d)$. But the family $\{S_d : d|(p-1)\}$ forms a partition of Z_p^*. It follows from Euler's theorem that

$$p - 1 = \sum_{d|(p-1)} \varphi(d) = \sum_{d|(p-1)} |S_d|.$$

Consequently, for all $d|(p-1)$, $|S_d| = \varphi(d)$, and Z_p^* must be a cyclic group.

The following claim will be useful in the sequel:

Claim 1: There exists a primitive root g modulo p such that for all $k > 1$, $g^{\varphi(p^{k-1})} \not\equiv 1 \bmod p^k$.

Proof of claim 1: Let g be a primitive root modulo p. Then notice that $(g+p)^{p-1} \equiv g^{p-1} + (p-1)pg^{p-2} \equiv g^{p-1} - pg^{p-2} \bmod p^2$. Hence, at least one of the two primitive roots $g, g+p$, say g_0, must satisfy $x^{p-1} \not\equiv 1 \bmod p^2$. The rest of the proof of the claim is by induction on k. It will be shown that g_0 satisfies the requirements of the claim. The proof in case $k = 2$ has already been completed. Assume by induction that $g_0^{\varphi(p^{k-1})} \not\equiv 1 \bmod p^k$. By the theorem of Euler-Fermat there exists an integer t such that $g_0^{\varphi(p^{k-1})} = 1 + tp^{k-1}$. By the induction hypothesis p does not divide t. It follows that $g_0^{\varphi(p^k)} \equiv (1 + tp^{k-1})^p \equiv 1 + tp^k + (1/2)p(p-1)t^2 p^{2k-2} \equiv 1 + tp^k \not\equiv 1 \bmod p^{k+1}$. This completes the proof of claim 1.

$Z_{p^k}^*$ is cyclic:

Let g be a primitive root modulo p which satisfies the condition of claim 1. It will be shown that for all $k > 0$, g is a primitive root modulo p^k. Let $k > 1$ be fixed, and let $e = $ least exponent such that $g^e \equiv 1 \bmod p^k$. Clearly $g^e \equiv 1 \bmod p$, and hence $(p-1)|e$. However, $e|\varphi(p^k) = (p-1)p^{k-1}$. It follows that $e = \varphi(p^t) = (p-1)p^{t-1}$, for some $t \leq k$. But it is clear from the choice of g that t must be equal to k i.e. $e = \varphi(p^k)$.

$Z_{2p^k}^*$ is cyclic:

Let g be a primitive root modulo p^k, where k is positive. Let g_0 be the odd number among the two integers $g, g + p^k$. It will be showm that g_0 is a primitive root modulo $2p^k$. Indeed, $\varphi(2p^k) = \varphi(p^k)$. If one defines $e = $ least exponent such that $g_0^e \equiv 1 \bmod (2p^k)$, then it follows from the Euler-Fermat theorem that $e|\varphi(2p^k)$, and hence $e \leq \varphi(2p^k)$. But g_0 is a primitive root modulo p^k, and hence $e \geq \varphi(p^k)$. Hence $e = \varphi(p^k)$. This completes the proof of ($\Leftarrow$).

($\Rightarrow$)

Suppose that m is not of the form $1, 2, 4, p^k, 2p^k$, where p is an odd prime and $k > 0$. Clearly the theorem is an immediate consequence of the following:

Claim 2: For all $a \in Z_m^*$, $a^{\varphi(m)/2} \equiv 1 \bmod m$.

Proof of claim 2: If $m = 2^k$, then $\varphi(m)/2 = 2^{k-2}$. The claim will be proved by induction on k. The initial step $k = 3$ is trivial. Assume $a^{2^{k-2}} \equiv 1 \bmod 2^k$ is true. Then $a^{2^{k-2}} = 1 + t2^k$, for some t. Hence, $a^{2^{k-1}} \equiv$

$(1 + t2^k)^2 \equiv 1 + t2^{k+1} + t^2 2^{2k} \equiv 1 \bmod 2^{k+1}.$

If $m = 2^k p^n$, where $k > 1$ and $n > 0$, then $\varphi(m)/2 = 2^{k-2} p^{n-1}(p-1)$ is divisible by both $\varphi(2^k)$ and $\varphi(p^n)$. Hence, the claim follows in this case easily, using the result in case $m = 2^k$ and the Euler-Fermat theorem.

If $m = 2^k p_1^{n_1} \cdots p_r^{n_r}$ where $k > 1, r > 0$ then it is clear that $\varphi(m)/2 = 2^{k-2} \varphi(p_1^{n_1}) \cdots \varphi(p_r^{n_r})$. It follows that $\varphi(m)/2$ is divisible by each of the integers $\varphi(2^k), \varphi(p_1^{n_1}), \ldots, \varphi(p_r^{n_r})$, and the rest of the proof can be completed exactly as before. This completes the proof of the claim, and hence of the theorem •

Figure 3 displays a table of the first ten odd primes and their corresponding least primitive root:

p	3	5	7	11	13	17	19	23	29	31
g	2	2	3	2	2	3	2	5	2	3

Figure 3: Table of primitive roots.

EXERCISES

1: Let g be a primitive root modulo m. Then for all nonnegative integers t, $g^t \bmod m$ is a primitive root modulo m if and only if $\gcd(t, \varphi(m)) = 1$. In particular, there exist exactly $\varphi(\varphi(m))$ primitive roots modulo m, provided there exists at least one primitive root modulo m.

2: Show that the groups Z_1^*, Z_2^*, Z_4^* are cyclic.

3: If $m = p_1^{e_1} \cdots p_r^{e_r}$ is the prime factorization of m, and $q_i = p_i^{e_i}$ for $i = 1, \ldots, r$, then the group Z_m^* and the product group $Z_{q_1}^* \times \cdots \times Z_{q_r}^*$ are isomorphic.

4: Show that for each odd a and each $r \geq 3$, $a^{2^{r-2}} \equiv 1 \bmod 2^r$.

5: Use exercise 4 to show that if $r \geq 3$ then $Z_{2^r}^*$ is isomorphic to the product of a cyclic group of order 2 and a cyclic group of order 2^{r-2}. **Hint:** -1 generates the group of order 2, and 5 the group of order 2^{r-2}.

6: Any polynomial of degree n over a field has at most n roots in this field. **Hint:** Use induction on n.

1.8   Artin's Conjecture

Theorem 1.9 gives a complete characterization of those m for which the multiplicative group, Z_m^*, is cyclic, i.e. Z_m^* has a generator. However, the following questions arise:

Question 1: Is there an efficient algorithm which, when given as input a prime number p, will output a primitive root modulo p?

Question 2: Given a specific integer g, determine the primes p such that g is a primitive root modulo p.

The second question is also mentioned by Gauss in [G3] for the special case $g = 10$. The results of section 4 make the importance of these questions apparent for the construction of pseudorandom generators. Nevertheless, to this date both questions are open. Some empirical data are provided in the table of figure 4 (see [S3], pp. 80 - 83, for additional empirical data). Let $\nu_g(n) = $ the number of primes $p \leq n$ such that g is a primitive root modulo p, and let $\pi(n) = $ the number of primes $\leq n$.

g	$\nu_g(10^4)$	$\nu_g(10^4)/\pi(10^4)$
2	470	.382
3	476	.387
5	492	.400
6	470	.382
7	465	.378

Figure 4: Artin's Constant

Based on probalistic heuristic considerations (see [S3], pp. 82), Artin has conjectured that:

Conjecture 1: (Artin) Every integer $g \neq -1, 1$ which is not a complete square is a primitive root of infinitely many primes.

More exactly it is conjectured that:

Conjecture 2: For every integer $g \neq -1, 1$ which is not a complete square,

$$\nu_g(n) \approx F_g \cdot A \cdot \pi(n),$$

where A is Artin's constant (approximately equal to .37395 ...). A is independent of n, g, and the (rational) number F_g is given in [H8]. For many values of g (e.g. $g = 2, 3, 6$) $F_g = 1$.

It is significant to note that Hooley in [H8] has confirmed Conjecture 2 under the assumption that Riemann's hypothesis holds for certain Dedekind functions (see [S3], pp. 222 - 225).

| EXERCISES |

1: (Lucas) The following result can be useful to test if a given g is a primitive root modulo n, providing that the prime factors of $n - 1$ are known. Prove the following statement: g is a primitive root modulo $n \Leftrightarrow$ for all prime factors p of $n - 1$, $g^{(n-1)/p} \not\equiv 1 \bmod n$.

1.9   The Carmichael Function

A useful generalization of the theorem of Euler - Fermat is given through the Carmichael function λ. For each integer m, $\lambda(m)$ is defined as follows:

$$\lambda(2^t) = \begin{cases} 2^{t-1} & \text{if } t < 3 \\ 2^{t-2} & \text{if } t \geq 3, \end{cases}$$

and for any given integer $m = 2^{a_0} p_1^{a_1} \cdots p_r^{a_r}$, where $p_1, \ldots, p_r$ are the distinct odd prime factors of m, one defines

$$\lambda(m) = \text{lcm}(\lambda(2^{a_0}), \varphi(p_1^{a_1}), \ldots, \varphi(p_r^{a_r})).$$

The intended improvement of the Euler-Fermat theorem (see theorem 1.3) is given in the theorem below.

Theorem 1.10 (Carmichael) *For all* $a \in Z_m^*$, $a^{\lambda(m)} \equiv 1 \bmod m$.

Proof: It has been shown in the proof of theorem 1.9 that for any integer m which is not of the form $1, 2, 4, p^k, 2p^k$, where p is an odd prime, $k > 0$, and for all a in Z_m^*,

$$a^{\varphi(m)/2} \equiv 1 \bmod m. \tag{3}$$

Let $p_0, p_1, \ldots, p_r$ be the distinct prime divisors of m in ascending order and for each i let q_i be the largest power of p_i dividing m. Hence, $m = q_0 \cdot q_1 \cdots q_r$. By the theorem of Euler-Fermat and the observation in congruence (3), it is true that for all $a \in Z_m^*$, and all $i = 0, \ldots, r$, $a^{\varphi(q_i)} \equiv 1 \bmod q_i$, and if $p_0 = 2$ then $a^{\lambda(q_0)} \equiv 1 \bmod q_0$. But this is enough to complete the proof of the theorem $\bullet$

| EXERCISES |

1: Let m be odd. Show that $\lambda(m)$ is the least exponent e such that for all $a \in Z_m^*, a^e \equiv 1 \bmod m$. **Hint:** Let $p_1, \ldots, p_r$ be the distinct prime divisors of m, and for each i let q_i be the largest power of p_i dividing m. For each i, let g_i be a primitive root modulo q_i. Fix an $i = 1, \ldots, r$. Use the Chinese remainder theorem to find an $a_i \in Z_m^*$ such that $a_i \equiv g_i \bmod q_i$ and $a_i \equiv 1 \bmod q_j$ for all $j \neq i$. Let e be the least exponent e such that for all $a \in Z_m^*$, $a^e \equiv 1 \bmod m$. By assumption, $a_i^e \equiv 1 \bmod m$ and hence $g_i^e \equiv 1 \bmod q_i$. But g_i is a primitive root modulo q_i. Thus, $\varphi(q_i)|e$.

1.10   The Legendre Symbol

Call an x in Z_m^* a **quadratic residue** modulo m, if $x \equiv y^2 \bmod m$ for some $y \in Z_m^*$; otherwise x is called a **quadratic nonresidue** modulo m. Let QR_m (respectively QNR_m) be the set of all quadratic residues (respectively nonresidues) modulo m.

For each prime number p, and any $x \in Z_m^*$ let

$$(x|p) = \begin{cases} 1 & \text{if } x \in QR_p \\ -1 & \text{if } x \in QNR_p. \end{cases}$$

$(x|p)$ is called the **Legendre symbol** of x modulo p.

Remark: The symbol $\left(\frac{x}{p}\right)$ is also widely used in the literature as identical to the symbol $(x|p)$. The symbol $(x|p)$ is used here for typographical convenience.

One of the most useful properties of the Legendre symbol is conveyed in the following:

Theorem 1.11 *(Euler's Criterion) For all primes $p > 2$, and all $x \in Z_p^*$,*

$$x^{(p-1)/2} \equiv (x|p) \bmod p.$$

Proof: Let $x \in Z_p^*$. Then $x^{p-1} \equiv 1 \bmod p$, and hence either $x^{(p-1)/2} \equiv 1 \bmod p$ or $x^{(p-1)/2} \equiv -1 \bmod p$. The mapping $f : Z_p^* \longrightarrow \{-1, 1\}$ such that $f(x) = x^{(p-1)/2} \bmod p$, is a group homomorphism. Since for any primitive root g of Z_p^*, $g^{(p-1)/2} \equiv -1 \bmod p$, the mapping f is onto, and consequently, the kernel K of f is a proper subgroup of Z_p^* of size $(p-1)/2$ (see theorem 1.1).

If $(x|p) = 1$, then $x \in QR_p$. Thus, $x \equiv y^2 \bmod p$ for some $y \in Z_p^*$. It follows that $x^{(p-1)/2} \equiv y^{p-1} \equiv 1 \bmod p$, by the theorem of Euler-Fermat (see theorem 1.3.) Thus, $x \in QR_p \Rightarrow x^{(p-1)/2} \equiv 1 \bmod p \Rightarrow x \in K$.

However, $QR_p = \{1^2 \bmod p, 2^2 \bmod p, \ldots, (p-1)^2 \bmod p\}$. Moreover, $(p-x)^2 \equiv p^2 - 2px + x^2 \equiv x^2 \bmod p$, for all $x \in Z_p^*$. Thus, exactly one half the numbers in Z_p^* are quadratic residues, and the other half are quadratic nonresidues modulo p. Since $K \supseteq QR_p$, and both K, QR_p have exactly the same size $(p-1)/2$, it follows that $K = QR_p$.

If $(x|p) = -1$, then $x \in QNR_p$. It follows from the above remarks that $x \notin K$ and $x^{(p-1)/2} \equiv -1 \bmod p$. Thus, $x \notin K \Rightarrow x^{(p-1)/2} \equiv -1 \bmod p$, which completes the proof of the theorem •

EXERCISES

1: The following result is a generalization of Euler's criterion (see theorem 1.11): for all primes $p > 2$, for all $k > 0$, and all $x \in Z_{p^k}^*$, $x^{\varphi(p^k)/2} \equiv 1 \bmod p \Leftrightarrow x \in QR_{p^k}$. **Hint:** Argue as in the above proof to show that the mapping $f : Z_{p^k}^* \longrightarrow \{-1, 1\}$, such that $f(x) = x^{\varphi(p^k)/2} \bmod p^k$, is a group epimorphism, whose kernel K equals QR_{p^k}.

2: Use exercise 1 to show that for all integers $x \in Z_{p^k}^*$, $x \in QR_p \Leftrightarrow x \in QR_{p^k}$. **Hint:** ($\Rightarrow$) Let $x \in QR_p$ and put $a = x^{\varphi(p)/2}$. Then $p | (x^{\varphi(p)/2} - 1)$. Hence, $x^{\varphi(p^k)/2} - 1 = a^{p^{k-1}} - 1 = (a-1)(a^{p^{k-1}-1} + a^{p^{k-1}-2} + \cdots + a + 1)$. Notice that the second factor of the last product is divisable by p^{k-1}.

3: If both $x, y \in QNR_p$, then $x \cdot y \in QR_p$.

1.11   The Legendre-Jacobi Symbol

The definition of the Legendre symbol can be extended to all m and all x in Z_m^*. Indeed, let $m = p_1 \cdots p_r$, where $p_1, \ldots, p_r$ are primes. Then the **Legendre-Jacobi symbol** is defined by $(x|m) = (x|p_1) \cdots (x|p_r)$. One also defines the sets $Z_m^*(+1) = \{x \in Z_m^* : (x|m) = 1\}$, and $Z_m^*(-1) = \{x \in Z_m^* : (x|m) = -1\}$.

In determining whether a given $x \in Z_p^*$ is a quadratic residue modulo a prime p one needs to compute $(x|p)$. This is in fact done using the next two theorems.

Theorem 1.12 *(Evaluating $(x|m)$)* Let $x, y \in Z_m^*$.
  (i) If $x \equiv y \bmod m$ then $(x|m) = (y|m)$.
  (ii) $(x|m) \cdot (y|m) = (x \cdot y|m)$.
  (iii) $(-1|m) = (-1)^{(m-1)/2}$.
  (iv) $(2|m) = (-1)^{(m^2-1)/8}$, where m is odd.

Proof: The proofs of (i), (ii) are easy and are left as an exercise to the reader. As a first step, parts (iii), (iv) of the theorem will be reduced to the case of the Legendre symbol, i.e. m is prime. This reduction is based on the following lemma whose proof is straightforward:

Lemma 1.1 *If both s and t are odd, then*

$$\frac{s-1}{2} + \frac{t-1}{2} \equiv \frac{st-1}{2} \mod 2, \text{ and}$$

$$\frac{s^2-1}{8} + \frac{t^2-1}{8} \equiv \frac{s^2 t^2-1}{8} \mod 2.$$

Using the definition of the Legendre-Jacobi symbol, the reduction to the case of the Legendre symbol is an immediate consequence of congruences (4), (5) below. Let $m = p_1 \cdots p_r$ be the prime number factorization of m. Then the lemma above implies that

$$\frac{p_1-1}{2} + \cdots + \frac{p_r-1}{2} \equiv \frac{m-1}{2} \mod 2, \tag{4}$$

$$\frac{p_1^2-1}{8} + \cdots + \frac{p_r^2-1}{8} \equiv \frac{m^2-1}{8} \mod 2. \tag{5}$$

So from now on it will be assumed that $m = p$ is a prime. It is now obvious that (iii) is an immediate consequence of Euler's criterion. Hence it only remains to give the proof of (iv).

Since $((p-1)/2)!$ is the product of numbers all of which are less than p, it is clear that p does not divide $((p-1)/2)!$. Also notice that

$$(-1)^k \cdot k \equiv \begin{cases} k \mod p & \text{if } k \text{ is even} \\ (p-k) \mod p & \text{if } k \text{ is odd} \end{cases}$$

It follows that, on the one hand,

$$(-1)^1 1 (-1)^2 2 \cdots (-1)^{(p-1)/2} \frac{p-1}{2} = \tag{6}$$

$$\left(\frac{p-1}{2}\right)! (-1)^{1+2+\cdots+(p-1)/2} = \left(\frac{p-1}{2}\right)! (-1)^{(p^2-1)/8}, \tag{7}$$

and, on the other hand, using Euler's criterion,

$$(-1)^1 1 (-1)^2 2 \cdots (-1)^{(p-1)/2} \frac{p-1}{2} \equiv 2 \cdot 4 \cdot 6 \cdots (p-1) \equiv \tag{8}$$

$$2^{(p-1)/2}\left(\frac{p-1}{2}\right)! \equiv (2|p)\left(\frac{p-1}{2}\right)! \bmod p. \tag{9}$$

The result now follows by combining congruences (6-9) and the fact that p does not divide $((p-1)/2)!$ •

Theorem 1.13 (**Law of Quadratic Reciprocity, Gauss**) *For all odd* $m, n > 2$ *which are relatively prime the following equation holds:*

$$(n|m) \cdot (m|n) = (-1)^{(m-1)\cdot(n-1)/4}.$$

   Proof: Using the first part of lemma 1.1 it can be assumed without loss of generality that $m = p$, $n = q$ are primes. For any set $M \subseteq Z_m^*$ define the set $-M = \{-a : a \in M\}$. For the given primes p, q, let $P = \{1, 2, \dots, (p-1)/2\}$ and $Q = \{1, 2, \dots, (q-1)/2\}$. It is clear that for any $c \in Q$ there exists $b \in Q$ such that either $pc \equiv b \bmod q$ or $pc \equiv -b \bmod q$ (a similar property holds for P). Define $n(p, q) =$ the number of times that pc is congruent modulo q to an integer in $-Q$, as c runs through Q. The proof is based on the following:

Lemma 1.2 (**Gauss's Lemma**) $(p|q) = (-1)^{n(p,q)}$.

   Proof of the Lemma: For each $c \in Q$, one can find s_c, b_c such that

$$pc \equiv s_c b_c \bmod q, \tag{10}$$

where $b_c \in Q$ and $s_c = +1$ or -1. The mapping $c \longrightarrow b_c (c \in Q, b_c \in Q)$ is $1 - 1$ (and hence also onto). Indeed, assume that $b_c = b_d$. Hence, either $pc \equiv pd \bmod q$ or $pc \equiv -pd \bmod q$. But p, q are relatively prime. It follows from the definition of Q that $c = d$. Hence, the mapping $c \longrightarrow b_c$ is a permutation of Q and

$$\left(\frac{q-1}{2}\right)! = b_1 b_2 \cdots b_{(q-1)/2}. \tag{11}$$

   Multiplying the congruences (10) as c ranges over Q and using (11), one obtains that

$$p^{(q-1)/2} \equiv (-1)^{n(p,q)} \bmod q.$$

The proof of the lemma can now be completed using Euler's criterion •

   Returning to the proof of the theorem, let $\vartheta = e^{2\pi i/p}$ (respectively $\varrho = e^{2\pi i/q}$) be the primitive p-th (respectively q-th) root of unity. Together,

Gauss's Lemma and the fact that for all $a \in Q$ there exists $b \in Q \cup (-Q)$ such that $pa \equiv b \bmod q$, imply that

$$(p|q) = (-1)^{n(p,q)} = \prod_{a \in Q} \frac{\varrho^{pa} - \varrho^{-pa}}{\varrho^a - \varrho^{-a}}. \tag{12}$$

However, the following identity holds for all $x \neq 0$:

$$x^p - x^{-p} = \prod_{b \in Z_p} (x\vartheta^b - x^{-1}\vartheta^{-b}). \tag{13}$$

(To see this, multiply both sides of (13) by x^p and use $\vartheta^p = 1$ to show that the resulting polynomials have the same leading coefficient 1 and the same zeroes: $\vartheta^b, -\vartheta^b$, where $b = 0, \ldots, p-1$.) Combining (12) and (13) one easily obtains that

$$(p|q) = \left(\prod_{a \in Q} \prod_{b \in Z_p} (\varrho^a \vartheta^b - \varrho^{-a} \vartheta^{-b}) \right) \Bigg/ \left(\prod_{a \in Q} (\varrho^a - \varrho^{-a}) \right)$$

$$= \prod_{a \in Q} \prod_{b \in Z_p^*} (\varrho^a \vartheta^b - \varrho^{-a} \vartheta^{-b})$$

$$= \prod_{a \in Q} \prod_{b \in P} (\varrho^a \vartheta^b - \varrho^{-a} \vartheta^{-b}) \cdot (\varrho^a \vartheta^{-b} - \varrho^{-a} \vartheta^b).$$

Hence,

$$(p|q) = \prod_{a \in Q, b \in P} ((\varrho^{2a} + \varrho^{-2a})) - (\vartheta^{2b} + \vartheta^{-2b})).$$

Interchanging the roles of p and q one also obtains:

$$(q|p) = \prod_{a \in Q, b \in P} ((\vartheta^{2b} + \vartheta^{-2b}) - (\varrho^{2a} + \varrho^{-2a})).$$

Since each of the last two products has $(p-1)(q-1)/4$ factors, the proof of the Law of Quadratic Reciprocity is complete ●

It is not hard to see that computing the Legendre-Jacobi symbol $(x|m)$ of two relatively prime integers x, m is similar to computing the greatest common divisor of x, m. This is illustrated in the example below.

Example 1.5 *Show that* $76 \notin QR_{131}$. *Indeed,*
$(76|131) = (2|131) \cdot (2|131) \cdot (19|131) =$
$(19|131) = (131|19) \cdot (-1)^{(131-1)/2 \cdot (19-1)/2} =$
$(17|19) \cdot (-1) = -(19|17) \cdot (-1)^{(19-1)/2 \cdot (17-1)/2} =$
$-(19|17) = -(2|17) = -(-1)^{(17^2-1)/8} = -1$

An analysis similar to that in the proof of Lamé's theorem, (see theorem 1.2) shows that:

Theorem 1.14 *If $N \geq a, b > 0$ are integers, with a, b relatively prime, then the number of steps required to compute $(a|b)$ is $O(\log_R N)$, where R is the golden mean* •

EXERCISES

1: Prove parts (i) and (ii), as well as the lemma used in the proof of theorem 1.12.

2: Compute $(56|39)$.

3: Determine $(3|p)$, where p is a prime > 3.

4: For $k > 2$ and a odd, $a \in QR_{2^k} \Leftrightarrow a \equiv 1 \bmod 8$. **Hint:** ($\Rightarrow$) See the proof of claim 2 in theorem 1.9; ($\Leftarrow$) use exercise 5 of subsection 1.7.

From now on assume that p is an odd prime and $k > 1$.

5: Show that $(1 + p)^{p^{k-1}} \equiv 1 \bmod p^k$ and $(1 + p)^{p^{k-2}} \equiv (1 + p^{k-1}) \not\equiv 1 \bmod p^k$. Hence, $(1 + p)$ generates in $Z_{p^k}^*$ a cyclic subgroup H of $Z_{p^k}^*$ of order p^{k-1}.

6: (This is a continuation of exercise 5.) Let g be a primitive root modulo p. Then $g_0 = g^{p^{k-1}}$ is a primitive root modulo p and g_0 generates a cyclic subgroup G of $Z_{p^k}^*$ of order $p - 1$. Moreover, $G \times H$ is isomorphic to $Z_{p^k}^*$. Every element $a \in Z_{p^k}^*$ can be written uniquely in the form $a \equiv g_0^t(1 + p)^r \bmod p^k$, where $0 \leq t < p - 1$ and $0 \leq r < p^{k-1}$. (Exercise 6 gives a new proof of the cyclicity of $Z_{p^k}^*$, for $k > 1$.)

7: For all a, if a is relatively prime to p then $a \in QR_p \Leftrightarrow a \in QR_{p^k}$ **Hint:** ($\Rightarrow$) Write a in the form $a = g_0^t(1 + p)^r \bmod p^k$, where $0 \leq t < p - 1$ and $0 \leq r < p^{k-1}$. Notice that t is even. Find c such that $2c \equiv 1 \bmod p^{k-1}$ and let $b \equiv g_0^{t/2}(1 + p)^{cr} \bmod p^k$. Show that $a \equiv b^2 \bmod p^k$. (Exercise 7 gives a new proof of exercise 2 in subsection 1.10.)

8: Give the proof of theorem 1.14.

1.12 Computing Square Roots

One of the most important problems in complexity theory is to find an efficient algorithm which, given as input an $x \in QR_n$ and an integer n, it will output a square root of x modulo n. It will be seen in the sequel that such an algorithm exists if n is prime. It will be shown later (see theorem 4.7) that, for composite n, the preceding problem is equivalent to the problem of finding an efficient algorithm, which given n as input will output the factors of n.

If p is an odd prime number, then such an efficient probabilistic procedure to compute square roots modulo p is given in the theorem below.

Theorem 1.15 *(Adleman-Manders-Miller) There exists a probabilistic polynomial time algorithm which when given an odd prime p and an $a \in QR_p$ as inputs, will output a square root of a modulo p.*

Proof: Let p be a prime and $a \in QR_p$. Write $p-1$ in the form $p-1 = 2^e P$, where P is odd. Choose any random $b \in QNR_p$. Define a sequence $a_1, a_2, \ldots, a_n, \ldots$ of quadratic residues modulo p and a sequence of indices $e \geq k_1 > \cdots > k_n > \cdots$ as follows, by induction on n:

$$a_1 = a,$$

$$k_{n-1} = \text{least } k \geq 0 \text{ such that } a_{n-1}^{2^k P} \equiv 1 \bmod p,$$

$$a_n \equiv a_{n-1} b^{2^{e-k_{n-1}}} \bmod p, \text{for } n \geq 2.$$

However, it is true that

$$a_n^{2^{k_{n-1}-1}P} \equiv \left(a_{n-1}b^{2^{e-k_{n-1}}}\right)^{2^{k_{n-1}-1}P} \equiv$$

$$a_{n-1}^{2^{k_{n-1}-1}P} b^{2^{e-1}P} \equiv (-1)(-1) \equiv 1 \bmod p.$$

The proof of the last congruence uses the fact that $b^{2^{e-1}P} \equiv b^{(p-1)/2} \equiv (b|p) \equiv -1 \bmod p$. Using the minimality of k_{n-1}, the preceding congruences, and the Euler-Fermat theorem, it follows that, for all integers n, if $k_{n-1} > 0$, then $k_n < k_{n-1}$. Hence, there exists an $n \leq e$ such that $k_n = 0$, and for such an n, $a_n^{(P+1)/2}$ is a square root of a_n. Next, one defines by reverse induction a sequence $r_1, \ldots, r_n$ such that, for all i, $r_i^2 \equiv a_i \bmod p$. Indeed, let $r_n \equiv a_n^{(P+1)/2} \bmod p$. Assume that r_{i+1} has already been defined and let $r_i \equiv r_{i+1}(b^{2^{e-k_i-1}})^{-1} \bmod p$. It is straightforward to see that for all i, $a_i \equiv r_i^2 \bmod p$. Moreover, $n \leq \log_2 p$.

The foregoing observations provide an efficient algorithm, described more explicitly below, to compute square roots modulo a prime number p. One merely chooses a random b such that $(b|p) = -1$ and then follows the procedure described above with input p, a.

Input: p (prime), $a \in QR_p$.

Step 1: Compute an odd P, and e such that $p - 1 = 2^e P$.
Step 2: Choose random b such that $(b|p) = -1$.
Step 3: Set $y = a, r = a^{(P+1)/2} \bmod p$.
Step 4: Find the least k such that $y^{2^k P} \equiv 1 \bmod p$.
Step 5: **If** $k = 0$ **then** output r; **else** set

$$y \equiv yb^{2^{e-k}} \bmod p, \quad r \equiv r(b^{2^{e-k-1}})^{-1} \bmod p$$

and **go to** step 4.
Output: r.

The running time of the algorithm is polynomial in the lengths of p and a, plus the time required to find an integer b such that $(b|p) = -1$ •

The case of composite n is studied in the theorem below.

Theorem 1.16 *For all $x \in Z_{pq}^*$, where p, q are distinct odd primes, $x \in QR_{pq} \Leftrightarrow x \in QR_p$ and $x \in QR_q$. Moreover there is an efficient algorithm which, given x, u, v, p, q as inputs, where p and q are distinct odd primes and $x \equiv u^2 \bmod p$ and $x \equiv v^2 \bmod q$, will output a w such that $x \equiv w^2 \bmod (pq)$.*

Proof: The first part of the theorem is easy. To prove the second part suppose that x, u, v, p, q are as in the hypothesis of the theorem. Since p, q are relatively prime one can efficiently compute integers a, b such that $1 = ap + bq$. Put $c = bq = 1 - ap$ and $d = ap = 1 - bq$. It is then clear that

$$c \equiv 0 \bmod q, \ c \equiv 1 \bmod p, \ d \equiv 0 \bmod p, \ d \equiv 1 \bmod q.$$

It will be shown that $w = cu + dv$ is a quadratic residue modulo n. It is enough to show that w is a quadratic residue both modulo p and modulo q. Indeed,

$$w^2 \equiv (cu + dv)^2 \equiv (c^2 u^2 + d^2 v^2 + 2cduv) \equiv u^2 \equiv x \bmod p.$$

A similar calculation shows that $w^2 \equiv x \bmod q$. This completes the proof of the theorem •

EXERCISES

In exercises 1 and 2 below, $f(x)$ denotes a polynomial with integer coefficients.

1: Use Hensel's Lemma (see [K3], theorem 3, page 16 or [K2], exercise 22, page 439) to show that if one has a solution of the congruence $f(x) \equiv$

0 mod$p$, where p is prime, then for any $e \geq 1$ one can lift it to a solution of $f(x) \equiv 0 \bmod p^e$ in polynomial time.

2: Use Exercise 1 and the Chinese remainder theorem to show that if the factorization of n is known, then one can take solutions of $f(x) \equiv 0 \bmod p$ for $p|n$ to produce a solution of $f(x) \equiv 0 \bmod n$ in polynomial time.

3: If $p = 4n + 3$ is prime and $a \in QR_p$, then $a^{n+1} \bmod p$ is a square root of a modulo p (see also [S3], page 47).

1.13   Indices

Let p be a prime and let g be a primitive root modulo p. It is known that $Z_p^* = \{g^0 \bmod p, g^1 \bmod p, \ldots, g^{p-2} \bmod p\}$, and hence for any $x \in Z_p^*$, one can define the **index** or **discrete logarithm** of x with respect to g, abbreviated index$_{p,g}(x)$, as the unique $m \leq p - 1$ such that $x \equiv g^m \bmod p$.

The following theorem gives a very useful characterization of quadratic residues in terms of the index defined above.

Theorem 1.17 *(Characterization of Quadratic Residues) Let p be an odd prime, and let g be a primitive root modulo p. Then, for any $x \in Z_p^*$, $x \in QR_p \Leftrightarrow$ index$_{p,g}(x)$ is even.*

Proof: The proof of ($\Leftarrow$) is easy and is left to the reader.

($\Rightarrow$) Let x be a quadratic residue modulo p. There exists an integer u such that $x \equiv u^2 \bmod p$. Let $t = $ index$_{p,g}(u) < p - 1$. Then $u \equiv g^t \bmod p$ and $x \equiv g^{2t} \bmod p$. It follows that index$_{p,g}(x) \equiv 2t \bmod(p - 1)$, and hence index$_{p,g}(x)$ is even •

Using the multiplication table of Z_{11}^* one can compute the table of indices given in figure 5.

x	1	2	3	4	5	6	7	8	9	10
index$_{11,2}(x)$	0	1	8	2	4	9	7	3	6	5

Figure 5: Table of values of index$_{11,2}(x)$.

If $n = pq$ is the product of two distinct primes, then the product mapping $< x, y > \longrightarrow xy$ is an isomorphism between the groups $Z_p^* \times Z_q^*$ and Z_n^*. Let g (respectively h) be a primitive root modulo p (respectively q). Then any element in Z_n^* can be written in a unique way in the form $z = g^r h^t$. As before, let the index of z with respect to g, h, abbreviated $\text{index}_{n,g,h}(z)$, be the pair $< r, t >$.

1: Prove ($\Leftarrow$) in theorem 1.17.

2: Let $n = pq$ be the product of two distinct odd primes such that g (respectively h) is a primitive root modulo p (respectively q). For any $z \in Z_n^*$, $z \in QR_n \Leftrightarrow$ both components of $\text{index}_{n,g,h}(z)$ are even.

3: Let g be a primitive root modulo the prime $p > 2$. Show that for all $a, b \in Z_p^*$, and all $n > 0$,

(1) $\text{index}_{p,g}(ab) \equiv \text{index}_{p,g}(a) + \text{index}_{p,g}(b) \bmod (p - 1)$.

(2) $\text{index}_{p,g}(a^n) \equiv n \cdot \text{index}_{p,g}(a) \bmod (p - 1)$.

(3) $\text{index}_{p,g}(1) = 0$.

(4) $\text{index}_{p,g}(g) = 1$.

(5) $\text{index}_{p,g}(-1) = (p - 1)/2$.

4: If g is a primitive root modulo p, then $g \notin QR_p$.

1.14   Computing Indices

Another important problem in complexity theory is to find an efficient algorithm A such that, for any prime p, any primitive root g modulo p, and any $x \in Z_p^*$, $A(p, g, x) = \text{index}_{p,g}(x)$. This problem is very significant for the construction of secure pseudorandom generators. In general, no such algorithm is known. However, the theorem below provides an efficient algorithm in the case where the prime factors of $p - 1$ are known and are *small* with respect to p. For each integer n, $|n|$ denotes the binary length of n.

Theorem 1.18 (Pohlig-Hellman) *For any polynomial $P(\cdot)$ there exists an efficient algorithm A such that if p is a prime such that the prime factors $p_1, \ldots, p_r$ of $p - 1$ satisfy $p_1, \ldots, p_r \leq P(|p|), g$ is a generator of Z_p^*, and $y \in Z_p^*$ then $A(p, g, p_1, \ldots, p_r, y) = \text{index}_{p,g}(y)$. Moreover, A runs in time polunomial (which depends on the polynomial P) in the length $|p|$ of p.*

Proof: Let p be a prime number such that the prime factors $p_1, \ldots, p_r$ of $p - 1$ satisfy $p_1, \ldots, p_r \leq P(|p|)$. Let g be a generator of Z_p^*, and let $y \in Z_p^*$. For each $j = 1, \ldots, r$, let $e_j =$ the largest exponent e such that $p_j^e | (p - 1)$ and let $q_j = p_j^{e_j}$. For each $j = 1, \ldots, r$ define $y_j \equiv y^{(p-1)/q_j} \bmod p$, $g_j \equiv g^{(p-1)/q_j} \bmod p$, $x_j =$ the unique x such that $g_j^x \equiv y_j \bmod p$. Notice that

$x_j < q_j$. Thus, x_j can be represented in the number base p_j as follows:

$$x_j = x_{j,0} + x_{j,1}p_j + x_{j,2}p_j^2 + \cdots + x_{j,e_j-1}p_j^{e_j-1}, \text{ where } x_{j,i} < p_j. \quad (14)$$

The idea of the proof is as follows: first, one gives an algorithm A_1 that, on input p, p_j, g, y, computes $x_{j,0}$ as above; second, one extends A_1 to give an algorithm A_2 that, on input p, p_j, g, y, computes x_j; third, one uses the Chinese remainder theorem to compute the $\text{index}_{p,g}(y)$ from the previously computed x_j.

The algorithm A_1 is given below.

Input: p, p_j, g, y.

Step 1: Compute q_j, g_j, y_j as above.

Step 2: Compute $z_j \equiv y_j^{(p-1)/p_j} \bmod p$.

Step 3: Compute $i_0 =$ the first $i < p_j$ such that $z_j \equiv g_j^{i(p-1)/p_j} \bmod p$.

Output: i_0.

It is a consequence of the Euler-Fermat theorem that $i_0 = x_{j,0}$. Indeed, using (14) one obtains $i_0 = x_{j,0}$ through the following congruences: $z_j \equiv g_j^{i_0(p-1)/p_j} \equiv y_j^{(p-1)/p_j} \equiv g_j^{x_j(p-1)/p_j} \equiv g_j^{x_{j,0}(p-1)/p_j} \bmod p$.

An easy extension of the preceding algorithm gives a new algorithm to compute x_j. Indeed, consider the following algorithm A_2 defined by:

Input: p, p_j, g, y.

Step 1: Compute q_j, e_j, g_j, y_j.

Step 2: Compute $A_1(p, p_j, g, y)$.

Step 3: Put $g_{j,0} = g_j$, $y_{j,0} = y_j$, $c_{j,0} = A_1(p, p_j, g, y)$.

Step 4: For $i = 0$ to $e_j - 1$ **do:**

Compute the following:

$$g_{j,i+1} \equiv g_{j,i}^{p_j} \bmod p, y_{j,i+1} \equiv y_{j,i}g_{j,i}^{-c_{j,i}} \bmod p.$$

Step 5: Compute $c_{j,i+1} = A_1(p, p_j, g_{j,i+1}, y_{j,i+1})$.

Output: $c_{j,0} + c_{j,1}p_j + c_{j,2}p_j^2 + \cdots + c_{j,e_j-1}p_j^{e_j-1}$.

To prove the correctness of A_2 one shows by induction on $i \leq e_j$ that $c_{j,i} = x_{j,i}$. For example, it has already been shown that $x_{j,0} = c_{j,0}$. Thus,

$$y_{j,1} \equiv y_{j,0}g_{j,0}^{-c_{j,0}} \equiv$$

$$g_j^{x_{j,1}p_j + \cdots + x_{j,e_j-1}p_j^{e_j-1}} \equiv (g_j^{p_j})^{x_{j,1} + \cdots + x_{j,e_j-1}p_j^{e_j-2}}.$$

Consequently,

$$x_{j,1} = A_1\left(p, p_j, g_j^{p_j}, y_j g_j^{-x_{j,0}}\right) = A_1\left(p, p_j, g_{j,1}, y_{j,1}\right) = c_{j,1}.$$

The proof of $c_{j,i} = x_{j,i}$ $(i > 1)$ is similar.

The rest of the proof is an application of the Chinese remainder theorem. Indeed, consider the following algorithm A:

Input: $p, g, p_1, \ldots, p_r, y$.
Step 1: Compute $x_j = A_2(p, p_j, g, y)$.
Output: The unique x such that for all $j = 1, \ldots, r$,

$$x \equiv x_j \bmod (q_1 \ldots q_r).$$

To see that A works, notice that for all $j = 1, \ldots, r$,

$$y^{(p-1)/q_j} \equiv g^{x_j(p-1)/q_j} \bmod p \text{ and } x \equiv x_j \bmod (p-1).$$

Since $\gcd((p-1)/q_1, \ldots, (p-1)/q_r) = 1$, there exist $t_1, \ldots, t_r$ such that

$$t_1(p-1)/q_1 + \cdots + t_r(p-1)/q_r = 1.$$

It follows from the Euler-Fermat theorem that

$$y \equiv y^1 \equiv y^{t_1(p-1)/q_1 + \cdots + t_r(p-1)/q_r} \equiv y^{t_1(p-1)/q_1} \ldots y^{t_r(p-1)/q_r} \equiv$$

$$g^{x_1 t_1(p-1)/q_1} \ldots g^{x_r t_r(p-1)/q_r} \equiv g^{x_1 t_1(p-1)/q_1 + \cdots + x_r t_r(p-1)/q_r} \equiv g^x \bmod p,$$

which completes the proof of the theorem •

Remark: Clearly the running time of the above algorithm is polynomial and depends on the given polynomial $P(\cdot)$. In general, however, no such efficient algorithm is known. Recently E. Bach has shown (see [B1], exercise 2) that if one can solve $a^x \equiv b \bmod n$ in polynomial time, then one can find a proper factor of n with high probability, in polynomial time. (If the Extended Riemann Hypothesis holds, then this algorithm can in fact be made deterministic.) Conversely, if $a^x \equiv b \bmod p$ can be solved efficiently for prime p, so can $a^x \equiv b \bmod n$, for any modulus n, provided the factorization of n is known.

| EXERCISES |

1: Complete the proof of $c_{j,i} = x_{j,i}, i > 1$ in algorithm A_2 of theorem 1.18.

2: (**Miller-Bach**) Assume that the congruence $a^x \equiv 1 \bmod n$, $x \neq 0$, can be solved in plynomial time (in the length of a and n). If a is a random integer such that

$$a^{\lambda(n)/2} \not\equiv 1 \bmod n, \text{ and } a^{\lambda(n)/2} \not\equiv -1 \bmod n,$$

then a can be used to factor n. **Hint:** Compute an x such that $a^x \equiv 1 \bmod n$ and let k be minimal with $a^{x/2^k} \not\equiv +1 \bmod n$ and $a^{x/2^k} \not\equiv -1 \bmod n$. Show that $\gcd(n, (a^{x/2^k} + 1) \bmod n)$ is a proper factor of n.

1.15   The Prime Number Theorem

Let b, c be relatively prime positive integers, and let $\pi_{b,c}(x) =$ the number of primes $p \leq x$ such that p is of the form $p = bk + c$. If $b = 1$, $c = 0$, then $\pi(x) = \pi_{1,0}(x) =$ the number of primes $p \leq x$. The **prime number theorem** is the following statement (where the logarithm is taken with respect to the base e) :

Theorem 1.19 *(***Dirichlet, Hadamard, de la Vallée Poussin***)*
If $\gcd(b, c) = 1$, *then*

$$\pi_{b,c}(x) \sim \frac{1}{\varphi(b)} \cdot \frac{x}{\log x} \quad \bullet$$

In particular, as a special case of theorem 1.19, one obtains that

$$\pi(x) \sim \frac{x}{\log x}.$$

The table of figure 6 gives some values of $\pi(n)$.

n	10^1	10^2	10^3	10^4	10^5	10^6	10^7
$\pi(n)$	4	25	168	1,229	9,592	78,498	664,579

Figure 6: Table of values of $\pi(n)$.

A proof of theorem 1.19 would lie outside the scope of the present book. However, a proof of the following weaker version of the prime number theorem will be sufficient for most applications. Its proof is due to Zagier (see [Z1]) and is partly based on ideas of Chebyshev.

Theorem 1.20 *(Chebyshev) For all $x > 200$,*

$$\frac{2}{3} \cdot \frac{x}{\log x} < \pi(x). \tag{15}$$

Proof: **(Zagier)** For simplicity, p will range over prime numbers through-out the present proof. For each real r, let $[r]$ denote the integral part of r. The following claim will be useful in the sequel.

Claim: For all x, k the following holds:

$$\binom{x}{k} \leq x^{\pi(x)}. \tag{16}$$

Proof: Let x be fixed. It is clear that for any power p^t of the prime p, the number of integers among $1, 2, \ldots, x - 1, x$ divisable by p^t is exactly $[x/p^t]$. For each integer n let

$$\nu_p(n) = \text{the largest exponent } e \text{ such that } p^e | n.$$

Further, let

$$\Delta_e = \{1 \leq d \leq x : p^e | d\}.$$

It is then clear that

$$|\Delta_e| = \left[\frac{x}{p^e}\right].$$

Moreover,

$$\Delta_1 \supseteq \Delta_2 \supseteq \cdots \supseteq \Delta_e \supseteq \Delta_{e+1} \supseteq \cdots.$$

However, for any $1 \leq d \leq x$,

$$d \notin \Delta_{\nu_x(d)+1}, d \in \Delta_{\nu_x(d)} \subseteq \cdots \subseteq \Delta_1.$$

Hence, each $1 \leq d \leq x$ is counted in the sum $\sum_{e \geq 1} |\Delta_e|$ exactly $\nu_x(d)$ times. It follows that

$$\nu_p(x!) = \sum_{d=1}^{x} \nu_p(d) = \sum_{e \geq 1} |\Delta_e| = \sum_{e \geq 1} \left[\frac{x}{p^e}\right].$$

It follows from the last equation and the definition of the binomial coefficient that

$$\nu_p\left(\binom{x}{k}\right) = \nu_p(x!) - \nu_p((x - k)!) - \nu_p(k!) =$$

$$\sum_{e \geq 1} \left(\left[\frac{x}{p^e} \right] - \left[\frac{x-k}{p^e} \right] - \left[\frac{k}{p^e} \right] \right). \tag{17}$$

Since each of the summands in (17) is either 0 or 1, and all summands vanish if $e > \log x / \log p$, it is clear that $\nu_p \left(\binom{x}{k} \right) \leq [\log x / \log p]$ and hence, $p^{\nu_p} \left(\binom{x}{k} \right) \leq x$. Now the claim follows from the fact that

$$\binom{x}{k} = \prod_{p \leq x} p^{\nu_p} \left(\binom{x}{k} \right) \leq x^{\pi(x)}.$$

This completes the proof of the claim. To complete the proof of the theorem, apply (16) to $k = 0, 1, \ldots, x$, and add the resulting inequalities to obtain:

$$2^x = \sum_{k=0}^{x} \binom{x}{k} \leq (x+1) \cdot x^{\pi(x)}.$$

Taking the logarithm of both sides of the inequality above one obtains that

$$\pi(x) \geq \frac{x \log 2}{\log x} - \frac{\log (x+1)}{\log x} > \frac{2x}{3 \log x} \tag{18}$$

(it is easy to verify that the right-hand side of the last inequality is valid for $x > 200$) •

Remark: Zagier in [Z1] also proves that

$$\pi(x) < \frac{17}{10} \cdot \frac{x}{\log x}$$

holds for $x > 2,400$. For more information the reader should consult [E2] (pp. 23 - 25, and exercises 1.8 - 1.13 in pages 30 - 31). Better upper and lower bounds of the quantity $\pi(x)$ are known, e.g. it is known that for all $x \geq 114$,

$$\frac{x}{\log x} < \pi(x) < \frac{5}{4} \cdot \frac{x}{\log x}$$

(see [R11]).

EXERCISES

1: Use $\varphi(4) = 2$ to show that, asymptotically for all x, half the primes $p \leq x$ satisfy $p \equiv 3 \bmod 4$.

2: How many primes of a given length k exist? **Hint:** Use theorem 1.19.

3: The result of the present exercise is used in the proof of theorem 1.7. Let p_n be the n-th prime and let $0 < \alpha < 1$ be any real number. Let $\pi(n, \alpha)$ denote the number of primes in the interval $(p_n^\alpha, p_n]$. Use the prime number theorem to show that for all large enough n, t,

$$\pi(n + t, \alpha) \approx (n + t) \cdot \left(1 - \frac{1}{\alpha p_{n+t}^{1-\alpha}} \right).$$

In particular, for any $2 \le k \le n$ there exist arbitrarily large integers t such that

$$\pi\left(t, \frac{k^2 - 1}{k^2} \right) > n. \tag{19}$$

4: Prove that the right hand side of inequality (18) holds, for all $x > 200$. **Hint:** Reduce to a simpler inequality and use a hand calculator.

1.16   Continued Fractions

For any two positive real numbers α, β, let $[\alpha, \beta] = \alpha + 1/\beta$. This notation is extended by induction to sequences $\alpha_1, \ldots, \alpha_n, \ldots$ of positive real numbers by the equation:

$$[\alpha_1, \ldots, \alpha_{n+1}] = [\alpha_1, [\alpha_2, \ldots, \alpha_{n+1}]].$$

For any real number $\alpha > 0$, define the sequence $\alpha_1, \alpha_2, \ldots, \alpha_n, \ldots$ of reals and the sequence $a_1, a_2, \ldots, a_n, \ldots$ of nonnegative integers as follows: $\alpha_1 = \alpha$, $a_n = \lfloor \alpha_n \rfloor = $ the greatest integer $\le \alpha_n$, and

$$\alpha_{n+1} = \frac{1}{\alpha_n - a_n},$$

i.e $\alpha_n = [a_n, \alpha_{n+1}]$. The sequence $[a_1], [a_1, a_2], \ldots, [a_1, \ldots, a_n], \ldots$, defined as above from the given real number α, is called **the continued fraction expansion** of α.

   Remark 1: Notice that if $\alpha_n = a_n$, then α_{n+i} is undefined for all $i > 0$.
   Remark 2: For all n,

$$\alpha_n = [a_n, \alpha_{n+1}] = [a_n, a_{n+1}, \alpha_{n+2}] = \cdots.$$

In particular,

$$\alpha = [a_1, \alpha_2] = [a_1, a_2, \alpha_3] = \cdots.$$

The continued fraction expansion $[a_1], [a_1, a_2], \ldots, [a_1, \ldots, a_n], \ldots$ of the real number α **breaks-up** if for some n, $\alpha_n = a_n$.

The following observation, which is an immediate consequence of the definitions above and of the Euclidean algorithm, will be useful in the sequel: if d is the divisor and r is the remainder in the Euclidean division $x = yd + r$, where $x > y > r > 0$ and $\gcd(x, y) = 1$, then

$$d = \left\lfloor \frac{x}{y} \right\rfloor \text{ and } \left[d, \frac{y}{r} \right] = \frac{x}{y}.$$

Theorem 1.21 *A real number > 0 is rational if and only if its continued fraction expansion breaks-up.*

Proof: Let $\alpha > 0$ be a real number with continued fraction expansion $[a_1, a_2], \ldots, [a_1, \ldots, a_n], \ldots$. If for some n, $a_n = \alpha_n$, then an easy computation shows that $\alpha = [a_1, \ldots, a_{n-1}, \alpha_n] = [a_1, \ldots, a_{n-1}, a_n]$ is rational.

Conversely, assume that $\alpha = a/b$ is rational. Use the Euclidean algorithm to define sequences

$$0 < r_n < r_{n-1} < \cdots < r_1 < r_0 = b < r_{-1} = a, d_1, d_2, \ldots, d_n, d_{n+1}$$

such that

$$a = d_1 b + r_1, b = d_2 r_1 + r_2,$$

$$r_1 = d_3 r_2 + r_3, \ldots, r_{n-2} = d_n r_{n-1} + r_n, r_{n-1} = d_{n+1} r_n.$$

It follows by induction on i that

$$\alpha_i = \frac{r_{i-2}}{r_{i-1}}, \ a_i = d_i, \text{ for } i = 1, \ldots, n + 1.$$

In particular,

$$\alpha_{n+1} = \frac{r_{n-1}}{r_n} = d_{n+1} = a_{n+1} \bullet$$

Let $[a_1, a_2], \ldots, [a_1, \ldots, a_n], \ldots$ be the continued fraction expansion of the real number $\alpha > 1$; define the sequences

$$A_{-1}, A_0, A_1, \ldots, A_n, \ldots, B_{-1}, B_0, B_1, \ldots, B_n, \ldots,$$

as follows:

$$A_{-1} = 0, A_0 = 1, B_{-1} = 1, B_0 = 0 \text{ and}$$

$$A_n = a_n A_{n-1} + A_{n-2}, B_n = a_n B_{n-1} + B_{n-2}.$$

The fraction A_n/B_n is called the n-th **convergent** of α.

The basic properties of the convergents can be found in the theorem below.

Theorem 1.22 *Let $\alpha > 0$ be a real number with continued fraction expansion $[a_1, a_2], \ldots, [a_1, \ldots, a_n], \ldots$ and convergents A_n/B_n. For any integer $n \geq 0$ for which α_{n+1} is defined, the following hold*

(i) $A_n B_{n-1} - A_{n-1} B_n = (-1)^n$.

(ii) $\gcd(A_n, B_n) = 1$.

(iii) $A_0 < A_1 < \cdots < A_n < \cdots, \quad B_0 < B_1 < \cdots < B_n < \cdots$.

(iv) $\alpha = (A_n \alpha_{n+1} + A_{n-1})/(B_n \alpha_{n+1} + B_{n-1}), n \geq 1$.

(v) $|\alpha - A_n/B_n| < 1/(B_n B_{n+1}) < 1/B_n^2$.

(vi) $A_n/B_n - A_{n-1}/B_{n-1} = (-1)^n/(B_n B_{n-1}), n > 1$.

(vii) $A_n/B_n - A_{n-2}/B_{n-2} = a_n(-1)^{n-1}/(B_n B_{n-2}), n > 2$.

(viii) $A_{2n-1}/B_{2n-1} < A_{2n+1}/B_{2n+1} < \alpha < A_{2n}/B_{2n} < A_{2n-2}/B_{2n-2}$.

(ix) $\lim_{n \to \infty} A_n/B_n = \alpha$.

Proof: The proof of the theorem, although long and detailed, is straightforward by induction on n and is left as an exercise to the reader. Notice that (ix) follows from (v) and the fact that the sequence B_n has exponential growth. In fact, an easy induction on n, using the definitions of A_n, B_n, will show that $A_n, B_n \geq f_n \geq R^{n-2}$, where R is the golden mean. Hence, $n \leq 2 + \log_R B_n$, $2 + \log_R A_n$, where $n > 1$, and the number of steps needed to compute A_n (respectively B_n) is equal to $O($number of steps needed to compute $f_n)$ •

Theorem 1.23 *For any reals $\alpha > 0$ and $r \geq 1$, there exist integers A, B such that $1 \leq B \leq r$ and*

$$\left| \frac{A}{B} - \alpha \right| < \frac{1}{rB}.$$

Proof: Let A_n/B_n denote the n-th convergent of α. Without loss of generality it can be assumed that if $\alpha = a/b$ is rational, then $b > r$ (otherwise the theorem is trivial). In this case one can choose n large enough such that $B_n \leq r \leq B_{n+1}$. Setting $A = A_n, B = B_n$, the theorem follows easily from part (v) of theorem 1.22 •

A rational A/B is called a **Diophantine approximation** of the real number $\alpha > 0$ if and only if $B > 0$, $\gcd(A, B) = 1$, and for all integers C, D with $D \leq B$ and $C/D \neq A/B$, the inequality $|A - B\alpha| < |C - D\alpha|$ holds. It is easy to see that if A/B is a Diophantine approximation of $\alpha > 0$, then for all integers C, D,

$$D \leq B \text{ and } C/D \neq A/B \Rightarrow \left| \frac{A}{B} - \alpha \right| < \left| \frac{C}{D} - \alpha \right|.$$

The following theorem will be essential in the study of the $1/p$ pseudorandom generator.

Theorem 1.24 *Let A, B be positive integers such that $\gcd(A, B) = 1$ and let α be a positive real. Then the following statements hold:*

(i) A/B is a Diophantine approximation of $\alpha \Rightarrow A/B$ is a convergent of α.

(ii) $|\alpha - A/B| < 1/(2B^2) \Rightarrow A/B$ is a Diophantine approximation of α.

Proof: (i) First notice that

$$\frac{A_2}{B_2} < \frac{A_4}{B_4} < \cdots < \alpha < \cdots < \frac{A_3}{B_3} < \frac{A_1}{B_1}.$$

At first it will be shown that A/B is either a convergent or else lies between two convergents of α. Indeed, assume on the contrary

$$\frac{A_1}{B_1} < \frac{A}{B}.$$

Recall that $a_1/1 = A_1/B_1$. It follows from the definition of Diophantine approximation that

$$\left|\frac{a_1}{1} - \alpha\right| < \left|\frac{A}{B} - \alpha\right| = \frac{|A - \alpha B|}{B} \leq |A - \alpha B| < \left|\frac{a_1}{1} - \alpha\right|,$$

which is a contradiction. Hence, $A_1/B_1 \geq A/B$. Next, assume on the contrary that

$$\frac{A_2}{B_2} > \frac{A}{B}.$$

Recall that $B_2 = a_2$. It follows that

$$\left|\frac{A}{B} - \alpha\right| > \left|\frac{A}{B} - \frac{A_2}{B_2}\right| \geq \frac{1}{B_2 B}.$$

Thus,

$$|A - \alpha B| > \frac{1}{B_2} = \frac{1}{a_2} \geq \frac{1}{\alpha_2} = |a_1 - \alpha| = |A_1 - \alpha B_1|,$$

which contradicts the definition of Diophantine approximation. It follows that

$$\frac{A_2}{B_2} \leq \frac{A}{B} \leq \frac{A_1}{B_1}.$$

Now it can be shown that A/B is a convergent. Indeed, assume on the contrary that A/B lies strictly between two convergents, i.e.

$$\frac{A_{n+1}}{B_{n+1}} < \frac{A}{B} < \frac{A_{n-1}}{B_{n-1}}.$$

A contradiction will be derived by distinguishing two cases.

Case 1: n is odd (see figure 7).

$$\frac{A_2}{B_2} \ \frac{A_4}{B_4} \ \cdots \ \frac{A_{n-1}}{B_{n-1}} \ \frac{A}{B} \ \frac{A_{n+1}}{B_{n+1}} \ \cdots \ \alpha \ \cdots \ \frac{A_n}{B_n} \ \frac{A_{n-2}}{B_{n-2}} \ \cdots \ \frac{A_3}{B_3} \ \frac{A_1}{B_1}$$

Figure 7: The Convergents of α

$$\left| \frac{A_n}{B_n} - \frac{A_{n-1}}{B_{n-1}} \right| = \frac{|(-1)^n|}{B_n B_{n-1}} =$$

$$\frac{1}{B_n B_{n-1}} > \left| \frac{A}{B} - \frac{A_{n-1}}{B_{n-1}} \right| \geq \frac{1}{B B_{n-1}}.$$

It follows that $B \geq B_n$. Moreover,

$$\left| \frac{A}{B} - \alpha \right| \geq \left| \frac{A}{B} - \frac{A_{n+1}}{B_{n+1}} \right| \geq \frac{1}{B B_{n+1}} \geq \frac{1}{(B_n \alpha_{n+1} + B_{n-1}) B}$$

and

$$\left| \alpha - \frac{A_n}{B_n} \right| = \left| \frac{A_n \alpha_{n+1} + A_{n-1}}{B_n \alpha_{n+1} + B_{n-1}} - \frac{A_n}{B_n} \right| = \frac{1}{(B_n \alpha_{n+1} + B_{n-1}) B_n}.$$

It follows that

$$|A_n - \alpha B_n| = \frac{1}{B_{n+1}} \leq |A - \alpha B| < |A_n - \alpha B_n|,$$

since $B_n \leq B$, and A/B is a Diophantine approximation of α, which is a contradiction.

Case 2: n is even.

This is omitted because it is similar to the proof of case 1. Hence the proof of (i) is complete.

(ii) Assume on the contrary that A/B is not a Diophantine approximation of α. This means that there exist integers C, D with $D \leq B$ and
$C/D \neq A/B$ such that the following inequality holds:

$$|A - B\alpha| \geq |C - D\alpha|. \tag{20}$$

In the proof below it will be assumed that $\alpha < A/B$. The case $\alpha > A/B$
is treated similarly. Notice that $|AD - CB| \geq 1$, and hence,

$$\left| \frac{A}{B} - \frac{C}{D} \right| \geq \frac{1}{BD}. \tag{21}$$

Case 1: $C/D < A/B < \alpha$.
In this case one has

$$0 < \frac{A}{B} - \frac{C}{D} < \alpha - \frac{C}{D} = \frac{D\alpha - C}{D} \leq \frac{B\alpha - A}{D} =$$

$$\left(\alpha - \frac{A}{B} \right) \cdot \frac{B}{D} < \frac{B}{D} \cdot \frac{1}{2B^2} = \frac{1}{2BD},$$

which contradicts inequality (21).
Case 2: $A/B < C/D < \alpha$.
In this case one uses $D \leq B$ to obtain

$$0 < \frac{C}{D} - \frac{A}{B} < \alpha - \frac{A}{B} < \frac{1}{2B^2} \leq \frac{1}{2BD},$$

which contradicts inequality (21).
Case 3: $\alpha < C/D$.

$$0 < \frac{C}{D} - \alpha = \frac{C - D\alpha}{D} \leq \frac{A - B\alpha}{D} = -\frac{B}{D}\left(\alpha - \frac{A}{B} \right).$$

Consequently,

$$0 < \frac{C}{D} - \frac{A}{B} = \frac{C}{D} - \alpha + \alpha - \frac{A}{B} \leq -\frac{B}{D}\left(\alpha - \frac{A}{B} \right) + \left(\alpha - \frac{A}{B} \right)$$

$$= \left(1 - \frac{B}{D} \right)\left(\alpha - \frac{A}{B} \right) = \frac{D - B}{D}\left(\alpha - \frac{A}{B} \right) < \frac{D - B}{D} \cdot \frac{1}{2B^2}$$

$$\leq \frac{B}{D} \cdot \frac{1}{2B^2} = \frac{1}{2BD},$$

which contradicts inequality (21). This completes the proof •

EXERCISES

1: Give the details of the proof of Theorem 1.22.

2: What is the limit of the sequence $[1, 1], [1, 1, 1], \ldots$?

3: Give the details of the proof of case 2 of part (i) of theorem 1.24.

4: Give the details of the proof of part (ii) of theorem 1.24 in the case where $\alpha > A/B$.

1.17 Bibliographical Remarks

The approach taken in this section is to provide a self-contained introduction to all the material on number theory necessary to understand the results on the security of pseudorandom generators (section 4) and public key cryptosystems (section 5). There are many nice introductory and advanced books in number theory, including [W1], [V2], [L14], [N3], [K9], and [S3]. Since the present chapter is intended to empasize techniques useful to understand the security of public key cryptosystems, the material presented is combined with the study of the complexity of certain problems in number theory. Several more algorithms in computational number theory can be found in [K2], as well as in [A8].

Example 1.3 is the modern reformulation of a problem posed by Sun Tzu[1] in the fourth century AD:

> We have a number of things but we do not know exactly how many. If we count them by threes we have two left over. If we count them by fives we have three left over. If we count them by sevens we have two left over. How many things are there?

For more information on Lamé's theorem (1.2) see [K2] (page 343). The result on (k, n) threshold schemes is originally due to [S9]. However, the construction of (k, n) threshold schemes from (k, n) threshold sequences given in theorem 1.7 follows the presentation of [M8]. In addition, [M8] gives a different way to construct (k, n) threshold sequences.

The publication of Gauss's monumental *Disquisitiones Arithmeticae* (see [G3]) in 1801 opened a new era for number theory. The wealth and elegance of this work, which he completed between 1796 and 1798 while a student in Göttingen, influenced the development of number theory for centuries to come. The characterization in theorem 1.9 of those m for which Z_m^* is

---

[1]See J. Needham, Science and Civilization in China, Vol. 3, pp. 119 - 122, Cambridge University Press, 1959.

cyclic, as well as the Law of Quadratic Reciprocity (theorem 1.13) were first
proved by Gauss in [G3]. The interested reader can find more information
on Artin's conjecture in [S3], pp. 80 - 83, 222 - 225, as well as in [H2], pp.
74 - 75.

The Law of Quadratic Reciprocity is very useful in solving Diophantine
equations. According to Gesternhaber more than 150 proofs of the Law of
Quadratic Reciprocity have so far appeared in the literature, including 8
given by Gauss himself. The present simple proof appears in [G4]. Some
interesting proofs and comments on the law of Quadratic Reciprocity can
also be found in [P3].

A procedure for finding square roots modulo a prime number first appeared in [B3]. The present proof of theorem 1.15 is from [A4].

The algorithm given in theorem 1.18 is from [P6]. The problem of computing efficiently the index of a number x modulo a prime number p is
in general open. However, the fastest known algorithm for computing the
$\text{index}_{p,g}$, which runs in time

$$O\left(2^{\sqrt{\log p \cdot \log \log p}}\right),$$

is due to Adleman (see [A1]).

A complete proof of theorem 1.19 can be found in [L2] (part 6) or [P10]
(pp. 131 - 139). A further generalization of the prime number theorem was
given by E. Landau in 1911: if $\pi_r(n) =$ the number of integers $\leq n$ which
can be expressed as the product of r pairwise distinct primes then

$$\pi_r(n) \sim \frac{1}{(r-1)!} \cdot \frac{n(\log \log n)^{r-1}}{\log n}.$$

The proof of the weaker version of the prime number theorem 1.20 presented in subsection 1.15 is due to Chebyshev and follows closely the presentation of Zagier in [Z1]. For more information the reader can consult the
beautiful expository articles: *Prime Numbers*, by Mardzanisvili and Postnikov in [M2] and *Die ersten 50 Millionen Primzahlen*, by Zagier in [Z1].

For a more thorough study of the theory of continued fractions the reader
should consult [P2] or the number theory books cited above.

2   PRIMALITY TESTS

There are problems that one poses,
and there are problems that pose themselves.
(H. Poincaré)

2.1   Introduction

Prime numbers have fascinated mathematicians at least since Euclid's time. Primality testing from its outset in ancient Greece to the 1st World War was limited mostly to calculations done by hand. Then, in 1926 D. H. Lehmer built a machine for factoring and primality testing (which is known as the *Bicycle-chain Sieve*), using *a sawhorse, bicycle chains and other readily available materials*.[1] The advent of electronic computers since the 2nd World War has changed all this and has brought to the forefront the problem of how to test the primality of a given integer efficiently. In recent years, prime numbers and primality testing have become very important for the construction of secure pseudorandom generators and public key cryptosystems.

This section attempts to give an account of recent work on primality testing. The sieve of Eratosthenes (subsection 2.2) is still useful in listing all the primes less than or equal a given integer. Subsections 2.3, 2.4 give two tests of theoretical significance: Wilson's and Lucas's tests. Subsection 2.5 includes the Sum of Two Squares test. Subsection 2.6 studies the number of steps needed to prove the primality of a given prime, using only the converse of Fermat's theorem. Subsections 2.7, 2.8 and 2.9 study the primality of integers of specific forms, including Fermat and Mersenne numbers. The Extended Riemann Hypothesis (abbreviated ERH) is explained in subsection 2.10. Subsections 2.11, 2.12, 2.13 and 2.14 give three tests which prove that, assuming ERH, primality can be tested in polynomial time.

It is still an open problem to determine whether the set of binary representations of prime numbers is computable in deterministic polynomial time. Thus, it is useful to look for efficient probabilistic primality tests. Two *probabilistic (Monte Carlo)* primality tests are given in subsections 2.17 (Solovay

---

[1]See C. Pomerance, *The Search for Prime Numbers*, Scientific American, Dec. 1982, pp. 136 - 147.

- Strassen) and 2.18 (Rabin). In practice, to test the primality of a given integer n, it is convenient to apply a Monte Carlo test. If n is composite this might be detected in short time; otherwise, there is strong evidence that n might be prime, in which case one applies any of the known fast (non polynomial) deterministic tests.

The test in subsection 2.15 is inspired from the tests based on ERH and is of practical value. The section concludes with an account of the Rumeley - Adleman algorithm in subsection 2.19.

2.2   The Sieve of Eratosthenes

The sieve of Eratosthenes can be useful if one wants to determine all the primes less than or equal a given positive integer x, assuming that x is relatively small. To do this list all the numbers from 2 up to x in their natural order in the sequence

$$2, 3, 4, 5, 6, 7, 8, 9, 10, 11, 12, 13, 14, 15, \ldots, x.$$

Starting from 2, the first prime in the sequence, delete all the multiples $2m$ of 2 such that $2 < 2m \leq x$. The resulting sequence is

$$2, 3, 5, 7, 9, 11, 13, 15, \ldots, x.$$

Next, starting from 3, the next prime in the sequence, delete all the multiples $3m$ of 3 such that $3 < 3m \leq x$. The resulting sequence is

$$2, 3, 5, 7, 11, 13, \ldots, x.$$

In general, if the resulting sequence at the $t-$th stage is

$$2, 3, 5, 7, 11, 13, \ldots, p, \ldots, x,$$

where p is the $t-$th prime, then delete all the multiples pm of p such that $p < pm \leq x$. Continue in this manner untill you exhaust all primes less than or equal to x. If at some stage in the course of this procedure a number k has dropped then k is composite, else it is prime. It is clear that the above procedure will give a list of all the primes less than or equal to x.

With minor alterations in this procedure, it is easy to see that in order to check the primality of x one only needs to continue the process up to the t-th stage, where if p is the t-th prime, then $p \leq \sqrt{x}$; moreover at the t-th stage one need only delete all multiples pm such that $p^2 \leq pm \leq x$.

EXERCISES

1: Prove the assertions made in the last paragraph of the subsection above.

2.3   Wilson's Test

The following test requires computation of factorials and is not of practical significance.

Theorem 2.1 *For any positive integer n the following are equivalent:*
(1) n is prime
(2) $(n-1)! \equiv -1 \bmod n$.

Proof: Without loss of generality it can be assumed that $n > 2$.
$(1) \Rightarrow (2)$
For each $a \in Z_n^*$, the congruence $ax \equiv 1 \bmod n$ has a unique solution modulo n, say a^{-1} (here one uses the primality of n). Since

$$a^2 \equiv 1 \bmod n \Leftrightarrow a \equiv 1 \bmod n \text{ or } a \equiv (n-1) \bmod n,$$

it follows that the only fixed points of the mapping $a \to a^{-1}$ are the numbers $1, n-1$. Thus, after writing all the factors of the product $(n-1)! = 1 \cdot 2 \cdot 3 \cdots (n-1)$ (except for $1, n-1$) in pairs a, a^{-1} and cancelling out, it will follow that $(n-1)! \equiv (n-1) \equiv -1 \bmod n$.
$(2) \Rightarrow (1)$
Assume on the contrary that n is composite. Let $n = ab$, where $a, b > 1$. Then it is clear that $a|(n-1)!$. Hence, by assumption $a|(n-1)$. But this is a contradiction since $a|n$ •

It appears that Wilson's test has only theoretical value. However it can be used to obtain a list of all the primes. Indeed, for each integer n let $r(n) = $ the remainder in the division of $(n-1)!$ by $n(n-1)/2$. It is clear that if n is composite then $r(n) = 0$. On the other hand, if $n > 2$ is prime, then by Wilson's theorem $n|(n-1)! + 1$. It follows that $(n-1)/2|r(n)$, $n|r(n) + 1$ and $r(n) < n(n-1)/2$. Hence there exist $s \geq 2$ and $t \geq 0$ such that $r(n) = s(n-1)/2$ and $r(n) + 1 = tn$. It is now easy to see that $2tn = sn - s + 2$. This in turn implies $n|s - 2$, and hence, $s = 2$ and $r(n) = n - 1$. Hence, the following theorem has been proved (see [D5], page 428).

Theorem 2.2 *(Barinaga)* $\{r(n) + 1 : r(n) > 0\}$ *is exactly the set of odd prime numbers* •

EXERCISES

1: For any positive integer $n > 4$ the following are equivalent:
(1) n is composite
(2) $(n - 1)! \equiv 0 \bmod n$.
(3) $(n - 1)! \not\equiv -1 \bmod n$.

2.4   Lucas's Test

Theorem 2.3 *For any positive integer n the following are equivalent:*
(1) n is prime
(2) There exists $g \in Z_n^*$ such that $g^{n-1} \equiv 1 \bmod n$, but for all primes $p|(n-1)$, $g^{(n-1)/p} \not\equiv 1 \bmod n$.

Proof: $(1) \Rightarrow (2)$
If n is prime then the proof follows from Gauss's theorem on the cyclicity of the multiplicative group Z_n^*. Let g be a generator of this group. It can be verified easily that this g satisfies (2).
$(2) \Rightarrow (1)$
Let g satisfy (2) and let m be the order of g in the group Z_n^* i.e. m = the least t such that $g^t \equiv 1 \bmod n$. Since $g^{n-1} \equiv 1 \bmod n$, it follows that $m|(n-1)$. On the other hand, the second part of (2) implies that m cannot be a proper divisor of $n-1$. It follows that $m = n-1$. Further, the theorem of Euler-Fermat implies that $g^{\varphi(n)} \equiv 1 \bmod n$. Hence, $m = n - 1|\varphi(n)$ and consequently $n - 1 = \varphi(n)$. It follows that n is prime •

Lucas's test like Wilson's test does not provide any efficient algorithm to test the primality of a given integer n. However, the following corollary of the proof of theorem 2.3 shows that if the factorization of $n-1$ is known, then it can be used to test if a given $g \in Z_n^*$ generates the multiplicative group Z_n^*.

Theorem 2.4 *For any positive integer n and any $g \in Z_n^*$ the following are equivalent:*
(1) g generates Z_n^*.
(2) $g^{n-1} \equiv 1 \bmod n$ and for all primes $p|(n-1)$, $g^{(n-1)/p} \not\equiv 1 \bmod n$ •

EXERCISES

1: Show that for any positive integer n the following statements are equivalent:

(1) n is prime.

(2) $\varphi(n) = n - 1$.

2: Complete the details of the proof of theorem 2.4.

2.5   Sum of Two Squares Test

Let $\nu_m(t) = $ largest k such that $m^k | t$. The following lemma will be essential for the present as well as for later subsections.

Lemma 2.1 *Let* $n = p_1^{k_1} \cdots p_r^{k_r}$ *be the prime factorization of an odd integer* n, *where* $p_1, \ldots, p_r$ *are distinct primes. Put* $\nu = \min\{\nu_2(p_i - 1) : i = 1, \ldots, r\}$ *and* $s = \prod_{i=1}^{r} \gcd(m, \varphi(p_i^{k_i}))$. *Then it can be shown that*

(1) $x^m \equiv 1 \bmod n$ *has exactly* s *solutions.*

(2) $(\exists x)(x^m \equiv -1 \bmod n) \Leftrightarrow \nu_2(m) < \min\{\nu_2(p_i - 1) : i = 1, \ldots, r\}$.

(3) If $x^m \equiv -1 \bmod n$ *has a solution then it must have exactly* s *solutions.*

Proof: For each $i = 1, \ldots, r$ let g_i be a generator of $Z^*_{p_i^{k_i}}$. Taking the indices of both sides of the congruence $x^m \equiv a \bmod n$ one obtains the congruences

$$m \cdot \text{index}_{g_i}(x) \equiv \text{index}_{g_i}(a) \bmod \varphi(p_i^{k_i}), \text{ for } i = 1, \ldots, r. \qquad (1)$$

If $a = 1$, then $\text{index}_{g_i}(1) = 0$, and hence congruences (1) become

$$m \cdot \text{index}_{g_i}(x) \equiv 0 \bmod \varphi(p_i^{k_i}), \text{ for } i = 1, \ldots, r. \qquad (2)$$

If $a = -1$, then $\text{index}_{g_i}(-1) = \varphi(p_i^{k_i})/2$, and hence congruences (1) become

$$m \cdot \text{index}_{g_i}(x) \equiv \frac{\varphi(p_i^{k_i})}{2} \bmod \varphi(p_i^{k_i}), \text{ for } i = 1, \ldots, r. \qquad (3)$$

Part (1) of the lemma follows from congruences (2) and the theorem on solving linear congruences. On the other hand the same theorem implies that congruences (3) have a solution if and only if $\gcd(m, \varphi(p_i^{k_i})) | \varphi(p_i^{k_i})/2$, for each $i = 1, \ldots, r$. However, it is easy to see that this last equivalence holds exactly when $\nu_2(m) < \min\{\nu_2(p_i - 1) : i = 1, \ldots, r\}$ •

For each n let $r(n)$ denote the number of distinct prime factors of n and let $\rho(n) = |\{a \in Z_n^* : a^2 \equiv -1 \bmod n\}|$. It is an immediate consequence of lemma 2.1 that for all odd integers $n > 2$,

$$\rho(n) = \begin{cases} 2^{r(n)} & \text{if } \exists x(x^2 \equiv -1 \bmod n) \\ 0 & \text{if } \forall x(x^2 \not\equiv -1 \bmod n) \end{cases}$$

The main result leading to the Sum of Two Squares test is the following:

Theorem 2.5 *For all odd integers $n > 2$ the following statements are equivalent:*

(1) $\exists x(x^2 \equiv -1 \bmod n)$.
(2) $\exists a, b(n = a^2 + b^2 \text{ and } \gcd(a, b) = 1)$.

Proof: $(2) \Rightarrow (1)$
Let $n = a^2 + b^2$, $\gcd(a, b) = 1$. It is clear that $\gcd(b, n) = 1$. Hence, b is invertible modulo n and $a \cdot b^{-1} \bmod n$ is a solution of the congruence $x^2 \equiv -1 \bmod n$.
$(1) \Rightarrow (2)$
Let z be an arbitrary solution of $x^2 \equiv -1 \bmod n$. It follows from the theory of continued fractions that there exists a rational k/b with $\gcd(k, b) = 1, 1 \le b \le \sqrt{n}$ such that

$$\left| \frac{z}{n} + \frac{k}{b} \right| < \frac{1}{b\sqrt{n}} \tag{4}$$

(see theorem 1.23). Put $a = zb + kn$ and use equation (4) to show that $|a| < \sqrt{n}$. It is clear from the definition of a that $a^2 + b^2 \equiv 0 \bmod n$. Since $0 < a^2 + b^2 < 2n$, it follows that $a^2 + b^2 = n$. Substituting the value of $a = zb + kn$ in the last equation, using the congruence $z^2 \equiv -1 \bmod n$ and dividing through by n one obtains that

$$1 = \left(\frac{z^2 + 1}{n} b + kz \right) b + ka.$$

However the last equation implies that $\gcd(a, b) = 1$ •
A more careful analysis of the proof of theorem 2.5 shows that

Theorem 2.6 *For all odd integers $n > 2$ if z is a solution of the congruence $x^2 \equiv -1 \bmod n$ then there exists exactly one ordered pair (a, b) such that*

$$a, b > 0, \ \gcd(a, b) = 1, \ n = a^2 + b^2, \ bz \equiv a \bmod n.$$

Proof:

Existence:

Consider the integers a, b defined in the course of the proof of $(1) \Rightarrow (2)$ in theorem 2.5. If $a > 0$ then all the conditions of the theorem are satisfied by the pair (a, b). If $a < 0$, then $(-a)z \equiv (-b)z^2 \equiv b \bmod n$. Hence, all the conditions of the theorem are satisfied by the pair $(b, -a)$.

Uniqueness:

Let $(a, b), (a_1, b_1)$ be two pairs satisfying the conclusion of the theorem. Using Diophantus's identity (see exercise 2) it follows that $n^2 = (aa_1 + bb_1)^2 + (ab_1 - ba_1)^2$ and $aa_1 + bb_1 \equiv (1 + z^2)bb_1 \equiv 0 \bmod n$. These imply that $aa_1 + bb_1 = n$ and $ab_1 - ba_1 = 0$. Thus, $a = a_1, b = b_1$ •

If n can be represented as the sum of the squares of the components of the pair (a, b) then it can also be represented as the sum of squares of the components of each of the pairs

$$(a, b), (-a, b), (a, -b), (-a, -b), (b, a), (-b, a), (b, -a), (-b, -a).$$

It follows from theorem 2.6 that for any odd $n > 2$ there exist exactly $4\rho(n)$ pairs (a, b) such that $\gcd(a, b) = 1, n = a^2 + b^2$.

If $n = a^2 + b^2 = a_1^2 + b_1^2$, with $\gcd(a, b) = \gcd(a_1, b_1) = 1$, then the pairs $(a, b), (a_1, b_1)$ are called **essentially identical** if and only if $\{a^2, b^2\} = \{a_1^2, b_1^2\}$. The integer n is said to have an **essentially unique representation** as a sum of two squares if n is the sum of two nonzero squares $n = a^2 + b^2$, with $\gcd(a, b) = 1$, and all such representations of n are essentially identical. It is now easy to prove the following:

Theorem 2.7 *(Sum of Two Squares Test, Euler) For any odd $n > 2$ the following statements are equivalent:*

(1) n is prime

(2)(a) n is not a nontrivial power of a prime

(b) n has an essentially unique representation as a sum of two squares of integers •

EXERCISES

1: Show that a prime $n > 2$ can be written as a sum of two squares if and only if $n \equiv 1 \bmod 4$.

2: Prove the following identity of Diophantus:

$$(a^2 + b^2)(a_1^2 + b_1^2) = (aa_1 + bb_1)^2 + (ab_1 - ba_1)^2.$$

Conclude that if each of n, m is a sum of two squares, so is their product.

3: Show that for any odd $n > 2$ there exist exactly $4\rho(n)$ pairs (a, b) such that $\gcd(a, b) = 1, n = a^2 + b^2$.

4: Determine all the integers that can be expressed as a sum of two squares. **Hint:** Use lemma 2.1 and theorem 2.5.

5: (**Euler**) Show that the Fermat number $F_5 = 2^{2^5} + 1$ is not prime. **Hint:** $F_5 = (62, 264)^2 + (20, 449)^2 = (2^{16})^2 + 1^2$. In fact, it is also known that $F_5 = 641 \cdot 6, 700, 417$ (see also [S3], page 58).

2.6   Pratt's Test

Fermat's theorem asserts that if n is prime then $a^{n-1} \equiv 1 \bmod n$, for all $a \in Z_n^*$. Pratt's test is concerned with the number of steps needed to verify that a given integer n is prime, using only the converse of Fermat's theorem. Call (a, n), where n is a positive integer and $a \in Z_n^*$, a **Fermat pair** if and only if either $(a, n) = (1, 2)$ or $a \geq 2$ and $a^{n-1} \equiv 1 \bmod n$.

Example 2.1 *(1) If p is prime then (a, p) is a Fermat pair, for all $a \in Z_p^*$.*
(2) None of $(5, 12), (7, 12), (11, 12)$ is a Fermat pair.
(3) $(2, 341)$ is a Fermat pair, while $(3, 341)$ is not (see [S3], page 118).

Define a partial ordering $\prec$ on Fermat pairs by

$$(b, m) \prec (a, n) \Leftrightarrow m | (n - 1) \text{ and } a^{(n-1)/m} \not\equiv 1 \bmod n.$$

It is clear from the definition of $\prec$ above that there are no infinite $\prec$ descending sequences, i.e. infinite sequences $(a_1, n_1), (a_2, n_2), \ldots, (a_k, n_k), \ldots$ such that

$$\cdots \prec (a_k, n_k) \prec \cdots \prec (a_1, n_1)$$

For such a partial ordering it makes sense to define for each Fermat pair (a, n) the rank of (a, n) by

$$\text{rank}(a, n) = \sup\{\text{rank}(b, m) + 1 : (b, m) \prec (a, n)\}.$$

Call a sequence $(a_1, n_1), \ldots, (a_k, n_k)$ of Fermat pairs, where $k > 1$, a **Pratt sequence** for the Fermat pair (a, n) if and only if for each $i = 1, \ldots, k$, $(a_i, n_i) \prec (a, n)$ and $n - 1 = n_1 \cdots n_k$.

For any (possibly empty) set S of Fermat pairs, let $\Gamma(S)$ denote the set of Fermat pairs (a, n) such that either (a, n) has no $\prec$ predecessor or else there exists a Pratt sequence $(a_1, n_1), \ldots, (a_k, n_k)$ for (a, n) such that for all

$i = 1, \ldots, k$, $(a_i, n_i) \in S$. Finally, for each $t \geq 0$ let the sets $\Gamma^{<t}$ and Γ^t of Fermat pairs be defined by induction on t as follows:

$$\Gamma^{<t} = \bigcup_{r<t} \Gamma^r \text{ and } \Gamma^t = \Gamma(\Gamma^{<t}).$$

In addition, let

$$\Gamma^\infty = \bigcup_{t\geq 0} \Gamma^t.$$

It is an immediate consequence of the definition that the operator Γ is monotone i.e. $S \subseteq S' \Rightarrow \Gamma(S) \subseteq \Gamma(S')$. Using this, and $\prec$ induction it can be shown easily that the sequence Γ^t satisfies the following properties:
(1) $t < t' \Rightarrow \Gamma^t \subseteq \Gamma^{t'}$.
(2) For all t, $\Gamma^t \subseteq \Gamma(\Gamma^t)$.
(3) $\Gamma(\Gamma^\infty) = \Gamma^\infty$.

Theorem 2.8 *For any Fermat pair (a, n) the following are equivalent:*
(1) $(a, n) \in \Gamma^\infty$.
(2) n is prime and a generates Z_n^*.

Proof: $(1) \Rightarrow (2)$
It will be shown by induction on t that for all Fermat pairs (a, n),

$$(a, n) \in \Gamma^t \Rightarrow n \text{ is prime and } a \text{ generates } Z_n^*.$$

If $t = 0$, then it will be shown that $\Gamma^0 = \{(1, 2)\}$. Indeed, let $(a, n) \in \Gamma^0$. By definition of Γ, (a, n) does not have an $\prec$ predecessor. If $n > 2$, then write $n - 1 = q_1 \cdots q_k$, where $q_1, \ldots, q_k$ are the distinct prime powers dividing $(n - 1)$. For each $i = 1, \ldots, k$, let a_i be a generator of $Z_{q_i}^*$. Then it is clear that $(a_i, q_i) \not\prec (a, n)$. This however implies that $a^{(n-1)/q_i} \equiv 1 \bmod n$ for all $i = 1, \ldots, k$. Consequently, $a = 1$, which is a contradiction. Hence, $(a, n) = (1, 2)$. In the general case where $t > 0$, let $(a, n) \in \Gamma^t$. By definition of Γ^t, $(a, n) \in \Gamma(\bigcup_{r<t} \Gamma^r)$. Hence, there exists an $r < t$ and a Pratt sequence $(a_1, n_1), \ldots, (a_k, n_k)$ for (a, n) such that for all $i = 1, \ldots, k$, $(a_i, n_i) \in \Gamma^r$ and $n - 1 = n_1 \cdots n_k$. It follows from the induction hypothesis that for each $i = 1, \ldots, k$, n_i is prime and a_i generates $Z_{n_i}^*$. Moreover, each $(a_i, n_i) \prec (a, n)$, and hence $a^{(n-1)/n_i} \not\equiv 1 \bmod n$. It follows from Lucas's test that n is prime. In addition, a generates Z_n^*.
$(2) \Rightarrow (1)$
This direction will be proved by induction on the rank of the Fermat pair (a, n). If $\text{rank}(a, n) = 0$ then (a, n) has no $\prec$ predecessor. Hence, as

in the proof of $(1) \Rightarrow (2)$ it can be shown that $(a, n) = (1, 2)$. In general, if $n > 2$, write $n - 1 = p_1 \cdots p_k$, where $p_1, \ldots, p_k$ are primes. For each $i = 1, \ldots, k$, let a_i be a generator of $Z^*_{p_i}$. It is then clear that $(a_i, p_i) \prec (a, n)$, and hence $\text{rank}(a_i, p_i) < \text{rank}(a, n)$, for all $i = 1, \ldots, k$. It follows from the induction hypothesis that for all $i = 1, \ldots, k$, $(a_i, p_i) \in \Gamma^\infty$. Hence, $(a, n) \in \Gamma(\Gamma^\infty) = \Gamma^\infty$, and the proof of the theorem is complete $\bullet$

Example 2.2 *Consider the Fermat pair* $(6, 971)$. *Notice that* $971 - 1 = 2 \cdot 5 \cdot 97$, $97 - 1 = 2^5 \cdot 3$, $5 - 1 = 2^2$, $3 - 1 = 2$. $\prec$ *predecessors of* $(6, 971)$ *are* $(1, 2), (2, 5), (5, 97)$; $\prec$ *predecessors of* $(5, 97)$ *are* $(1, 2), (2, 3)$; *the only* $\prec$ *predecessor of* $(2, 5)$ *and* $(2, 3)$ *is* $(1, 2)$. *It is clear that* $\text{rank}(1, 2) = 0$, $\text{rank}(2, 3) = \text{rank}(2, 5) = 1$, $\text{rank}(5, 97) = 2$, $\text{rank}(6, 971) = 3$. *Moreover,* $(6, 971) \in \Gamma^3$.

For each Fermat pair $(a, n) \in \Gamma^\infty$ let

$$|a, n|_\Gamma = \text{ smallest } t \geq 0 \text{ such that } (a, n) \in \Gamma^t.$$

In the next result an upper bound of the quantity $|a, n|_\Gamma$ will be determined which depends only on n. Let $(a, n) \in \Gamma^\infty$ such that $(a, n) \neq (1, 2)$. Then there exists a Pratt sequence $(a_1, n_1), \ldots, (a_k, n_k)$ for (a, n) such that $n - 1 = n_1 \cdots n_k$ and

$$|a, n|_\Gamma = \max\{|a_i, n_i|_\Gamma + 1 : i = 1, \ldots, k\}.$$

It follows by induction that

$$|a, n|_\Gamma \leq \max\{\log_2 n_i + 1 : i = 1, \ldots, k\} \leq$$

$$\log_2(n_1 \cdots n_k) = \log_2(n - 1) < \log_2 n.$$

Thus, the following theorem has been proved:

Theorem 2.9 *For any prime* n *and any generator* a *of the group* Z^*_n,

$$|a, n|_\Gamma \leq \log_2 n \bullet$$

An immediate consequence of the above results is also the following:

Theorem 2.10 *For any integer* $n > 1$ *the following statements are equivalent:*
   (1) n *is prime.*
   (2) $\exists a((a, n)$ *is a Fermat pair and* $(a, n) \in \Gamma^{\lfloor \log_2 n \rfloor})$ $\bullet$

For each prime n let $\Pi(n)$ be the number of divisions and exponentiations needed to prove the primality of n. To test the primality of n write $n - 1 = p_1 \cdots p_k$, where $p_1, \ldots, p_r$ are primes. Consider a generator a of Z_n^* and verify the following two properties:

(1) each p_i is prime

(2) $a^{(n-1)/p_i} \not\equiv 1 \bmod n$, for $i = 1, \ldots, k$,

where property (1) is of course proved recursively. It is now easy to show by induction on n that

$$\Pi(n) \leq 2k + \sum_{i=1}^{k} \Pi(p_i) \leq 2k + \sum_{i=1}^{k}(-2 + 3\log_2 p_i) \leq -2 + 3\log_2 n.$$

Hence it has been shown that

Theorem 2.11 *For any prime n the number of divisions and exponentiations needed to prove the primality of n, using only the converse of Fermat's theorem, is at most $-2 + 3\log_2 n$* •

EXERCISES

1: Show that $2^{340} \equiv 1 \bmod 341$, but $3^{340} \equiv 56 \bmod 341$.

2: Show that $\prec$ has no infinite descending sequences.

3: Show that the operator Γ defined above satisfies:

(1) $t < t' \Rightarrow \Gamma^t \subseteq \Gamma^{t'}$.

(2) For all t, $\Gamma^t \subseteq \Gamma(\Gamma^t)$.

(3 $\Gamma(\Gamma^\infty) = \Gamma^\infty$.

4: Let **NP** (respectively **Co-NP**) be the class of problems which are solvable (respectively whose complements are solvable) in nondeterministic polynomial time (see [G2] for more details on the classes **NP, Co-NP**). Let PR be the set of binary representations of prime numbers. Show that $PR \in$ **NP∩Co-NP**. **Hint:** Given n, guess a generator a of Z_n^* and a prime factorization of $n - 1$. Then use the proof of theorem 2.11 (see also [A8], page 23).

2.7 Proth's Test

This and the next two tests can be used to verify the primality of positive integers of specific forms. Proth's test is concerned with numbers of the form $k2^n + 1$. Its proof requires the following lemma.

Lemma 2.2 (Pocklington) *Let $n = ab + 1 > 1$, where $0 < a \le b + 1$. Assume that for any prime divisor p of b there exists an integer x such that $x^{n-1} \equiv 1 \bmod n$ and $\gcd(x^{(n-1)/p} - 1, n) = 1$. Then n is prime.*

Proof: Assume on the contrary that n is not prime and let q be a prime factor of n which is $\le \sqrt{n}$. By assumption, for every prime factor p of b there exists an integer x_p such that

$$\mathrm{order}_q(x_p) | (n-1) \text{ and } \mathrm{order}_q(x_p) \nmid \frac{n-1}{p},$$

where $\mathrm{order}_q(x) = $ least t such that $x^t \equiv 1 \bmod q$. Let p^k be the largest power of the prime p such that $p^k | b$. Then $\mathrm{order}_q(x_p) = sp^k$, for some integer s. Considering the prime factorization of b and using the last assertion one can find an integer x such that $\mathrm{order}_q(x) = b$. It follows that $q - 1 \ge b$ and hence,

$$q^2 \ge (b+1)^2 \ge a(b+1) = ab + a \ge n.$$

In particular, $q^2 = n$, $a = 1$ and $a = b + 1$, which is a contradiction •

It is now easy to prove Proth's theorem.

Theorem 2.12 (Proth) *Assume $3 \nmid k$, $k \le 2^n + 1$ and $3 < 2^n + 1$. Then the following statements are equivalent:*
(1) $k2^n + 1$ is prime.
(2) $3^{k2^{n-1}} \equiv -1 \bmod(k2^n + 1)$.

Proof: $(2) \Rightarrow (1)$

This is immediate from the previous lemma, with $a = k$, $b = 2^n + 1$ and $x = 3$.

$(1) \Rightarrow (2)$

Using Euler's criterion, it is enough to show that 3 is a quadratic non-residue modulo $k2^n + 1$. Since $3 \nmid k$, $k2^n + 1 \equiv 2 \bmod 3$. Hence,

$$(k2^n + 1 | 3) = (2|3) = -1.$$

Using Gauss's law of quadratic reciprocity one easily obtains that

$$(3|k2^n + 1) = (-1)^{k2^{n-1}} \cdot (k2^n + 1|3) = -1 \; \bullet$$

EXERCISES

1: Let $n = ap^k + 1 > 1$, where p is prime, $a \le p^k + 1$ and $p \nmid a$. If x is such that $x^{n-1} \equiv 1 \bmod n$ and $\gcd(x^{(n-1)/p} - 1, n) = 1$ then each prime factor q of n satisfies $q \equiv 1 \bmod p^k$. **Hint:** Imitate the proof of lemma 2.2.

2.8 Pepin's Test

Suppose that $2^n + 1$ is prime. It will be shown that $n = 2^m$, for some integer $m \geq 0$. Indeed, assume on the contrary that $n = k \cdot 2^m$, where k is odd > 1. Put $a = 2^{2^m}$. Then

$$2^n + 1 = a^k + 1 = (a+1)(a^{k-1} - a^{k-2} + a^{k-3} - \cdots + 1),$$

which contradicts the primality of $2^n + 1$.

For each $n \geq 0$, let the n−th **Fermat number** be defined by

$$F_n = 2^{2^n} + 1.$$

Pepin's test is used to verify the primality of Fermat numbers, and is an immediate consequence of Proth's theorem.

Theorem 2.13 *(Pepin) For each $n \geq 1$, the following are equivalent:*
(1) F_n is prime.
(2) $3^{(F_n - 1)/2} \equiv -1 \bmod F_n$ •

According to [S3], page 80, [W2], page 134, and [B8], the Fermat numbers F_0, F_1, F_2, F_3, F_4 are primes, but all of $F_5, \ldots, F_{19}, F_{21}$ are composite. The status of F_{20} is not known. Other Fermat composites, for $n \geq 23$, are listed in [W2] . Moreover no other Fermat prime seems to be known.

EXERCISES

1: Show that for all $k \geq 0$, $F_{k+1} = F_0 \cdots F_k + 2$. Hence, the Fermat numbers are relatively prime to each other.

2: Show that the Fermat numbers F_0, F_1, F_2, F_3, F_4 are primes.

2.9 Lucas-Lehmer Test

It is easy to show that if $2^n - 1$ is prime so is n. Indeed, assume on the contrary that $2^n - 1$ is prime but n is composite. Let $n = ab$ be two nontrivial factors of n and put $x = 2^a$. Then one can show that

$$2^n - 1 = x^b - 1 = (x-1)(x^{b-1} + x^{b-2} + \cdots + x + 1),$$

which is a contradiction.

The Lucas-Lehmer test can be used to determine the primality of the so called **Mersenne integers**, i.e. integers of the form $2^p - 1$, where p is prime. For each prime p, let the Mersenne number corresponding to p be defined by

$$M_p = 2^p - 1.$$

Remark 1: It is not known if there exist infinitely many Mersenne primes or infinitely many Mersenne composites. $M_2, M_3, M_5, M_7, M_{13}, M_{17}$ are primes. All the remaining known Mersenne primes are listed in the table of Figure 1.

p with $2^p - 1$ prime	Discoverer	Year	Machine
19	Cataldi	1588	–
31	Euler	1722	–
61	Pervushin	1883	–
89	Powers	1911	–
107	Powers	1914	–
127	Lucas	1876	–
521 607 1,279 2,203 2,281	Lehmer − Robinson	1952	SWAC
3,217	Riesel	1957	BESK
4,253 4,423	Hurwitz − Selfridge	1961	IBM 7090
9,689 9,941 11,213	Gillies	1963	ILIAC 2
19,937	Tuckerman	1971	IBM 360
21,701	Nickel − Noll	1978	CYBER 174
23,209	Noll	1978	CYBER 174
44,497	Slowinsky − Nelson	1979	CRAY−1
86,243	Slowinsky	1982	CRAY

Figure 1: Table of Mersenne Primes

The main result to be used in the proof of the Lucas-Lehmer test is the following:

Lemma 2.3 (**H. W. Lenstra**) *Let A be a commutative ring with unit, which includes Z_n as a subring. Let $s > 0$ be an integer. Further, assume that there exists an $\alpha \in A$ such that $\alpha^s = 1$ but for all prime $q|s$, $\alpha^{s/q} - 1$ is invertible in A. If for some integer $t > 0$,*

$$\prod_{i=0}^{t-1} \left(x - \alpha^{n^i}\right)$$

is a polynomial with coefficients in Z_n then for any $r|s$, there exists an i such that $r \equiv n^i$ mod$s$.

Proof: Assume that the hypothesis of the lemma is true. Let r be a divisor of n. It is required to show that $r \equiv n^i$ mod$s$, for some i. Without loss of generality it can be assumed that r is prime. Since $r|n$, $n = rk = 0$, for some k, and hence r is a zero divisor in A. Clearly, $I = \{x \in A : xk = 0\}$ is an ideal of A such that $r \in I$. Let M be a maximal ideal containing r and consider the field $B = A/M$. The hypothesis of the lemma implies that the multiplicative order of $\beta \equiv \alpha$ mod$M$ in B is exactly s (this is because no invertible element can belong to a maximal ideal). By assumption, the polynomial

$$p(x) = \prod_{i=0}^{t-1} \left(x - \beta^{n^i} \right)$$

has coefficients in Z_n. Since $r \equiv 0$ mod$M$ and $r|n$, it can also be assumed without loss of generality that $p(x) \in Z_r[x]$. Moreover, $p(\beta) = 0$. The mapping $x \to x^r$ is a homomorphism of B which leaves Z_r fixed. It follows that $p(\beta^r) = 0$, and hence $\beta^r = \beta^{n^i}$ for some $0 \le i < t$. The rest of the proof follows from the fact that the multiplicative order of β in B is exactly s •

Define the sequence e_k by induction on k as follows:

$$e_1 = 4 \text{ and } e_{k+1} = e_k^2 - 2.$$

Theorem 2.14 *(Lucas-Lehmer) For all $m > 2$ the following statements are equivalent:*

(1) $M_m = 2^m - 1$ is prime.

(2) $e_{m-1} \equiv 0$ modM_m.

Proof: (H. W. Lenstra) If $m = 2k$ is even, then $M_m = 2^{2k} - 1 = 3(4^{k-1} + 4^{k-2} + \cdots + 1)$ and hence M_m is not prime. In addition, it can be shown by induction on $t > 2$ that $e_{t-1} \equiv -1$ mod3. In particular, $e_{m-1} \not\equiv 0$ modM_m (since $3|M_m$). Thus, without loss of generality it can be assumed that m is odd.

Put $n = M_m$ and consider the element $a \equiv 2^{(m+1)/2}$ mod$n$ of Z_n^*. It is then clear that

$$a^2 \equiv 2^{m+1} \equiv (2^m - 1) + (2^m + 1) \equiv 2 \text{ mod}n.$$

Consider the quotient ring

$$A = \frac{Z_n^*[x]}{(x^2 - ax - 1)},$$

where $(x^2 - ax - 1)$ is the ideal generated from the polynomial $x^2 - ax - 1$ and let α be the image of x in A. Since $x^2 - ax - 1$ is of degree 2 it is clear that

$$A = \{s + t\alpha : s, t \in Z_n^*\}, \quad \alpha^2 = a\alpha + 1.$$

It follows that $\beta = a - \alpha = -\alpha^{-1}$ is the other root of $x^2 - ax - 1$ in A. Moreover, $\alpha + \beta = a$ and $\alpha\beta = -1$. Using this and induction on $k \geq 1$ it follows that

$$\alpha^{2^k} + \beta^{2^k} \equiv e_k \bmod n. \tag{5}$$

Now the proof of the main theorem can be completed easily.

$(1) \Rightarrow (2)$

Assume n is prime. It follows easily from $n = 2^m - 1$, that $n \equiv 1 \bmod 3$ and $n \equiv -1 \bmod 8$. Using the last two congruences, quadratic reciprocity and the formula $(2|n) = (-1)^{(n^2-1)/8}$, it can be shown that $(2|n) = -(3|n) = 1$, and hence $(6|n) = -1$. Since the discriminant of the polynomial $x^2 - ax - 1$ is equal to 6, it follows that A is a quadratic field extension of Z_n^*. Moreover, α, β are conjugate over Z_n^*, being roots of the same polynomial. Considering the automorphism $x \to x^n$ it follows easily that $\alpha^n = \beta$. Thus, $\alpha^{n+1} = \alpha\beta = -1$ and $\beta^{2^{m-1}} = \alpha^{-2^{m-1}}$ (since $\beta = \alpha^{-1}$). It follows from equation (5) that

$$e_{m-1} \equiv \alpha^{2^{m-1}} + \beta^{2^{m-1}} = \alpha^{2^{m-1}} + \alpha^{-2^{m-1}} = 0 \bmod n.$$

$(2) \Rightarrow (1)$

Since $e_{m-1} \equiv 0 \bmod n$ and $\beta^{2^{m-1}} = \alpha^{-2^{m-1}}$, it follows from equation (5) that

$$\alpha^{2^m} \equiv -1 \bmod n \text{ and } \alpha^{2^{m+1}} \equiv 1 \bmod n.$$

The idea is to apply lemma 2.3 to $s = 2^{m+1}$ and the ring $A = Z_n$. The lemma applies because $\alpha^n = \beta$, and hence $x^2 - ax - 1 = (x - \alpha)(x - \alpha^n)$. It follows that for any $r|s$, there exists an i such that $r \equiv n^i \bmod s$. But, $n^2 \equiv (2^m - 1)^2 \equiv 1 \bmod 2^{m+1}$. Hence, for every $r|n$, either $r \equiv 1 \bmod 2^{m+1}$ or $r \equiv n \bmod 2^{m+1}$. It follows that n is prime $\bullet$

Remark 2: A different proof of the Lucas - Lehmer test can be given using the so called **Lucas - Lehmer functions**, which for any two relatively prime integers p, q are defined as follows:

$$u_n(p, q) = \frac{\alpha^n - \beta^n}{\alpha - \beta}, \quad v_n(p, q) = \alpha^n + \beta^n,$$

where α, β are the two roots of the quadratic $x^2 - px + q$ and $n \geq 0$. Many of the properties of the Lucas - Lehmer functions can be found in [W2]. In section 4.5.4. of [K2] the Lucas - Lehmer functions $u_n(4, 1), v_n(4, 1)$ are used to derive theorem 2.14 .

EXERCISES

1: Show that for all n, m, $\gcd(2^n - 1, 2^m - 1) = 2^{\gcd(n,m)} - 1$ (see [S3] theorem 10). Hence, the Mersenne numbers $\{M_p : p$ is prime $\}$ are relatively prime to each other.

2: In the proof of $(1) \Rightarrow (2)$ in theorem 2.14 show that $n \equiv 1 \bmod 3, n \equiv -1 \bmod 8$ as well as $(2|n) = -(3|n) = 1$.

2.10   Extended Riemann Hypothesis

Let C^* denote the multiplicative group of the field of complex numbers. A **character** modulo n is a function $\chi : Z_n^* \to C^*$ which is a group homomorphism between Z_n^* and C^*. Any character χ can be extended to a function $\chi' : Z^* \to C^*$ as follows:

$$\chi'(a) = \begin{cases} \chi(a \bmod n) & \text{if } \gcd(a, n) = 1 \\ 0 & \text{if } \gcd(a, n) \neq 1, \end{cases}$$

where $Z^* = \{n \in Z : n > 0\}$. For simplicity the same symbol will be used for χ, χ'.

For any character χ the **Dirichlet L–function** corresponding to χ is a function L_χ of a single complex variable z defined by the following infinite series:

$$L_\chi(z) = \sum_{n=1}^{\infty} \frac{\chi(n)}{n^z}.$$

Let χ_1 be the character which is identically equal to 1. L_{χ_1} can be meromorphically extended to a unique analytic function defined in the region $\Re(z) > 0$; $z = 1$ is its unique pole with residue 1 ($\Re(z)$ denotes the **real part** of the complex number z). If $\chi \neq \chi_1$ then the series $L_\chi(z)$ converges for $\Re(z) > 0$ and converges absolutely for $\Re(z) > 1$ (e.g. see [K4] theorems 6.10 and 6.25). **The Riemann Hypothesis for the L function L_χ**, abbreviated $RH[L_\chi]$, is the statement: all the zeroes of the function L_χ in the critical strip $0 < \Re(z) \leq 1$ must lie on the line $\Re(z) = 1/2$. **The Extended Riemann Hypothesis**, abbreviated ERH is the statement: for all characters χ, $RH[L_\chi]$ holds.

The following theorem will be essential in understanding the primality tests that follow (see [M11] theorems 13.1 and 13.2).

Theorem 2.15 *(Ankeny-Montgomery) There exists a constant $C > 0$ such that if χ is a nontrivial character modulo n and $RH[L_\chi]$ holds then there exists a prime $p < C \cdot (\log n)^2$ for which $\chi(p) \neq 1$* •

It is a well known result from the theory of finite abelian groups that every finite abelian group G is the direct product of cyclic groups, say $G_1, \ldots, G_r$ (see [K13], part II, chapter VI). For each $i = 1, \ldots, r$, put $e_i = |G_i|$ and let

$$\xi_i = \exp\left(\frac{2\pi i}{e_i}\right)$$

be an e_i-th root of unity. Clearly, each cyclic group G_i is isomorphic to the cyclic group $\{\xi_i^j : j = 0, \ldots, e_i - 1\}$. It follows that the group G can be embedded into the group C^*.

Let $f : Z_n^* \to G$ be a nontrivial abelian group homomorphism. The **image** $Im(f) = \{f(a) : a \in Z_n^*\}$ of Z_n^* under f is also an abelian group and as such it can be embedded into C^*; let $g : Im(f) \to C^*$ be the embedding thus defined and let χ be the modulo n character $g \circ f$. It is then clear that for any $a \in Z_n^*$, $\chi(a) \neq 1$ if and only if $f(a) \neq 1$.

As an immediate consequence of the remarks above and theorem 2.15 it can be shown that

Theorem 2.16 *(Assume ERH) There exists a constant $C > 0$ such that if $f : Z_n^* \to G$ is a nontrivial homomorphism between the abelian groups Z_n^* and G, then there exists a prime $p < C \cdot (\log n)^2$ for which $f(p) \neq 1$* •

 EXERCISES

1: Show that every finite abelian group can be embedded into the multiplicative group C^* of complex numbers.

2.11   Solovay-Strassen Deterministic Test

This test is based on the following theorem:

Theorem 2.17 *For any odd integer $n > 1$ the following statements are equivalent:*
   (1) n is prime.
   (2) $(\forall a \in Z_n^*)(a^{(n-1)/2} \equiv (a|n) \bmod n)$.

Proof: (1) $\Rightarrow$ (2) is an immediate consequence of Euler's criterion. For each $a \in Z_m^*$ let the **order** of a modulo m, abbreviated $\text{order}_m(a)$, be the least nonegative integer t such that $a^t \equiv 1 \bmod m$. Call n **square free** if $(\forall p)(p|n \Rightarrow p^2 \nmid n)$. To prove (2) $\Rightarrow$ (1) the following lemma will be used.

Lemma 2.4 *If* $(\forall a \in Z_n^*)(a^{n-1} \equiv 1 \bmod n)$, *then n is square-free.*

Proof of the lemma: Let p be a prime dividing n and let p^t be the largest power of p dividing n. Let g be a generator of $Z_{p^t}^*$. Use the Chinese remainder theorem to find an $a \in Z_n^*$ such that

$$a \equiv g \bmod p^t \text{ and } a \equiv 1 \bmod(n/p^t).$$

It follows from the hypothesis that $a^{n-1} \equiv g^{n-1} \equiv 1 \bmod p^t$. Hence,

$$\text{order}_{p^t}(g) = \varphi(p^t) = p^{t-1}(p-1)|(n-1).$$

Thus, $t = 1$, as desired $\bullet$

Proof of the main theorem:

The lemma above implies that if n is composite then it must be of the form $n = p_1 \cdots p_r$, where $p_1, \ldots, p_r$ are distinct primes and $r \geq 2$. Let a be a quadratic nonresidue modulo p_1. Use the Chinese remainder theorem to find an $x \in Z_n^*$ such that $x \equiv a \bmod p_1$ and $x \equiv 1 \bmod(n/p_1)$. Hypothesis (2) of the theorem implies that

$$(x|n) = (x|p_1) \cdots (x|p_r) = (a|p_1) = -1 \equiv x^{(n-1)/2} \bmod n.$$

However, this contradicts $x \equiv 1 \bmod p_2$ $\bullet$

Using theorems 2.17 and 2.16 it can be shown that

Theorem 2.18 *(Assume ERH) There exists a constant $C > 0$ such that for any odd integer $n > 1$ the following statements are equivalent:*
(1) n is prime.
(2) For all $a \in Z_n^*$ such that $a < C \cdot (\log n)^2$, $a^{(n-1)/2} \equiv (a|n) \bmod n$.

Proof: (1) $\Rightarrow$ (2) is trivial. To prove the converse assume (2) is true, but n is composite. Let $C > 0$ be the constant of theorem 2.16. Consider the abelian group $G = \{a^{(n-1)/2} \cdot (a|n) \bmod n : a \in Z_n^*\}$ and the group homomorphism $\chi : Z_n^* \to G$ such that $\chi(a) = a^{(n-1)/2} \cdot (a|n) \bmod n$. Theorem 2.17 implies that χ is nontrivial. A contradiction follows easily from theorem 2.16 $\bullet$

2.12   A Variant of the Solovay-Strassen Test

This test constitutes a simplification of the Solovay-Strassen deterministic test because it makes no mention of the Langrange-Jacobi symbol. It is based on the following theorem.

Theorem 2.19 *For any odd integer $n > 1$ the following statements are equivalent:*

   (1) n is prime.
   (2) $(\forall a \in Z_n^*)(a^{(n-1)/2} \equiv \pm\, 1 \bmod n)$ and $(\exists a \in Z_n^*)(a^{(n-1)/2} \equiv -1 \bmod n)$.

Proof: $(1) \Rightarrow (2)$

This is an immediate consequence of Euler's criterion and the primality of n.

$(2) \Rightarrow (1)$

It follows from lemma 2.4 that n is square free i.e. $(\forall p)(p|n \Rightarrow p^2 \nmid n)$. Hence, without loss of generality it can be assumed that n is the product of the distinct primes $p_1, \ldots, p_r$. The groups Z_n^* and $Z_{p_1}^* \times \cdots \times Z_{p_r}^*$ are isomporphic. Since there exists an $a \in Z_n^*$ such that $a^{(n-1)/2} \equiv -1 \bmod n$, there exist $a_i \in Z_{p_i}^*$ such that $a_i^{(n-1)/2} \equiv -1 \bmod p_i$, for $i = 1, \ldots, r$. Consider the nontrivial characters

$$\chi(a) = a^{(n-1)/2} \bmod n, \quad \chi_i(a) = a^{(n-1)/2} \bmod p_i,$$

where $i = 1, \ldots, r$ and let $K, K_1, \ldots, K_r$ be their respective kernels. It is then clear that K is isomorphic to $K_1 \times \cdots \times K_r$ and hence,

$$\frac{\varphi(n)}{2} = |K| = |K_1| \cdots |K_r| = \frac{\varphi(p_1)}{2} \cdots \frac{\varphi(p_r)}{2} = \frac{\varphi(n)}{2^r}.$$

It follows that $r = 1$ and hence n is prime $\bullet$

Using theorem 2.16 the following result can be proved.

Theorem 2.20 *(Assume ERH) There exists a constant $C > 0$ such that for any odd integer $n > 1$ the following statements are equivalent:*
   (1) n is prime.
   (2) $(\forall a < C \cdot (\log n)^2 \text{ in } Z_n^*)(a^{(n-1)/2} \equiv \pm\, 1 \bmod n)$ and
       $(\exists a < C \cdot (\log n)^2 \text{ in } Z_n^*)(a^{(n-1)/2} \equiv -1 \bmod n)$.

Proof: $(1) \Rightarrow (2)$

Assume n is prime. The first part of (2) is an immediate consequence of theorem 2.19. To prove the second part use theorem 2.19 to conclude that the character $\chi(a) = a^{(n-1)/2} \bmod n$ is nontrivial and then use theorem 2.16.

(2) $\Rightarrow$ (1)

It is enough to prove that both conditions of part (2) of theorem 2.19 are true. The second part is immediate. To prove the first part assume on the contrary $(\exists a \in Z_n^*)a^{(n-1)/2} \not\equiv \pm 1 \bmod n$. Consider the quotient group G/H, where $G = Z_n^*$ and $H = \{1, -1\}$. Let $\chi : Z_n^* \to G/H$ be the character $\chi(a) = $ the equivalence class of $a^{(n-1)/2} \bmod n$ modulo H, which belongs to the group G/H. Using theorem 2.16 one easily obtains an $a < C \cdot (\log n)^2$ such that $\chi(a) \neq H$ (H is the unit of the group G/H). But this is a contradiction $\bullet$

2.13 Miller's Deterministic Test

Miller's deterministic test is based on the following theorem:

Theorem 2.21 *For any odd integer $n > 1$ write $n - 1 = 2^e u$, with u odd. Then the following statements are equivalent:*

(1) n is prime.

(2) $(\forall a \in Z_n^*)(a^u \not\equiv 1 \bmod n \Rightarrow \exists k < e(a^{2^k u} \equiv -1 \bmod n))$.

Proof: (1) $\Rightarrow$ (2) is an immediate consequence of the theorem of Euler-Fermat and the primality of n. The converse (2) $\Rightarrow$ (1) requires the following:

Lemma 2.5 *Assume that $n = p_1^{k_1} \cdots p_r^{k_r}$ is the prime factorization of n, where $p_1, \ldots, p_r$ are distinct primes. Write $n - 1 = 2^e u$, with u odd and put $\nu = \min\{\nu_2(p_i - 1) : i = 1, \ldots, r\}$. Then the following statements hold:*

(1) $e \geq \nu$.

(2) $e = \nu \Leftrightarrow |\{1 \leq i \leq r : k_i$ is odd and $\nu_2(p_i - 1) = \nu\}|$ is odd.

Proof of the lemma: Clearly $e \geq \nu$ follows easily from

$$n - 1 = (p_r^{k_r} - 1) + \sum_{i=1}^{r-1}(p_i^{k_i} - 1)p_{i+1}^{k_{i+1}} \cdots p_r^{k_r}. \tag{6}$$

Without loss of generality it can be assumed that $1, \ldots, h$ are the indices i for which k_i is odd and $\nu_2(p_i - 1) = \nu$. It is easy to see that

$$(\forall i \geq h + 1)(2^{\nu+1}|p_i^{k_i} - 1) \text{ and } (\forall i \leq h)(2^{\nu+1} \nmid p_i^{k_i} - 1).$$

Hence $p_i^{k_i} \equiv 1 \bmod 2^{\nu+1}$, for $i \geq h+1$. For $i \leq h$, let s_i be odd such that $p_i^{k_i} = 1 + s_i 2^\nu$. By substituting in equation (6) and multiplying out, it is easy to obtain

$$n - 1 \equiv (s_1 + \cdots + s_h)2^\nu \bmod 2^{\nu+1}. \tag{7}$$

It is now immediate from equation (7) that $e = \nu \Leftrightarrow s_1 + \cdots + s_h$ is odd. The result of the lemma follows easily ●

Proof of the theorem: Assume that hypothesis (2) of the theorem is true. Theorem 2.17 implies that it is enough to show $(\forall a \in Z_n^*)(a^{(n-1)/2} \equiv (a|n) \bmod n)$. Indeed, let $a \in Z_n^*$. If $a^u \equiv 1 \bmod n$, then $a^{(n-1)/2} \equiv 1 \bmod n$. Moreover, since u is odd

$$(a|n) = (a|n)^u = (a^u|n) = 1.$$

Hence without loss of generality it can be assumed that $a^u \not\equiv 1 \bmod n$. Hypothesis (2) of the theorem implies that there exists $k < e$ such that

$$a^{2^k u} \equiv -1 \bmod n \text{ and } a^{2^{k+1}u} \equiv 1 \bmod n. \tag{8}$$

Let $n = p_1^{k_1} \cdots p_r^{k_r}$ be the prime factorization of n, where $p_1, \ldots, p_r$ are distinct primes. For each $i = 1, \ldots, r$ let $\nu_i = \nu_2(p_i - 1)$; also let u_i be odd such that $p_i - 1 = 2^{\nu_i} u_i$. Then it is true that $(a|p_i) = (a|p_i)^u \equiv a^{u(p_i-1)/2} \equiv a^{2^{\nu_i - 1}u_i u} \bmod p_i$. Since both u, u_i are odd, it follows from (8) that

$$k = \nu_i - 1 \Rightarrow (a|p_i) = -1, \text{ and } k < \nu_i - 1 \Rightarrow (a|p_i) = 1. \tag{9}$$

Assume on the contrary that $k > \nu_i - 1$, for some $i = 1, \ldots, r$. Then $(a|p_i) \equiv a^{2^{\nu_i - 1}u_i u} \bmod p_i$, and hence $a^{2^{\nu_i}u_i u} \equiv 1 \bmod p_i$, which contradicts congruences (8). It follows that $k \leq \nu - 1 \leq e - 1$. If $k < \nu - 1$ then equations (9) imply that for all $i = 1, \ldots, r$, $(a|p_i) = 1$ and hence also $(a|n) = 1$. Since $k < e-1$ it follows that $a^{(n-1)/2} \equiv 1 \bmod n$. Consequently to complete the proof of the theorem it is enough to consider the case $k = \nu - 1$. Without loss of generality let $1, \ldots, h$ be the indices such that k_i is odd and $\nu_i = \nu$. It follows from equations (9) that $(a|n) = (-1)^{k_1 + \cdots + k_h}$. If $\nu = e$ then the above lemma implies that h is odd. Hence $(a|n) = -1$ and $a^{(n-1)/2} \equiv a^{2^k u} \equiv -1 \bmod n$. On the other hand if $\nu < e$, then h is even and $k + 1 < e$. Moreover, $(a|n) = 1$ and $a^{(n-1)/2} \equiv a^{2^{e-1}u} \equiv 1 \bmod n$. This completes the proof of the theorem ●

The theorem above and theorem 2.16 can be used to show:

Theorem 2.22 *(Assume ERH) There exists a constant $C > 0$ such that for any odd integer $n > 1$ if $n - 1 = 2^e u$, with u odd, then the following statements are equivalent:*

(1) n is prime.

(2) For all $a \in Z_n^*$ such that $a < C \cdot (\log n)^2$,

$$a^u \not\equiv 1 \bmod n \Rightarrow \exists k < e(a^{2^k u} \equiv -1 \bmod n).$$

Proof: $(1) \Rightarrow (2)$ is trivial. To prove the converse assume (2) is true but n is composite. Let $C > 0$ be the constant of theorem 2.16. Assume on the contrary that for some prime p, $p^2 | n$. Consider the abelian group $G = \{a^{p-1} \bmod p^2 : a \in Z_{p^2}^*\}$ and the group homomorphism $\chi : Z_{p^2}^* \to G$ such that $\chi(a) = a^{p-1} \bmod p^2$. The following lemma implies that χ is nontrivial.

Lemma 2.6 *The congruence $x^{p-1} \equiv 1 \bmod p^2$ has at most $p - 1$ solutions.*

Proof of the lemma: Let g be a generator of $Z_{p^2}^*$. Then it is easy to show that the only solutions of the above congruence are

$$g^p \bmod p^2, g^{2p} \bmod p^2, \ldots, g^{(p-1)p} \bmod p^2 \bullet$$

It follows from theorem 2.16 that there exists an integer $a < C \cdot (\log p^2)^2$ such that $a^{p-1} \not\equiv 1 \bmod p^2$. It will be shown that in fact $a^{n-1} \not\equiv 1 \bmod p^2$. Indeed, if $a^{n-1} \equiv 1 \bmod p^2$, then $\text{order}_{p^2}(a)|(n - 1)$ and $\text{order}_{p^2}(a)|\varphi(p^2) = p(p-1)$ imply that $\text{order}_{p^2}(a)|p-1$, which is a contradiction. Hence $a^{n-1} \not\equiv 1 \bmod p^2$, which contradicts the hypothesis of the theorem.

Thus it can be assumed that n is the product of distinct primes. Let p, q be two distinct prime factors of n. Without loss of generality it can be assumed that $\nu_2(p - 1) \geq \nu_2(q - 1)$. Define an integer $d \equiv 1 \bmod 4$ by:

$$d = \begin{cases} pq & \text{if } \nu_2(p - 1) = \nu_2(q - 1) \\ p & \text{if } \nu_2(p - 1) > \nu_2(q - 1) \end{cases}$$

It follows from theorem 2.16 that there exists an $a < C \cdot (\log d)^2 \leq C \cdot (\log n)^2$ such that $(a|d) = -1$. Put $b = a^u$. Since u is odd, it follows that $(b|d) = -1$, and hence $b \not\equiv 1 \bmod d$. It will be shown that for all $j < e$, $b^{2^j} \not\equiv -1 \bmod n$. This clearly contradicts hypothesis (2) of the theorem. Indeed, assume otherwise and let $j < e$ be maximal such that $b^{2^j} \equiv -1 \bmod n$. Then $\text{order}_p(b) = \text{order}_q(b) = 2^{j+1}$. One can now distinguish two cases:

Case 1: $\nu_2(p - 1) > \nu_2(q - 1)$

In this case $2^{j+1}|q-1$ and hence $2^{j+1}|(p-1)/2$. Thus, on the one hand $(b|d) = (b|p) = -1$ and on the other hand $b^{(p-1)/2} \equiv 1 \bmod p$, which contradicts the Euler-Fermat theorem.

Case 2: $\nu_2(p-1) = \nu_2(q-1)$

In this case $(b|d) = (b|p)(b|q) = -1$. It can be assumed, without loss of generality, that $(b|p) = -(b|q) = -1$. Hence $b^{(q-1)/2} \equiv 1 \bmod q$ and $\text{order}_p(b) = \text{order}_q(b)|(q-1)/2$. Since $\nu_2(p-1) = \nu_2(q-1)$, this implies that $\text{order}_p(b)|(p-1)/2$ and hence $b^{(p-1)/2} \equiv 1 \bmod p$, which is a contradiction, since it is true that $(b|p) = 1$ •

EXERCISES

1: (Assume ERH) Using the notation of theorem 2.22 show that if n is composite, then there exists a $k < e$ and an $a \in Z_n^*$ with $a < C \cdot (\log n)^2$ such that $\gcd(a^{2^k u} \bmod n - 1, n) > 1$. **Hint:** Use theorem 2.31.

2.14 An Improvement of Miller's Test

The proof of theorem 2.22 requires the Riemann hypothesis for the L functions corresponding to the characters:

$$\chi(a) = a^{p-1} \bmod p^2, p \text{ is prime and}$$

$$\chi(a) = (a|d),$$

where $d \equiv 1 \bmod 4$ and d is either a prime or the product of two primes. H.W. Lenstra in [L9] has observed that the Riemann hypothesis is not necessary for the characters $\chi(a) = a^{p-1} \bmod p^2$. In fact the following can be shown:

Theorem 2.23 *Assume that the Extended Riemann Hypothesis holds for all L functions of the form $L_d(z) = \sum_{k\geq 1}(k|d)k^{-z}$, where $d \equiv 1 \bmod 4$ and d is either a prime or the product of two primes. Then there exists a constant $C > 0$ such that for any odd integer $n > 1$ if $n - 1 = 2^e u$, with u odd, then the following statements are equivalent:*

(1) n is prime.

(2) For all $a \in Z_n^*$ such that $a < C \cdot (\log n)^2$,

$$a^u \not\equiv 1 \bmod n \Rightarrow \exists k < e(a^{2^k u} \equiv -1 \bmod n).$$

Proof: The proof of (2) $\Rightarrow$ (1) is exactly the same as the proof of theorem 2.22. However, to show that for all prime p, $p^2 \nmid n$, one does not use the ERH but instead the following lemma (due to H. W. Lenstra) which requires no unproved hypothesis.

Lemma 2.7 *For any odd prime p there exists a prime $a < 4(\log p)^2$ such that*

$$a^{p-1} \not\equiv 1 \bmod p^2.$$

This completes the proof of the theorem •

Details of the proof of lemma 2.7 can be found in [L9], page 87.

EXERCISES

1: (H. W. Lenstra) Use lemma 2.7 to give the following improvement of lemma 2.4, which requires no unproved hypothesis: if $n \neq 4$ and $(\forall a < (\log n)^2$ in $Z_n^*)(a^{n-1} \equiv 1 \bmod n)$, then n is square-free. **Hint:** Argue by contradiction. Assume that p is a prime such that $p^2 | n$. First show that n must be odd and then use lemma 2.7.

2.15 Selfridge-Weinberger Test

For each prime p let $F(p) = $ the least positive square-free integer n such that for all prime numbers $q \leq p$, $(q|n) = 1$.

A table of values of $F(p)$ can be found in [L7], from which the table in Figure 2 is extracted.

p	$F(p)$	p	$F(p)$
3	73	53	$22,000,801$
7	$1,009$	67	$175,244,281$
13	$8,089$	79	$898,716,289$
19	$53,881$	101	$10,310,263,441$
29	$117,049$	103	$23,616,331,489$
37	$1,083,289$	127	$196,265,095,009$

Figure 2: Table of Values of $F(p)$

Theorem 2.24 *Let $n > 1$ be an odd integer and suppose that p is a prime such that $p < n < F(p)$. Then the following statements are equivalent:*

(1) n is prime.

$(2)(a)$ $(\forall q \ prime \ \leq p) \gcd(q, n) = 1.$
   (b) *n is not a nontrivial power of a prime.*
   (c) $(\forall q \ prime \ \leq p)(q^{(n-1)/2} \equiv^{\pm} 1 \ \mathrm{mod} n).$
   (d) $(\exists q \ prime \ \leq p)(q^{(n-1)/2} \equiv -1 \ \mathrm{mod} n).$

Proof: $(1) \Rightarrow (2)$

This is an immediate consequence of Euler's criterion, the primality of n, and the minimality of $F(p)$.

$(2) \Rightarrow (1)$

Assume on the contrary that n is composite. Let $n = p_1^{k_1} \cdots p_r^{k_r}$ be the prime factorization of n, where $p_1, \ldots, p_r$ are distinct primes. By assumption $r \geq 2$. For $i = 1, \ldots, r$, write $n - 1 = 2^e u, p_i - 1 = 2^{\nu_i} u_i$, where $u, u_1, \ldots, u_r$ are odd. The basic step in the proof is the following

Claim: $\nu_i = e$, for all $i = 1, \ldots, r$.

Proof of the Claim: Consider an integer $i = 1, \ldots, r$. Since $p_i < n < F(p)$ there exists a prime $q \leq p$ such that $(q|p_i) = -1$. Let $d = \mathrm{order}_{p_i}(q)$. By Euler's criterion $q^{(p_i-1)/2} \equiv -1 \ \mathrm{mod} p_i$. By assumption, $q^{(n-1)/2} \equiv^{\pm} 1 \ \mathrm{mod} p_i$. It follows that $\nu_2(d) = \nu_i$ and $d|n-1$ and hence $\nu_i \leq e$. It remains to show that $\nu_i \geq e$. By assumption there exists a prime $q \leq p$ such that $q^{(n-1)/2} \equiv -1 \ \mathrm{mod} p_i$. On the other hand $q^{p_i-1} \equiv 1 \ \mathrm{mod} p_i$. It follows that $\nu_i \geq e$ and the proof of the claim is complete.

It follows from the claim and lemma 2.5 that there exist two distinct primes p_i, p_j such that $p_i \cdot p_j < n$ (assume for simplicity that $i = 1$ and $j = 2$). By assumption there exists a prime $q \leq p$ such that $(q|p_1 \cdot p_2) = -1$. Without loss of generality it can be assumed that $(q|p_1) = -(q|p_2) = 1$. Moreover it is true that

$$q^{(n-1)/2} \equiv +1 \ \mathrm{mod} n \ \text{or} \ q^{(n-1)/2} \equiv -1 \ \mathrm{mod} n. \tag{10}$$

For $i = 1, 2$ put $d_i = \mathrm{order}_{p_i}(q)$. Since $q^{(p_2-1)/2} \equiv -1 \ \mathrm{mod} p_2, 2^e|d_2$ and hence

$$q^{(n-1)/2} \equiv -1 \ \mathrm{mod} p_2. \tag{11}$$

Since $q^{(p_1-1)/2} \equiv 1 \ \mathrm{mod} p_1, d_1|2^{e-1}u_1$. It follows from congruence (10) that $d_1|(n-1)/2$. Hence,

$$q^{(n-1)/2} \equiv 1 \ \mathrm{mod} p_1. \tag{12}$$

However congruences (10), (11), (12) give a contradiction •

Besides its theoretical value the Selfridge-Weinberger test has practical significance as well. In applications one uses tables of values of the function

$F(p)$ (see the table in figure 2) and then tests the primality of a given integer $p < n < F(p)$ via theorem 2.24.

In addition, Weinberger has shown (unpublished) that assuming ERH there exist constants $c_1, c_2, c_3 > 0$ such that for all n and all primes p,

$$p > (c_1 \log n + c_2 \log\log n + c_3)^2 \Rightarrow n < F(p).$$

2.16 Probabilistic (Monte Carlo) Primality Tests

The main feature of a probabilistic (Monte Carlo) primality test is the construction of a family $P = \{P_n : n \geq 1\}$ of sets of integers such that the following properties hold:

(1) For each $n \geq 1$, $P_n \subseteq Z_n^*$.

(2) Given $b \in Z_n^*$ it is easy to check (i.e. in time polynomial in the length of the integer n) if $b \in P_n$.

(3) If n is prime then $P_n = \emptyset$.

(4) There is a constant $0 < \epsilon < 1$, which is indepedent of n, such that for all sufficiently large composite odd $n \geq 1$, $Pr[x \in Z_n^* : x \notin P_n] \leq \epsilon$.

Such a family $P = \{P_n : n \geq 1\}$ will be called a **primality sequence** and the constant ϵ satisfying condition (4) above is called the **primality constant** corresponding to the family P.

Remark: In practice property (4) above will be true for all $n > n_0$, where n_0 is small (e.g. $n_0 = 1$ in the Solovay-Strassen test and $n_0 = 9$ in the Rabin test).

To any primality sequence P one can associate a primality test, denoted by A_P and defined as follows:

Input: $n > 1$.

Step 1: Choose an integer $b \in Z_n^*$ at random.

Step 2: Check if $b \in P_n$.

Output:

$$A_P(n) = \begin{cases} \text{PRIME} & \text{if } b \notin P_n \\ \text{COMPOSITE} & \text{if } b \in P_n. \end{cases}$$

The following result is now an immediate consequence of the previous definitions.

Theorem 2.25 *Let ϵ be a primality constant corresponding to the primality sequence P. Then for any sufficiently large odd integer $n \geq 1$,*

(1) n is prime $\Rightarrow A_P(n) = PRIME$.

(2) n is odd and composite $\Rightarrow Pr[A_P(n) = PRIME] \leq \epsilon$ •

In other words, if n is prime the test A_P will output the correct answer (i.e. PRIME). However, if n is composite and odd the test A_P may not necessarily output COMPOSITE; in fact it may very well output PRIME. However, the probability of making such an error is less than or equal to ϵ.

If the random choices of b are independent in successive runs of the algorithm A_P then one can significantly improve the probability of error. In fact it is very easy to show the following:

Theorem 2.26 *Let ϵ be a primality constant corresponding to the primality sequence P. Then for any integer $m \geq 1$, and any sufficiently large odd integer n,*

$$n \text{ is composite} \Rightarrow Pr[A_P(n) = PRIME, \ m \ times] \leq \epsilon^m \ \bullet$$

The next two tests are probabilistic primality tests. In each case the primality sequence will be defined and the primality constant corresponding to this sequence will be determined. The probabilistic primality test corresponding to each such sequence P is A_P.

$\boxed{\textbf{EXERCISES}}$

1: Prove theorems 2.25 and 2.26.

2.17   Solovay-Strassen Test

The primality sequence of the Solovay-Strassen test is defined by

$$P_n = \{b \in Z_n^* : b^{(n-1)/2} \not\equiv (b|n) \bmod n\}.$$

It follows from Euler's criterion that $P = \{P_n : n \geq 1\}$ satisfies conditions $(1) - (3)$ of primality sequences. For each n consider the multiplicative group automorphisms $f_n, g_n, h_n : Z_n^* \rightarrow Z_n^*$ defined by

$$f_n(a) = a^{(n-1)/2} \bmod n, \ g_n(a) = (a|n) \bmod n, \ h_n(a) = (a|n) \cdot a^{(n-1)/2} \bmod n.$$

Let K_n, L_n, M_n denote the kernels of the homomorphisms f_n, g_n, h_n respectively. Put $K_n' = \{b \in Z_n^* : f_n(b) \equiv -1 \bmod n\}$, $L_n' = \{b \in Z_n^* : g_n(b) \equiv -1 \bmod n\}$ and $M_n' = \{b \in Z_n^* : h_n(b) \equiv -1 \bmod n\}$. It is clear that $M_n = Z_n^* - P_n$.

Theorem 2.27 *(Monier) For all odd n, if $p_1, \ldots, p_r$ are the distinct prime factors of n, then*

$$|Z_n^* - P_n| = \delta_n \cdot \prod_{i=1}^{r} \gcd\left(\frac{n-1}{2}, p_i - 1\right),$$

where δ_n has one of the values $1/2, 1, 2$.

Proof: It is clear from the definition of K_n and lemma 2.1 that

$$|K_n| = \prod_{i=1}^{r} \gcd\left(\frac{n-1}{2}, p_i - 1\right).$$

On the other hand it is true that $M_n = (K_n \cap L_n) \cup (K_n' \cap L_n')$. Hence,

$$|M_n| = \begin{cases} |K_n \cap L_n| & \text{if } K_n' \cap L_n' = \emptyset \\ 2|K_n \cap L_n| & \text{if } K_n' \cap L_n' \neq \emptyset \end{cases}$$

(if $K_n' \cap L_n' \neq \emptyset$ choose $b_0 \in K_n' \cap L_n'$ and consider the bijective function $b \to bb_0$ to show that $|K_n \cap L_n| = |K_n' \cap L_n'|$). A similar argument using $K_n = (K_n \cap L_n) \cup (K_n \cap L_n')$, the kernel of the homomorphism f_n shows that

$$|K_n \cap L_n| = \begin{cases} |K_n| & \text{if } K_n \cap L_n' = \emptyset \\ (1/2) \cdot |K_n| & \text{if } K_n \cap L_n' \neq \emptyset. \end{cases}$$

Hence $|M_n| = \delta_n |K_n|$ as desired •

Now it is not very difficult to determine the primality constant.

Theorem 2.28 *(Solovay-Strassen) For all composite odd integers n,*

$$\frac{|Z_n^* - P_n|}{\varphi(n)} \leq \frac{1}{2}.$$

Proof: Let $p_1, \ldots, p_r$ be the distinct prime factors of n and suppose that $p_i^{t_i}$ is the largest power of p_i dividing n. It follows from Monier's theorem and the properties of the function φ that

$$\frac{|Z_n^* - P_n|}{\varphi(n)} = \delta_n \cdot \prod_{i=1}^{r} \frac{\gcd\left(\frac{n-1}{2}, p_i - 1\right)}{p_i^{t_i-1}(p_i - 1)}. \tag{13}$$

If for some i, $t_i \geq 2$, then the righthand side of inequality (13) is $\leq \delta_n/3 \leq 2/3$. Hence, $Z_n^* - P_n$ is a proper subgroup of Z_n^* and as such it must be true that $|Z_n^* - P_n| \leq (1/2)\varphi(n)$.

Thus, without loss of generality it can be assumed that for all i, $t_i = 1$. In this case $n = p_1 \cdots p_r$. Assume on the contrary that $Z_n^* = M_n$. Since n is composite, $r \geq 2$. Let g be a generator of $Z_{p_1}^*$. Use the Chinese Remainder theorem to find an $a \in Z_n^*$ such that $a \equiv g \bmod p_1$ and $a \equiv 1 \bmod(n/p_1)$. Since $Z_n^* = M_n$ it is true that $a^{(n-1)/2} \equiv (a|n) \bmod n$. However, $(a|n) = (a|p_1) \cdots (a|p_r) = (a|p_1) = (g|p_1) = -1$. Hence, $a^{(n-1)/2} \equiv -1 \bmod(n/p_1)$, which contradicts $a \equiv 1 \bmod(n/p_1)$ •

As an immediate corollary of equality (13) one can also obtain that

Theorem 2.29 *For all composite odd integers n, if $(n-1)/2$ is odd and r is the number of distinct prime factors of n, then*

$$\frac{|Z_n^* - P_n|}{\varphi(n)} \leq \frac{1}{2^{r-1}} \bullet$$

EXERCISES

1: Show that the sequence $P = \{P_n : n \geq 0\}$ defined above satisfies conditions (1) - (3) of primality sequences.

2: Prove that for all composite odd integers n, if $(n-1)/2$ is odd, $p_1, \ldots, p_r$ are the distinct prime factors of n, and $e = \sum_{i=1}^{r} \nu_2(p_i - 1)$ then

$$\frac{|Z_n^* - P_n|}{\varphi(n)} \leq \frac{1}{2^{e-1}}.$$

Use this to deduce theorem 2.29.

2.18   Rabin's Test

The Rabin primality sequence is defined by

$$P_n = \{b \in Z_n^* : b^{(n-1)/2^e} \not\equiv 1 \bmod n \text{ and } (\forall t > 0)(b^{(n-1)/2^t} \not\equiv -1 \bmod n\},$$

where $e = \nu_2(n-1)$ and the quantifier $\forall t$ above is restricted to all $t \leq e$. It is easy to show that $P = \{P_n : n \geq 1\}$ satisfies conditions (1) - (3) of primality sequences. It is clear that $Z_n^* - P_n =$

$$\{b \in Z_n^* : b^{(n-1)/2^e} \equiv 1 \bmod n \text{ or } (\exists t > 0)(b^{(n-1)/2^t} \equiv -1 \bmod n)\}, \quad (14)$$

where the quantifier $\exists t$ above is restricted to $t \leq e$. The following theorem determines the exact size of this set:

Theorem 2.30 (**Monier**) *Let n be a composite odd integer, with prime factorization $n = p_1^{t_1} \cdots p_r^{t_r}$, where $p_1, \ldots, p_r$ are distinct primes. Write $n - 1 = 2^e u$, $p_i - 1 = 2^{\nu_i} u_i$, with u, u_i odd and let $\nu = \min\{\nu_i : i = 1, \ldots, r\}$. Then the following equality holds:*

$$|Z_n^* - P_n| = \left(1 + \frac{2^{r\nu} - 1}{2^r - 1}\right) \prod_{i=1}^{r} \gcd(u, u_i).$$

Proof: Put $s = \prod_{i=1}^{r} \gcd(u, u_i)$. The leftmost congruence of the set in (14) has exactly s solutions (see lemma 2.1). For any given $t > 0$ the other congruence has a solution if and only if $\nu_2((n-1)/2^t) = e - t < \nu$. Hence, for each $t > e - \nu$ the number of solutions of $b^{(n-1)/2^t} \equiv -1 \bmod n$ is

$$\prod_{i=1}^{r} \gcd\left(\frac{n-1}{2^t}, p_i - 1\right).$$

It follows that

$$|Z_n^* - P_n| = s + \sum_{e-\nu < t \le e} \prod_{i=1}^{r} \gcd\left(\frac{n-1}{2^t}, p_i - 1\right).$$

The theorem now follows easily from

$$\gcd\left(\frac{n-1}{2^t}, p_i - 1\right) = 2^{e-t} \cdot \gcd(u, u_i) \bullet$$

Let R_n be the set

$$\left\{b \in Z_n^* : b^{n-1} \not\equiv 1 \bmod n \text{ or } (\exists t \ge 0) \left[1 < \gcd\left(b^{(n-1)/2^t} - 1, n\right) < n\right]\right\},$$

where $n - 1 = 2^e u$, u is odd and the quantifier $\exists t$ above is restricted to $t \le e$. It is now easy to show that

Theorem 2.31 (**Miller-Rabin-Monier**) *For all odd integers $n > 2$, $P_n = R_n$.*

Proof: Let $b \in Z_n^*$ be arbitrary. For each t such that $2^t | n - 1$ let

$$d(t) = \frac{n-1}{2^t}, \quad x(t) = b^{d(t)}, \quad g(t) = \gcd(x(t) - 1, n).$$

It is very easy to show that for all t such that $2^t | n - 1$, the following hold:
(1) $g(t) = n \Leftrightarrow x(t) \equiv 1 \bmod n$,

(2) $g(t) = n \Rightarrow g(t-1) = n$,
(3) $x(t-1) = x(t)^2$.

Proof of $b \in P_n \Rightarrow b \in R_n$:

Assume on the contrary that $b \in P_n$ but $b \notin R_n$. It follows that there exists an integer $k \leq e$ such that $g(k) = n$. Since $b \in P_n$, $b^{d(e)} \not\equiv 1 \bmod n$ and hence $g(e) \neq n$. It follows that there exists $k < e$ such that

$$g(0) = g(1) = \cdots = g(k) = n > g(k+1) = \cdots = g(e) = 1.$$

But $g(k) = n$. Hence, $x(k+1)^2 \equiv 1 \bmod n$. Therefore $n|(x(k+1)-1)(x(k+1)+1)$. This and $g(k+1) = \gcd(x(k+1)-1, n) = 1$ imply that $x(k+1) \equiv -1 \bmod n$, which in turn contradicts $b \in P_n$.

Proof of $b \in R_n \Rightarrow b \in P_n$:

Assume that $b \notin P_n$. Then either $x(e) \equiv 1 \bmod n$ or $\exists t > 0(x(t) \equiv -1 \bmod n)$. In the first case $b \notin R_n$. Thus, without loss of generality it can be assumed that $x(e) \not\equiv 1 \bmod n$. Choose $k \leq e$ such that

$$x(0) \equiv x(1) \equiv \cdots \equiv x(k-1) \equiv 1, \; x(k) \equiv -1 \bmod n.$$

Using the fact that $x(k) \equiv x(k+j)^{2^j} \equiv -1 \bmod n$, it follows that

$$x(k) - 1 \equiv x(k+1)^2 - 1 \equiv x(k+2)^{2^2} - 1 \equiv \cdots \equiv x(e)^{2^{e-k}} - 1 \equiv -2 \bmod n.$$

However, for all $j \leq e-k$ there exists an integer b_j such that

$$x(k+j)^{2^{2^j}} - 1 \equiv (x(k+j) - 1)b_j \equiv -2 \bmod n.$$

Since n is odd > 2 it follows that $(\forall j \leq e-k)(g(k+j) = 1)$. Since $(\forall j < k)(g(j) = n)$ it follows that $(\forall t)(g(t) = 1 \text{ or } n)$. Hence, $b \notin R_n$ •

It remains to determine the primality constant of the Rabin sequence. Let n be an odd integer with $p_1, \ldots, p_r$ its distinct prime factors. Let $n = p_1^{k_1} \cdots p_r^{k_r}$ be the prime factorization of n and put $q_i = p_i^{k_i}$, where $i = 1, \ldots, r$. Let $t_i = \gcd(\varphi(q_i), n-1)$ and $m_i = \varphi(q_i)/t_i$. In addition put $e_i = \nu_2(t_i)$, $\alpha_i = \max\{e_i - e_j : j = 1, \ldots, r\}$. It is clear that if e_i is minimum among the $\{e_1, \ldots, e_r\}$ then $\alpha_i = 0$. Consider the sets

$$I = \{1 \leq i \leq r : \alpha_i > 0\}, \; J = \{1 \leq i \leq r : \alpha_i = 0\},$$

and put $\alpha = \alpha_1 + \cdots + \alpha_r$, $\beta = |J|$. It is clear that $\beta > 0$ and $\alpha + \beta \geq r$. The following result uses the notation above and is the main theorem of this subsection:

Theorem 2.32 *For any composite odd integer $n > 2$, if the number r of distinct prime factors of n is ≥ 2, then*

$$\frac{|Z_n^* - R_n|}{\varphi(n)} \leq \frac{1}{2^{\alpha+\beta-1}m_1 \cdots m_r}.$$

Proof: Let $b \in Z_n^* - R_n$. Then $b^{n-1} \equiv 1 \bmod n$. For each $i = 1, \ldots, r$ let a_i be a generator of $Z_{q_i}^*$. It follows that there exists an $s_i < \varphi(q_i)$ such that $b \equiv a_i^{s_i} \bmod q_i$. Thus, $b^{n-1} \equiv a_i^{s_i(n-1)} \equiv 1 \bmod q_i$ and $\varphi(q_i)|s_i(n-1)$. Since $\gcd(m_i, n-1) = 1$ and $m_i = \varphi(q_i)/t_i|s_i(n-1)$, it follows that $m_i|s_i$ and $s_i = m_i h_i$, for some $h_i < \varphi(q_i)/m_i$. So for all $i = 1, \ldots, r$,

$$b \equiv a_i^{m_i h_i} \bmod q_i \tag{15}$$

and $s_i(n-1) = m_i h_i(n-1) = \varphi(q_i)h_i\frac{n-1}{t_i}$. An essential step of the proof is the following

Claim: For all $i = 1, \ldots, r$, $2^{\alpha_i}|h_i$.

Proof of the Claim: Without loss of generality it can be assumed that $\alpha_i > 0$. Let j be an index such that $\alpha_i = e_i - e_j > 0$. Let $f_i \geq 0$ be such that $\nu_2(n-1) = e_i + f_i$. Put $\gamma_i = e_i - e_j + f_i$. Then $\nu_2(d(\gamma_i)) = e_j$. In addition, $t_j|d(\gamma_i)$. Hence, $\varphi(q_j) = t_j m_j|m_j d(\gamma_i)$. It follows from congruence (15) that $b^{d(\gamma_i)} \equiv a_j^{m_j h_j d(\gamma_i)} \equiv 1 \bmod q_j$. Hence, $1 < q_j \leq \gcd(b^{d(\gamma_i)} - 1, n)$. Since $b \notin R_n$, $\gcd(b^{d(\gamma_i)} - 1, n) = n$ and hence $b^{d(\gamma_i)} \equiv 1 \bmod n$. Using the last congruence, the fact that a_i generates $Z_{q_i}^*$ as well as congruence (15) it follows that $t_i|d(\gamma_i)h_i$. But this easily implies that $2^{e_i-e_j} = 2^{\alpha_i}|h_i$, which completes the proof of the claim.

Using the above claim and congruence (15) it follows easily that

$$|Z_n^* - R_n| \leq \frac{\varphi(q_1)}{2^{\alpha_1}m_1} \cdots \frac{\varphi(q_r)}{2^{\alpha_r}m_r} \leq \frac{\varphi(n)}{2^{\alpha}m_1 \cdots m_r}.$$

The inequality above shows that the proof of the theorem is complete, if $\beta = 1$. Hence, without loss of generality it can be assumed that $\beta \geq 2$. It follows from the definition of J that for all $i, j \in J$, $e_i = e_j$; let e^* be the common value of the e_j's, for $j \in J$. Put $\gamma_j' = f_j + 1$ (where f_j was defined above) and notice that for $j \in J$ the value of f_j, and hence of γ_j', does not depend on j; let γ be the common value of the γ_j''s, for $j \in J$. It is now clear that

$$\frac{t_j}{2}|d(\gamma) \text{ and } t_j \nmid d(\gamma).$$

On the other hand using congruence (15) it is true that for all $j \in J$,

$$b^{d(\gamma)} \equiv 1 \bmod q_j \Leftrightarrow \varphi(q_j)|h_j m_j d(\gamma) \Leftrightarrow t_j|h_j d(\gamma).$$

However, $b \in Z_n^* - R_n$ and hence $\gcd(b^{d(\gamma)} - 1, n) = 1$ or n. It follows that either $(\forall j \in J)(2|h_j)$ or $(\forall j \in J)(2 \nmid h_j)$. Since $(\forall i \in I)(2^{\alpha_i}|h_i)$, the proof of the theorem is complete •

As a first corollary it can be shown that

Theorem 2.33 *(Rabin) For all odd composite integers $n > 9$,*

$$\frac{|Z_n^* - R_n|}{\varphi(n)} \leq \frac{1}{4}.$$

Proof: If $r \geq 3$ the theorem follows from theorem 2.32. If $r = 2$ then $\alpha + \beta - 1 \geq 1$. Hence the theorem follows from theorem 2.32 if either $m_1 = 2$ or $m_2 = 2$. Assume on the contrary that $m_1 = m_2 = 1$. This last statement implies that $n = p_1 p_2$. Say $p_1 < p_2$. Then $p_2 - 1 = \varphi(p_2)|n - 1 = p_1(p_2 - 1) + (p_1 - 1)$, which is a contradiction. It remains to prove the theorem in the case $r = 1$. Let $n = p^t$, some $t \geq 2$. But,

$$|Z_n^* - R_n| \leq |\{b \in Z_n^* : b^{n-1} \equiv 1 \bmod n\}| \leq \gcd(n - 1, p - 1) = p - 1.$$

It follows that

$$\frac{|Z_n^* - R_n|}{\varphi(n)} \leq \frac{p - 1}{p^{t-1}(p - 1)} = \frac{1}{p^{t-1}}.$$

Since $n > 9$ the proof of the theorem is complete •

Another corollary is the following:

Theorem 2.34 *For all odd integers $n > 2$, if r is the number of distinct prime factors of n, then*

$$\frac{|Z_n^* - R_n|}{\varphi(n)} \leq \frac{1}{2^{r-1}} \bullet$$

EXERCISES

1: Show that the sequence $P = \{P_n : n \geq 0\}$ defined above satisfies conditions (1) - (3) of primality sequences.

2: Using the notation of the proof of theorem 2.32 one can show that

$$\frac{|Z_n^* - R_n|}{\varphi(n)} \geq \frac{1}{2^\delta m_1 \cdots m_r},$$

where $\delta = e_1 + \cdots + e_r$. **Hint:** Use lemma 2.1.

2.19   Rumeley-Adleman Test

The Rumeley-Adleman algorithm (abbreviated as RA) is different from the previously considered probabilistic primality tests. Given as input an odd integer $n > 1$, $RA(n)$ may not converge; however, if $RA(n)$ converges then the test gives the correct answer.

Throughout the proof below n will be an odd integer > 1. For each prime p let $\varsigma_p = \exp(2\pi i/p)$ be a primitive p–th root of unity and consider the cyclic group $G_p = \{\varsigma_p^i : 0 \le i \le p - 1\}$. Let p, q be primes such that $p|q - 1$ and consider a character $\chi_{p,q} = \chi : Z_q^* \to G_p$ of Z_q^* onto G_p. Such characters exist (e.g. let g be a generator of Z_q^* and put $\chi(g^x \bmod q) = \varsigma_p^x$, which is well defined since $p|q - 1$) and are called **characters of order p and conductor q**. Further, consider the ring $Z[\varsigma_p, \varsigma_q] = \{p(\varsigma_p, \varsigma_q) : p(x, y)$ is a polynomial in two variables x, y with integer coefficients $\}$.

For each character χ of order p and conductor q the **generalized Gaussian sum** corresponding to χ is defined by

$$G(a, \chi) = -\sum_{i=1}^{q-1} \chi(i)\varsigma_q^{ia}, \text{ where } a \in Z_q^*.$$

The **Gaussian sum** corresponding to χ is defined by $G(\chi) = G(1, \chi)$.

Now one can prove the following:

Lemma 2.8 *Let* $\chi : Z_q^* \to G_p$ *be a character of order p and conductor q, where $p|q - 1$. Then for any odd integer r the following statements hold:*
(1) $G(a, \chi) = \overline{\chi(a)} \cdot G(\chi)$, for $a \in Z_q^*$.
(2) $G(\chi) \cdot \overline{G(\chi)} = q$.
(3) $G(\chi)^r \equiv \chi(r)^{-r} \cdot G(\chi^r) \bmod(rZ[\varsigma_p, \varsigma_q])$.

Proof: The proof of (1) is immediate from the equations below:

$$G(a, \chi) = -\sum_{i=1}^{q-1} \chi(ia)\overline{\chi(a)}\varsigma_q^{ia} = \overline{\chi(a)}G(\chi).$$

To prove (2) notice that for $a \in Z_q^*$, $\sum_{i=0}^{q-1} \varsigma_q^{ia} = (\varsigma_q^{aq} - 1)/(\varsigma_q^a - 1) = 0$. Hence,

$$G(\chi)\overline{G(\chi)} = -G(\chi)\sum_{i=1}^{q-1} \overline{\chi(i)}\varsigma_q^{-i} = -\sum_{i=1}^{q-1} \varsigma_q^{-i}G(i, \chi) =$$

$$\sum_{i,j=1}^{q-1} \chi(j)\varsigma_q^{i(j-1)} = \sum_{j=1}^{q-1}[\chi(j)\sum_{i=1}^{q-1} \varsigma_q^{i(j-1)}] = q - 1 - \sum_{j=2}^{q-1} \chi(j) = q.$$

It is easy to show that if congruence (3) holds for each of the integers r, s then it must also hold for their product $r \cdot s$. Hence without loss of generality it is enough to prove (3) when r is prime. Using the binomial theorem it can be shown that

$$G(\chi)^r = -\left(\sum_{i=1}^{q-1} \chi(i)\varsigma_q^i\right)^r \equiv -\sum_{i=1}^{q-1} \chi(i)^r \varsigma_q^{ir} \equiv$$

$$-\chi(r)^{-r}\sum_{i=1}^{q-1} \chi(ir)^r \varsigma_q^{ir} \equiv \chi(r)^{-r} G(\chi^r) \bmod(rZ[\varsigma_p, \varsigma_q]) \bullet$$

The next lemma is basic for the proof of the Rumeley-Adleman test.

Lemma 2.9 Let $\chi : Z_q^* \to G_p$ be a character of order p and conductor q, where $p|q-1$. Then for any odd integer r one can show that
(1) If there exists an $\eta(\chi) \in G_p$ such that

$$G(\chi)^r \equiv \eta(\chi)^{-r} G(\chi^r) \bmod(rZ[\varsigma_p, \varsigma_q]), \qquad (16)$$

$$\text{then } \eta(\chi) \equiv G(\chi)^{r^{p-1}-1} \bmod(rZ[\varsigma_p, \varsigma_q]).$$

(2) In particular,

$$\chi(r) \equiv G(\chi)^{r^{p-1}-1} \bmod(rZ[\varsigma_p, \varsigma_q]).$$

Proof: Clearly (2) is an immediate consequence of (1) and part (3) of lemma 2.8. To prove part (1) apply the homomorphism of $Z[\varsigma_p, \varsigma_q]$, which carries ς_p to $\varsigma_p^{r^i}$ and ς_q to ς_q, to congruence (16) above to obtain:

$$G(\chi^{r^i})^r \equiv \eta(\chi)^{-r^{i+1}} G(\chi^{r^{i+1}}) \bmod(rZ[\varsigma_p, \varsigma_q]). \qquad (17)$$

Using this and induction on i it follows easily that

$$G(\chi)^{r^i} \equiv \eta(\chi)^{-ir^i} G(\chi^{r^i}) \bmod(rZ[\varsigma_p, \varsigma_q]). \qquad (18)$$

Now apply congruence (18) to the exponent $i = p-1$ in order to obtain the desired result $\bullet$

Let $r|n$ be such that $\nu_p(r^{p-1}-1) \geq \nu_p(n^{p-1}-1)$. Then $(r^{p-1}-1)/(n^{p-1}-1)$ is a fraction of the form $(p^k a)/b$, where a, b are relatively prime to p and $k \geq 0$. Hence b is invertible in Z_p^* and it makes sense to define

$$\ell_p(r) \equiv \frac{r^{p-1}-1}{n^{p-1}-1} \bmod p.$$

It is clear that $\ell_p(n) = 1$. If one uses the identity

$$(rs)^{p-1} - 1 = (r^{p-1} - 1)(s^{p-1} - 1) + (r^{p-1} - 1) + (s^{p-1} - 1),$$

then the following can be shown:

Lemma 2.10 *Assume that* $\gcd(p, n) = 1$ *and that for all primes* $r|n$,

$$\nu_p(r^{p-1} - 1) \geq \nu_p(n^{p-1} - 1). \tag{19}$$

Then for all integers $r, s|n$, $\ell_p(rs) \equiv \ell_p(r) + \ell_p(s) \bmod p$ •

Remark: If $n^{p-1} \not\equiv 1 \bmod p^2$, then for any $r|n$,

$$\nu_p(r^{p-1} - 1) \geq \nu_p(n^{p-1} - 1).$$

Lemma 2.11 *Let* p *be a prime such that* $\gcd(p, n) = 1$. *Assume there exists a character* $\chi : Z_q^* \to G_p$ *of order* p *and conductor* q *such that* $\gcd(q, n) = 1$ *and* $p|q - 1$. *If there exists an* $\eta(\chi) \in G_p$ *such that* $\eta(\chi) \neq 1$ *and*

$$G(\chi)^n \equiv \eta(\chi)^{-n} G(\chi^n) \bmod(nZ[\varsigma_p, \varsigma_q]), \tag{20}$$

then one can prove that for all $r|n$,
(1) $\nu_p(r^{p-1} - 1) \geq \nu_p(n^{p-1} - 1)$,
(2) $\chi(r) \equiv \eta(\chi)^{\ell_p(r)} \bmod(rZ[\varsigma_p, \varsigma_q])$,
(3) $\chi(n) = \eta(\chi)$ *and* $\chi(r) \equiv \chi(n)^{\ell_p(r)} \bmod(rZ[\varsigma_p, \varsigma_q])$

Proof: It follows from lemma 2.9 (for $r = n$) that

$$\eta(\chi) \equiv G(\chi)^{n^{p-1}-1} \bmod(nZ[\varsigma_p, \varsigma_q]).$$

Assume that $r|n$.
    Let a be the order of $G(\chi)$ in $Z[\varsigma_p, \varsigma_q]/nZ[\varsigma_p, \varsigma_q]$. Since $\eta(\chi) \neq 1$, a does not divide $n^{p-1} - 1$. Since $\eta(\chi)^p = 1$, $a|p(n^{p-1} - 1)$. In addition lemma 2.9 implies that

$$1 \equiv \chi(r)^p \equiv G(\chi)^{p(r^{p-1}-1)} \bmod(rZ[\varsigma_p, \varsigma_q]).$$

Hence it follows that $a = \nu_p(p(n^{p-1} - 1)) \leq \nu_p(p(r^{p-1} - 1))$ and the proof of (1) is complete.
    To prove part (2) write $(r^{p-1} - 1)/(n^{p-1} - 1) = a/b$, where $a, b > 0$ and $b \equiv 1 \bmod p$. It is then clear that $\ell_p(r) \equiv a \bmod p$ and hence

$$\chi(r) \equiv \chi(r)^b \equiv G(\chi)^{b(r^{p-1}-1)} \equiv G(\chi)^{a(n^{p-1}-1)} \equiv$$

$$\eta(\chi)^a \equiv \eta(\chi)^{\ell_p(r)} \operatorname{mod}(rZ[\varsigma_p, \varsigma_q]) \bullet$$

For each integer t put

$$s(t) = \prod \{q : q - 1 | t \text{ and } q \text{ is prime}\}.$$

To study the running time of the Rumeley-Adleman algorithm one needs the following result from analytic number theory (see [A5]).

Theorem 2.35 *(Odlyzko-Pomerance) There is a constant $c > 0$ which is effectively computable such that for all integers $n > e^e$, there is an integer*

$$0 < t < (\log n)^{c \log \log \log n}$$

(which is not actually constructed in the proof) such that $s(t) > \sqrt{n}$ $\bullet$

Now it is possible to state the Rumeley-Adleman algorithm.
Input: n odd > 1.
Step 1: Try the integers $t = 0, 1, \ldots$, until you compute an integer t such that $s(t) > \sqrt{n}$.
Step 2: Put $s = s(t)$ and confirm $\gcd(st, n) = 1$.
Step 3: If for any prime $p | t$ either
(1) $n^{p-1} \not\equiv 1 \operatorname{mod} p^2$ or
(2) $n^{p-1} \equiv 1 \operatorname{mod} p^2$ and a q can be selected with $q | s$ and $p | q - 1$, and also a character $\chi : Z_q^* \to G_p$ of order p and conductor q can be selected such that $G(\chi)^n \equiv \eta(\chi)^{-n} G(\chi^n) \operatorname{mod}(nZ[\varsigma_p, \varsigma_q])$ holds for some $\eta(\chi) \in G_p - \{1\}$,
then go to Step 4.
Step 4: For each $i = 0, 1, \ldots, s - 1$ compute $\gcd(n^i \operatorname{mod} s, n)$.
Output:

$$RA(n) = \begin{cases} \text{PRIME} & \text{if } (\forall i < s)(\gcd(n^i \operatorname{mod} s, n) = 1 \text{ or } n) \\ \text{COMPOSITE} & \text{if } (\exists i < s)(1 < \gcd(n^i \operatorname{mod} s, n) < n) \end{cases}$$

It is clear that the algorithm may not terminate but instead run forever in Step 3. However it can be shown that

Theorem 2.36 *(Rumeley-Adleman) For all odd integers $n > 1$, if the algorithm RA terminates on input n, then the following statements are equivalent:*

(1) *n is prime.*
(2) *$RA(n) = PRIME$.*

Moreover, if $RA(n)$ terminates, then the number of steps needed to output the answer is $O\left((\log n)^{c \log \log \log n}\right)$, where c is the constant of the previous theorem.

Proof: Assume on the contrary that $RA(n) = \text{PRIME}$, but that n is composite. Let r be a prime divisor of n such that $r \leq \sqrt{n}$. Let t be an integer such that $s = s(t) > \sqrt{n}$ and suppose that $\gcd(st, n) = 1$. Since $RA(n)$ converges the integer n passes the test in step 3. It follows from lemma 2.11 that $\nu_p(k^{p-1} - 1) \geq \nu_p(n^{p-1} - 1)$, for all $k|n$. Hence $\ell_p(k)$ is defined for all $k|n$. Use the Chinese Remainder theorem to find an integer $\ell(r) \in \{0, 1, \ldots, s - 1\}$ such that for all prime divisors p of t, $\ell(r) \equiv \ell_p(r) \bmod p$. It follows from parts $(2), (3)$ of lemma 2.11 that for any character $\chi : Z_q^* \to G_p$ of order p and conductor q (such that $p|q - 1$),

$$\chi(r) = \chi(n^{\ell(r)}).$$

However, such characters generate the group $Char(Z_s^*)$ of characters modulo s (which is isomorphic to Z_s^*). It follows from the duality theorem of the theory of characters (see [K4], page 129 or [C3], page 24) that $r \equiv n^{\ell(r)} \bmod s$. But this is a contradiction since $1 < r = \gcd(n^{\ell(r)} \bmod s, n) < n$. The other direction is easy. If the test declares n composite (i.e. $RA(n) = \text{COMPOSITE}$), then n must be composite •

Lenstra in [L10] has observed that the integer $s(t)$ used in the proof of the Rumeley - Adleman algorithm can in fact be replaced with

$$e(t) = 2 \cdot \prod \{q^{\nu_q(t)+1} : q - 1|t \text{ and } q \text{ is prime}\}.$$

Details of the proof (which is similar to the above proof) have been carried out by H. Cohen in [C2]. In addition, Lenstra has pointed out that condition $e(t) > \sqrt{n}$ can in fact be replaced by $e(t) > n^{1/3}$. Although both of these observations are useful for applications they do not alter the theoretical bound $O\left((\log n)^{c \log \log \log n}\right)$. In applying the Rumeley-Adleman test one need only form a table of values of $e(t)^2$ (see [C2], page 31).

The table in Figure 3 shows that to test the primality of a 200 digit integer one need only factor integers $t < 55,440$ (by all means an easy task) and then use the Rumeley - Adleman algorithm. According to [S6] this algorithm can be used to test the primality of an arbitrary 97 digit number in 78 seconds of computer time (see also [P8] for additional information).

EXERCISES

1: If p, q are primes such that $p|q - 1$, g is a generator of Z_q^*, and ς_p is a p-th root of unity then $\chi(g^x \bmod q) = \varsigma_p^x$ is an epimorphism of Z_q^* onto G_p.

2: For any character of order p and conductor q, $\sum_{j=1}^{q-1} \chi(j) = 0$.

t	$e(t)^2$
$60 = 2^2 3 \cdot 5$	4.64 E 19
$1,260 = 2^2 3^2 5 \cdot 7$	1.31 E 62
$10,080 = 2^5 3^2 5 \cdot 7$	1.83 E 128
$55,440 = 2^4 3^2 5 \cdot 7 \cdot 11$	2.42 E 213
$166,320 = 2^4 3^3 5 \cdot 7 \cdot 11$	4.88 E 313

Figure 3: Table of Values of $e(t)^2$

2.20   Bibliographical Remarks

According to definition 11 in book VII of *Euclid's Elements*:

Prime number is that which is measured by a unit alone.[2]

The existence of infinitely many primes is subsequently proved in proposition 20.[3] In modern terminology Euclid's proof runs as follows: assume there were only a finite number of primes, say $p_1, \ldots, p_n$. The integer $(1+p_1 \cdots p_n)$ must have a prime factor, say p. But this is a contradiction, since $p \neq p_1, \ldots, p \neq p_n$.

Eratosthenes developed the sieve method in the 3rd century BC. The observation that one need only run the algorithm for $p \leq \sqrt{n}$ in order to test the primality of n is due to Pisano (1202); this was also observed by Ibn Albanna (end of 13th century). For more details see [D5]. A discussion of the limits of the sieve method can be found in [S8]. In [R5] a double sieve method is applied to show that $\sum\{1/p + 1/(p+2)\}$ converges, where the sum ranges over primes p such that $p+2$ is also a prime. The reader should also consult [H3] for the notion of random sieve. In addition, exercise 8 in section 4.5.4 of [K2] is relevant. Barinaga's theorem is an immediate application of Wilson's theorem and is stated in page 428 of [D5]. Pratt's test was first proved in [P11]. For more information see [L12].

The Sum of Two Squares test is essentially due to Euler. His proof followed after Girard's determination of all integers which are expressible as the sum of two squares. This was also proved by Gauss using the theory of binary quadratic forms (see [G3], Art. 182). For more information the

[2]See Euclid's Elements, translated with an introduction by T. L. Heath, Vol. II, Books III - IX, Dover 1956

[3]Ibid, Book IX.

reader can consult [G11], pp. 265 - 277, [S3], pp. 159 - 163, and [K9], section 6.2.

Gauss was the first to state that Fermat's assertion on the primality of every F_n is false. It is not known if there exist infinitely many Fermat primes or infinitely many Fermat composites. Fermat numbers play an important role in Gauss's theorem: a regular polygon of m sides can be inscribed in a circle if and only if m is the product of distinct Fermat primes and a power of 2 (see [V1], page 196).

The present proof of the Lucas-Lehmer test is due to Lenstra (see [L12]). The traditional proof uses Lucas functions and can be found in [K2], page 391 or better yet in [W2]. In addition [W2] gives an excellent survey of Lehmer functions and generalized Lehmer sequences.

For more information on the Riemann Zeta function and the Extended Riemann Hypothesis the reader should consult [K4], [P10], [T1], [D1]. The proof of Ankeny-Montgomery's theorem can be found in [M11]. The idea of the proof of the Solovay-Strassen deterministic test is from [S15]. The deterministic test in subsection 2.12 is inspired from the Selfridge-Weinberger test and unlike the Solovay-Strassen test it makes no mention of the Legendre-Jacobi symbol. Miller was the first to show that under the Extended Riemann Hypothesis there is a polynomial time algorithm to test primality. The proofs of the tests given in subsections 2.12, 2.11 followed the proof of Miller's deterministic test. The original proof of Miller's test uses the Carmichael function (see [M9], [A8]). The present proof is from [M7] and [L9]; the last reference also includes the proof of lemma 2.7.

The probabilistic Solovay-Strassen test comes from [S15] and Rabin's test from [R2]. Theorem 2.32 is from [K10]. In addition, Monier in [M10] compares the performance of the last two probabilistic tests. The first proof of the Rumeley-Adleman test was published in [A2]. The proof given here is essentially due to Lenstra (see [L12], [L10], [C2]).

An interesting history of the machines used since 1925 for factoring and testing primality can be found in [B8] as well as the references cited there. A description of existing tables in number theory, as well as a guide to bibliography can be found in [L5]. In addition, [L4] gives a list of all prime numbers up to $10,006,721$.

3 PROBABILITY THEORY

The Truth is no more certain than the Probable.
(Ancient Greek Proverb)

3.1 Introduction

The concepts of probability theory presented in this section include only the material necessary to understand the proofs in the sections on pseudorandom generators and public key cryptosystems.

Subsection 3.2 includes all the necessary introductory notions, i.e. σ-algebra, probability space, product and sum of events. The notion of random variable is developed in subsection 3.3. Further, this subsection includes the fundamental theorems for computing expectations and variances of random variables. The binomial distribution, which is studied in subsection 3.4, will be the only probability distribution to be examined in the present book. Chebyshev's law of large numbers is proved in subsection 3.5. The strengthening of the weak law of large numbers, proved in subsection 3.6, will be very useful in the development of the general theory of the security of pseudorandom generators and public key cryptosystems. An introduction to the Monte Carlo method, is presented in subsection 3.7.

3.2 Basic Notions

A $\sigma-$**algebra** A on a nonempty set Ω is a nonempty set of subsets of Ω which satisfies the following three properties:
  (1) $\Omega \in A$.
  (2) If $E \in A$ then $\Omega - E \in A$.
  (3) If $\{E_n : n \geq 0\} \subseteq A$ then $\left(\bigcup_{n \geq 0} E_n\right) \in A$.

Example 3.1 *The set $\{\Omega, \emptyset\}$ is a $\sigma-$ algebra.*

Example 3.2 *The set of all subsets of a nonempty set Ω is a $\sigma-$ algebra.*

A **probability space** is a triple (Ω, A, Pr), where

  1. Ω is a nonempty set,

2. A is a $\sigma-$ algebra on the set Ω, and

3. Pr is an experiment on the $\sigma-$ algebra A, i.e. Pr is a function $Pr :$ $A \longrightarrow [0,1]$, with domain the $\sigma-$ algebra A and range a subset of the unit interval $[0,1]$ such that

   (a) $Pr[\Omega] = 1$ and $Pr[\emptyset] = 0$,

   (b) For any family $\{E_n : n \geq 0\} \subseteq A$ of pairwise disjoint subsets of Ω,

$$Pr\left[\bigcup_{n \geq 0} E_n\right] = \sum_{n=0}^{\infty} Pr[E_n].$$

The subsets of Ω are called **events**, while the subsets of Ω which belong to the $\sigma-$ algebra A are called **observed events**; the elements $\omega \in \Omega$ are called the **possible outcomes** of the experiment Pr. An event E is called **certain** (respectively **impossible**) if $Pr[E] = 1$ (respectively if $Pr[E] = 0$). The set Ω is called the **sample space** of the experiment.

Example 3.3 *The experiment determined by the flipping of a fair coin consists of the sample space $\Omega = \{H,T\}$, where $H = $ Head and $T = $ Tail, the $\sigma-$ algebra A of all subsets of Ω and the experiment Pr which satisfies:*

$$Pr[\{H,T\}] = 1, \; Pr[\{H\}] = Pr[\{T\}] = 1/2, \; Pr[\emptyset] = 0.$$

Example 3.4 *The experiment determined by the tossing of two fair dice consists of the sample space $\Omega = \{(i,j) : 1 \leq i, j \leq 6\}$, the $\sigma-$ algebra of all subsets of Ω, and the experiment Pr which satisfies*

$$Pr[E] = |E|/36, \text{ for all events } E.$$

Example 3.5 *In the previous experiment one can also consider the following $\sigma-$ algebra of observed events: an event $E \in A$ if and only if for all (i,j), if $(i,j) \in E$ then $(j,i) \in E$.*

Corresponding to the set-theoretic boolean operations of union, intersection and difference of sets, one can define respectively the sum, the product and the difference of events. Hence, given two events E, F one defines the **sum** (respectively **product**, **difference**) of the events E, F to be the event $E \cup F$ (respectively $E \cap F$, $E - F$).

Given a probability space (Ω, A, Pr) and an observed event K such that $Pr[K] > 0$, the **conditional probability space** with respect to K is the triple (Ω, A, Pr_K), where the new experiment Pr_K is defined by

$$Pr_K[E] = \frac{Pr[E \cap K]}{Pr[K]}.$$

In addition, the notation $Pr[E|K]$ will also be used as identical to $Pr_K[E]$.

Given a probability space (Ω, A, Pr) and two observed events E, F, the following three rules are very useful in the study of probability theory and can be derived easily from the defining properties of Pr:

(1) **Difference Rule:** If $E \subseteq F$ then $Pr[F - E] = Pr[F] - Pr[E]$.

(2) **Sum Rule:** $Pr[E \cup F] = Pr[E] + Pr[F] - Pr[E \cap F]$.

(3) **Product Rule:** If $Pr[F] > 0$ then $Pr[E \cap F] = Pr_F[E] \cdot Pr[F]$.

Events E, F are called **independent** with respect to the probability space (Ω, A, Pr) if $Pr[E \cap F] = Pr[E] \cdot Pr[F]$.

EXERCISES

1: Show that every $\sigma-$ algebra is closed under countable intersections.

2: Show that the empty set is a member of every $\sigma-$ algebra.

3: Prove in detail the difference, sum and product rules.

3.3 Random Variables

Let $\mathbf{R}$ be the set of all real numbers. **A random variable** on the probability space (Ω, A, Pr) is a real valued function $X : \Omega \longrightarrow \mathbf{R}$ such that for any open set I of real numbers,

$$X^{-1}[I] = \{\omega \in \Omega : X(\omega) \in I\} \in A.$$

A **vector random variable** on the probability space (Ω, A, Pr) is a real vector-valued function $X : \Omega \longrightarrow \mathbf{R}^n$ such that for any open subset I of the set $\mathbf{R}^n$ of n tuples of real numbers,

$$X^{-1}[I] = \{\omega \in \Omega : X(\omega) \in I\} \in A.$$

It is easy to see that if $X_1, \ldots, X_n$ are random variables on Ω, then the function $(X_1, \ldots, X_n)$ is a vector random variable on Ω.

For any random variable X on the probability space (Ω, A, Pr) and any real number k, let $X = k$ denote the event $\{\omega \in \Omega : X(\omega) = k\}$. A random variable is **finite** (respectively **discrete**) if it takes on only a finite (respectively countable) number of values.

For any random variables $X_1, \ldots, X_n$ on the probability space (Ω, A, Pr) and any function $f : \mathbf{R}^n \longrightarrow \mathbf{R}$, let $f(X_1, \ldots, X_n)$ denote the composition of the functions $f, (X_1, \ldots, X_n)$, i.e. for all $\omega \in \Omega$, $f(X_1, \ldots, X_n)(\omega) = f(X_1(\omega), \ldots, X_n(\omega))$. If f is continuous, then the inverse image under f of any open set is open. Hence, if all the $X_1, \ldots, X_n$ are random variables on the probability space (Ω, A, Pr) and f is continuous, then $f(X_1, \ldots, X_n)$ is a vector random variable on the probability space (Ω, A, Pr). In particular, if X, Y are random variables so are $X + Y$, $X \cdot Y$, $\exp(X)$, etc.

For any random variable X on the probability space (Ω, A, Pr), the **(probability) mass** or **(probability) distribution function** of the random variable X is the function p_X defined for all real numbers k by

$$p_X(k) = Pr[X = k].$$

Hence, if the random variable X takes on only the values $x_1, \ldots, x_n, \ldots$, then its corresponding probability distribution function p_X will take on only the values $p_X(x_1), \ldots, p_X(x_n), \ldots$.

The random variables X, Y on the probability space (Ω, A, Pr) are called **independent** if for all real numbers s, t the events $X = s, Y = t$ are independent.

For simplicity from now on and for the rest of this section all the random variables used will be discrete and bounded, i.e. there exists a real number B such that for all $\omega \in \Omega, |X(\omega)| \leq B$. Moreover, the probability space used in each particular case will not always be explicitly mentioned, unless there is cause for confusion.

Let X be a random variable which takes on only the pairwise distinct values $x_1, \ldots, x_n, \ldots$ and let $p_X(x_1) = p_1, \ldots, p_X(x_n) = p_n, \ldots$ be the corresponding values of its distribution function p_X (i.e. it is asssumed that $x_i \neq x_j$, for all $i \neq j$). The **expectation** of the random variable X, abbreviated $E[X]$, is defined by

$$E[X] = \sum_{n=0}^{\infty} x_n \cdot p_n. \tag{1}$$

The **variance** of the random variable X, abbreviated $Var[X]$, is defined by

$$Var[X] = E\left[(X - E[X])^2\right]. \tag{2}$$

It is easy to show (see theorem 3.1) that in fact

$$Var[X] = \sum_{n=0}^{\infty}(x_n - E[X])^2 \cdot p_n.$$

The square root of the variance of X is called the **standard deviation** of X and is denoted by $D[X]$, i.e.

$$D[X] = \sqrt{Var[X]}. \tag{3}$$

Remark: Since the random variable X is bounded, the infinite series in definition (1) is absolutely convergent. Hence, the definition of $E[X]$ does not depend on the given enumeration of the values taken on by X.

Example 3.6 *For the exact fitting of a certain part of a precision instrument, it is required to make $1, 2, \ldots, 5$ trials. The number of trials necessary to achieve exact fitting of the part is a random variable, denoted by X. Let $p_1 = .1, p_2 = .15, p_3 = .25, p_4 = .3, p_5 = .2$. The behavior of the probability distribution function of the random variable X is represented in the graph of figure 1.*
   The expectation of X is given by

$$E[X] = 1 \cdot .1 + 2 \cdot .15 + 3 \cdot .25 + 4 \cdot .3 + 5 \cdot .2 = 3.35.$$

Thus, the number of trials necessary to achieve exact fitting will be on the average 3.35, i.e. the exact fitting of 100 instruments will require on the average 335 trials.
   The variance of X is given by

$$Var[X] = (2.35)^2 \cdot .1 + (1.35)^2 \cdot .15 + (.35)^2 \cdot .25 + (.65)^2 \cdot .3 + (1.65)^2 \cdot .2 = 1.527.$$

The standard deviation of X will be

$$D[X] = \sqrt{1.795} = 1.236.$$

Thus, the standard deviation $D[X]$ gives the magnitude of the oscillations of X around the expectation $E[X]$.

The **covariance** of two random variables X, Y, abbreviated $Cov[X, Y]$, is defined by

$$Cov[X, Y] = E[(X - E[X]) \cdot (Y - E[Y])]. \tag{4}$$

The two theorems following will be useful in the sequel.

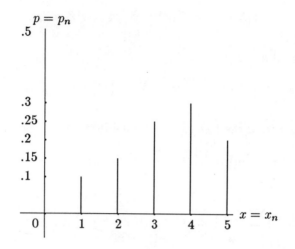

Figure 1: Graph of p_X

Theorem 3.1 (The Expectation Theorem) *Let X,Y be two random variables. Let the random variable X take on only the pairwise distinct values $x_0, \ldots, x_n, \ldots$ and let $p_X(x_0) = p_0, \ldots, p_X(x_n) = p_n, \ldots$ be the corresponding values of its distribution function p_X. Then*

(1) $E[a \cdot X + b \cdot Y] = a \cdot E[X] + b \cdot E[Y]$, where a, b are reals.
(2) If X, Y are indepedent then $E[X \cdot Y] = E[X] \cdot E[Y]$.
(3) For any continuous function $f : \mathbf{R} \longrightarrow \mathbf{R}$,

$$E[f(X)] = \sum_{n=0}^{\infty} f(x_n) \cdot p_n.$$

Proof of 1: Only the proof of $E[X + Y] = E[X] + E[Y]$ will be given; the rest will be left as an exercise for the reader. Suppose that the random variable Y takes on only the pairwise distinct values $y_0, \ldots, y_m, \ldots$ and let $p_Y(y_0) = q_0, \ldots, p_Y(y_m) = q_m, \ldots$ be the corresponding values of its distribution function p_Y. Let $Z = X + Y$ and suppose that $z_0, \ldots, z_k, \ldots$ are the pairwise distinct values taken on by the random variable Z. Finally, put $p_{n,m} = Pr[X = x_n \text{ and } Y = y_m]$.

From the definition of expectation,

$$E[X+Y] = E[Z] = \sum_{k\geq 0} z_k \cdot Pr[Z = z_k].$$

However, for all $k \geq 1$

$$z_k \cdot Pr[Z = z_k] = \sum_{x_n+y_m=z_k} (x_n + y_m) \cdot p_{n,m}.$$

It is then clear from the last two equations that

$$E[X+Y] = \sum_{n,m\geq 0} (x_n + y_m) \cdot p_{n,m} =$$

$$= \sum_{n\geq 0} x_n \cdot \left(\sum_{m\geq 0} p_{n,m}\right) + \sum_{m\geq 0} y_m \cdot \left(\sum_{n\geq 0} p_{n,m}\right).$$

On the other hand it is obvious that

$$p_n = \sum_{m\geq 0} p_{n,m}, \quad q_m = \sum_{n\geq 0} p_{n,m}.$$

The result now follows immediately from the definition of expectation and the last two equations.

Proof of 2: The notation of the proof of part (1) will be used in the proof of part (2) as well. Since the random variables X, Y are independent, it is clear that for all $n, m \geq 0$,

$$p_{n,m} = p_n \cdot q_m.$$

On the other hand using the definition of expectation, and arguing as in the proof of part (1) it can be shown that

$$E[X \cdot Y] = \sum_{n,m\geq 0} x_n \cdot y_m \cdot p_{n,m} = \sum_{n,m\geq 0} x_n \cdot y_m \cdot p_n \cdot q_m.$$

It follows that

$$E[X \cdot Y] = \left(\sum_{n\geq 0} x_n \cdot p_n\right) \cdot \left(\sum_{m\geq 0} y_m \cdot q_m\right) = E[X] \cdot E[Y],$$

which completes the proof of part (2).

Proof of 3:

Let $z_0, \ldots, z_k, \ldots$ be the pairwise distinct values taken on by the random variable $f(X)$. For each $k \geq 0$, let $I_k = \{n \geq 0 : f(x_n) = z_k\}$. Clearly, the event $f(X) = z_k$ occurs if and only if for some $n \in I_k$, the event $X = x_n$ occurs. Hence, the distribution function of $f(X)$ is given by

$$p_{f(X)}(z_k) = \sum_{n \in I_k} Pr[X = x_n] = \sum_{n \in I_k} p_n.$$

It follows from the definition of expectation that

$$E[f(X)] = \sum_{k \geq 0} z_k \cdot p_{f(X)}(z_k) =$$

$$\sum_{k \geq 0} z_k \cdot \left(\sum_{n \in I_k} p_n \right) = \sum_{n \geq 0} f(x_n) \cdot p_n.$$

This completes the proof of part (3) and hence of the theorem •

Theorem 3.2 (The Variance Theorem) *Let X, Y be two random variables. Then for all real numbers a, b,*

(1) $Var[a \cdot X + b \cdot Y] = a^2 \cdot Var[X] + b^2 \cdot Var[Y] + 2ab \cdot Cov[X, Y]$.

(2) If X, Y are independent then $Var[X + Y] = Var[X] + Var[Y]$.

Proof of 1: Only the proof of $Var[X + Y] = Var[X] + Var[Y] + 2Cov[X, Y]$ will be given; the rest will be left as an exercise to the reader. Let $E[X] = \mu, E[Y] = \nu$. Using the definition of the variance as well as the expectation theorem one can show that

$$Var[X + Y] = E[(X + Y - \mu - \nu)^2] =$$

$$E[(X - \mu)^2 + (Y - \nu)^2 + 2 \cdot (X - \mu) \cdot (Y - \nu)] =$$

$$= Var[X] + Var[Y] + 2Cov[X, Y].$$

Proof of 2: Using the definition of the covariance and the expectation theorem it is easy to see that

$$Cov[X, Y] = E[(X - E[X]) \cdot (Y - E[Y])] = E[X \cdot Y] - \mu \cdot \nu.$$

But the right side of the equality above is 0 because the random variables X, Y are independent. This completes the proof of (2) and hence of the theorem •

EXERCISES

1: If $X_1, \ldots, X_n$ are random variables, then $(X_1, \ldots, X_n)$ is a vector random variable.

2: If $(X_1, \ldots, X_n)$ is a vector random variable and the function $f : \mathbf{R}^n \longrightarrow \mathbf{R}$ is continuous, then $f(X_1, \ldots, X_n)$ is a random variable.

3: Let X be a random variable. Show that for all real numbers a, b,
(1) $E[a \cdot X + b] = a \cdot E[X] + b$.
(2) $Var[a \cdot X + b] = a^2 \cdot Var[X]$.
(3) $D[a \cdot X + b] = |a| \cdot D[X]$.

4: If the random variable X is bounded by the constant B, then $E[X] \leq B$.

3.4   The Binomial Distribution

A random variable X which takes on only the values $0, 1, \ldots, n$ is said to have the **binomial distribution** with parameters n, p if and only if for any $0 \leq k \leq n$,

$$Pr[X = k] = \binom{n}{k} p^k (1 - p)^{n-k}.$$

For any event E in a given probability space and any integer n, let the random variable $B_n(E)$ denote the number of occurrences of the event E in n trials (indepedent from one another). The n-th **relative frequency** of the event E, abbreviated $F_n(E)$, is the random variable

$$F_n(E) = \frac{B_n(E)}{n}.$$

The theorem following will be very useful in the sequel.

Theorem 3.3 *(The Binomial Distribution Theorem) For any event E in a given probability space such that $p = Pr[E]$ and any integer $n \geq 0$, the random variable $B_n(E)$ has the binomial distribution with parameters n, p. Moreover,*
(1) $E[B_n(E)] = n \cdot p, E[F_n(E)] = p$, and
(2) $Var[B_n(E)] = n \cdot p \cdot (1 - p), Var[F_n(E)] = (1/n) \cdot p \cdot (1 - p)$.

Proof: To see that $B_n(E)$ satisfies the binomial distribution, notice that the event $B_n(E) = k$ occurs exactly when the event E occurs k times and the event $\Omega - E$ occurs $(n - k)$ times. Each such event-sequence occurs with probability $p^k(1-p)^{n-k}$. Hence, the first part of the theorem follows from the fact that there exist exactly $\binom{n}{k}$ such sequences.

Proof of 1: Using the definition of expectation and trivial algebraic manipulations, one obtains that

$$E[B_n(E)] = \sum_{k=0}^{n} k \cdot \binom{n}{k} \cdot p^k \cdot (1-p)^{n-k} =$$

$$= np \cdot \sum_{k=1}^{n} \binom{n-1}{k-1} \cdot p^{k-1} \cdot (1-p)^{n-k} =$$

$$= np \cdot (p + (1-p))^{n-1} = np.$$

The evaluation of the quantity $E[F_n(E)]$ follows easily from the expectation theorem.

Proof of 2: Using the definition of variance, the result in part (1), and trivial algebraic manipulations, one obtains that

$$Var[B_n(E)] = \sum_{k=0}^{n} (k-np)^2 \cdot \binom{n}{k} \cdot p^k \cdot (1-p)^{n-k} =$$

$$= \sum_{k=0}^{n} k^2 \cdot \binom{n}{k} \cdot p^k \cdot (1-p)^{n-k} +$$

$$n^2 p^2 \cdot \sum_{k=0}^{n} \binom{n}{k} \cdot p^k \cdot (1-p)^{n-k} - 2np \cdot \sum_{k=0}^{n} k \cdot \binom{n}{k} \cdot p^k \cdot (1-p)^{n-k} =$$

$$-n^2 p^2 + \sum_{k=0}^{n} k^2 \cdot \binom{n}{k} \cdot p^k \cdot (1-p)^{n-k} =$$

$$-n^2 p^2 + \sum_{k=0}^{n} k(k-1) \cdot \binom{n}{k} \cdot p^k \cdot (1-p)^{n-k} + \sum_{k=0}^{n} k \cdot \binom{n}{k} \cdot p^k \cdot (1-p)^{n-k} =$$

$$-n^2 p^2 + n(n-1)p^2 + np = np(1-p).$$

The evaluation of the quantity $Var[F_n(E)]$ follows easily from the variance theorem ●

3.5   Chebyshev's Law of Large Numbers

In general, a law of large numbers gives a set of sufficient conditions such that
the arithmetic mean of a sequence of random variables will tend toward a
fixed constant number with high probability, when the number of summands
is increasing. The first such law to be proved is based on the following
inequality:

Lemma 3.1 *(Chebyshev's Inequality) For any random variable X, and
any real number $\epsilon > 0$,*

$$Pr[|X - E[X]| \geq \epsilon] \leq \frac{Var[X]}{\epsilon^2}.$$

Proof: Let the random variable X take on only the pairwise distinct
values $x_0, \ldots, x_n, \ldots$ and let $p_X(x_0) = p_0, \ldots, p_X(x_n) = p_n, \ldots$ be the corresponding values of its distribution function p_X. Put $\mu = E[X]$. Then

$$Var[X] = \sum_{n \geq 0} (x_n - \mu)^2 \cdot p_n.$$

It follows that

$$Var[X] \geq \sum_{|x_n - \mu| \geq \epsilon} (x_n - \mu)^2 \cdot p_n$$

$$\geq \sum_{|x_n - \mu| \geq \epsilon} \epsilon^2 \cdot p_n = \epsilon^2 \cdot \sum_{|x_n - \mu| \geq \epsilon} p_n =$$

$$\epsilon^2 \cdot \sum_{|x_n - \mu| \geq \epsilon} Pr[X = x_n] = \epsilon^2 \cdot Pr[|X - \mu| \geq \epsilon] \bullet$$

As an immediate application one obtains the following:

Theorem 3.4 *(Chebyshev's Law of Large Numbers) Let $X_1, \ldots, X_n$
be independent random variables and let the random variable X denote their
arithmetic mean, i.e.*

$$X = \frac{X_1 + \cdots + X_n}{n}.$$

Then for any $\epsilon > 0$,

$$Pr[|X - E[X]| \geq \epsilon] \leq \frac{\sum_{i=1}^{n} Var[X_i]}{n^2 \cdot \epsilon^2}.$$

Moreover,

$$Pr[|X - E[X]| \geq \epsilon] \leq \frac{\max_{1 \leq i \leq n} Var[X_i]}{n \cdot \epsilon^2}.$$

Proof: The proof is immediate from the variance theorem and Chebyshev's inequality •

The next theorem, which is an immediate consequence of Chebyshev's inequality, will be applied frequently in sections 4 through 6.

Theorem 3.5 *(Weak Law of Large Numbers, Bernoulli) Suppose that the event E occurs with probability p. Then for any integer n ≥ 1 and any ε > 0,*

$$Pr[|F_n(E) - p| \geq \epsilon] \leq \frac{p \cdot (1 - p)}{n \cdot \epsilon^2} \leq \frac{1}{4n \cdot \epsilon^2}.$$

Proof: This is an immediate consequence of the binomial distribution theorem, Chebyshev's inequality, and the fact that $4p(1 - p) \leq 1$ •

3.6   Bernshtein's Law of Large Numbers

The Bernoulli estimate for the weak law of large numbers given in theorem 3.5 can be substantially improved. The improvement is based on the inequality below.

Lemma 3.2 *(Markov's Inequality) For any random variable X, any real number ε > 0, and any nondecreasing continuous function f : R ⟶ R, which takes on only positive values,*

$$Pr[X \geq \epsilon] \leq \frac{E[f(X)]}{f(\epsilon)}.$$

In particular, if E[X] > 0, then

$$Pr[X \geq \epsilon \cdot E[X]] \leq \frac{1}{\epsilon}.$$

Proof: Let the random variable X take on only the pairwise distinct values $x_0, \ldots, x_n, \ldots$ and let $p_X(x_0) = p_0, \ldots, p_X(x_n) = p_n, \ldots$ be the corresponding values of its distribution function p_X. The expectation theorem implies that

$$E[f(X)] = \sum_{n=0}^{\infty} f(x_n) \cdot p_n \geq$$

$$\sum_{x_n \geq \epsilon} f(x_n) \cdot p_n \geq \sum_{x_n \geq \epsilon} f(\epsilon) \cdot p_n =$$

$$f(\epsilon) \cdot \sum_{x_n \geq \epsilon} p_n = f(\epsilon) \cdot Pr[X \geq \epsilon].$$

This completes the first part of the lemma. To prove the second part, apply the first part to the identity function and use $\epsilon' = \epsilon \cdot E[X]$ •

As an immediate consequence of the second part of Markov's inequality, with $X' = e^{\epsilon(X-E[X])}, \epsilon' = e^t$, one obtains that for all t,

$$Pr\left[e^{\epsilon(X-E[X])} \geq e^t E\left[e^{\epsilon(X-E[X])}\right]\right] \leq e^{-t}. \tag{5}$$

Clearly inequality (5) is equivalent to:

$$Pr\left[X \geq E[X] + \frac{t + \log E\left[e^{\epsilon(X-E[X])}\right]}{\epsilon}\right] \leq e^{-t}. \tag{6}$$

The next lemma constitutes the major step in proving Bernshtein's sharpening of the weak law of large numbers.

Lemma 3.3 *(Bernshtein) Let $X_1, \ldots, X_n$ be a sequence of independent random variables with zero expectations and which are bounded by the constant K. If $X = X_1 + \cdots + X_n$, then*

$$E\left[e^{\epsilon \cdot X}\right] \leq \exp\left[\frac{\epsilon^2 \cdot Var[X]}{2}\left(1 + \frac{\epsilon K}{3} \cdot e^{\epsilon K}\right)\right].$$

Proof: It is clear from the expectation theorem that

$$E\left[e^{\epsilon \cdot X}\right] = \prod_{i=1}^{n} E\left[e^{\epsilon \cdot X_i}\right]. \tag{7}$$

Hence, using the variance theorem and equation (7) it can be assumed without loss of generality that $n = 1, X = X_1$. Let $V = Var[X]$. It follows that

$$E\left[e^{\epsilon \cdot X}\right] = E\left[\sum_{k=o}^{\infty} \frac{\epsilon^k}{k!} X^k\right] = \sum_{k=0}^{\infty} \frac{\epsilon^k}{k!} E\left[X^k\right] =$$

$$1 + \epsilon E[X] + \frac{\epsilon^2}{2} E\left[X^2\right] + \sum_{k=3}^{\infty} \frac{\epsilon^k}{k!} E\left[X^k\right] \leq$$

$$1 + \frac{\epsilon^2}{2}V + \sum_{k=3}^{\infty} \frac{\epsilon^k}{k!} E\left[X^2\right] K^{k-2} =$$

$$1 + \frac{\epsilon^2}{2}V + \sum_{k=3}^{\infty} \frac{\epsilon^k}{k!}VK^{k-2} =$$

$$1 + \frac{\epsilon^2}{2}V + \frac{\epsilon^2}{6}V \sum_{k=3}^{\infty} \frac{(\epsilon K)^{k-2}}{(k-3)!} =$$

$$1 + \epsilon^2 V \left[\frac{1}{2} + \frac{\epsilon K e^{\epsilon K}}{6} \right]. \tag{8}$$

Using the inequality $1 + u < e^u$ and equation (8) one easily obtains that

$$E\left[e^{\epsilon \cdot X} \right] \le \exp\left[\epsilon^2 V \left(\frac{1}{2} + \frac{\epsilon K e^{\epsilon K}}{6} \right) \right].$$

Let $X_1, \ldots, X_n$ be a sequence of independent random variables with zero expectations and which are bounded by the constant K. Put $X = X_1 + \cdots + X_n$. Using inequality (6) to $X, -X$, applying lemma 3.3 to the random variables $X_1, \ldots, X_n$ and $-X_1, \ldots, -X_n$, and using the fact that $E[X] = 0$, it follows that for all t,

$$Pr\left[|X| \ge \frac{t + \epsilon^2 Var[X]\left(\frac{1}{2} + \frac{\epsilon K e^{\epsilon K}}{6} \right)}{\epsilon} \right] \le 2 \cdot e^{-t}. \tag{9}$$

Putting

$$D = D[X], \epsilon = \frac{\sqrt{2t}}{D}, \lambda = \sqrt{2t},$$

inequality (9) becomes

$$Pr\left[|X| \ge \lambda D \left(1 + \frac{\lambda K}{6D} e^{\frac{\lambda K}{D}} \right) \right] \le 2 \cdot e^{-\frac{\lambda^2}{2}}. \tag{10}$$

Assuming that $\frac{\lambda K}{D} \le 1$, one obtains that

$$e^{\frac{\lambda K}{D}} \le e < 3.$$

Putting

$$\mu = \lambda \cdot \left(1 + \frac{\lambda K}{2D} \right),$$

and using the fact that $\mu \ge \lambda$, inequality (10) becomes

$$Pr[|X| \ge \mu D] \le 2 \cdot e^{-\frac{\lambda^2}{2}} \le \exp\left[-\frac{\mu^2}{2\left(1 + \frac{\mu K}{2D} \right)^2} \right]. \tag{11}$$

To sum up, the following has been shown:

Lemma 3.4 *Let* $X_1, \ldots, X_n$ *be a sequence of independent random variables and let* K *be a constant such that for all* i, $|X_i - E[X_i]| \leq K$. *If* $X = X_1 + \cdots + X_n$, *then for all* $0 < \mu \leq \frac{D}{K}$,

$$Pr[|X - E[X]| \geq \mu D[X]] \leq 2 \cdot e^{-\frac{\lambda^2}{2}} \leq 2 \cdot \exp\left[-\frac{\mu^2}{2\left(1 + \frac{\mu K}{2D[X]}\right)^2}\right].$$

Proof: Immediate from the above, since $\mu \leq D/K \Rightarrow \lambda K/D \leq 1$ •

Using the last lemma and the binomial distribution theorem one easily obtains the following:

Theorem 3.6 *(Bernshtein's Law of Large Numbers) Suppose that the event* E *occurs with probability* p. *Then for any* $n \geq 1$ *and any* $0 < \epsilon \leq p(1-p)$,

$$Pr[|F_n[E] - p| \geq \epsilon] \leq 2 \cdot \exp\left[\frac{-n\epsilon^2}{4p(1-p)}\right] \leq 2 \cdot \exp[-n\epsilon^2] \bullet$$

EXERCISES

1: For any nonzero real number a, if $X_1, \ldots, X_n$ are independent random variables, so are $\exp[aX_1], \ldots, \exp[aX_n]$.

2: Derive theorem 3.6 from lemma 3.4 . **Hint:** Apply lemma 3.4 to the random variable $X = B_n(E)$, to $K = 1$ and $\mu = (n\epsilon)/D$.

3.7   The Monte Carlo Method

There are many computational problems whose solutions are cumbersome, or impossible, via deterministic procedures. For such problems it has been observed that statistical sampling methods can approximate solutions much faster than numerical methods based on classical analysis. An example of such a problem is the computation of π, the area of the unit circle.

Buffon's Needle Problem: Suppose that parallel lines are drawn on a plane surface at a distance d from one another. Let a needle of length ℓ less than d be thrown at random on the plane. What is the probability that the needle will touch one of the parallel lines?

Let the position of the needle be as in figure 2. Suppose that C is the center of the needle, x (respectively $d - x$) the distance of the center from

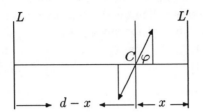

Figure 2: Buffon's Needle

the line L (respectively L'), and φ the angle between the needle and the line perpendicular to L (see figure 2). For the sake of the argument that follows, it will be assumed that the angle φ and the distance x are distributed uniformly over the respective ranges $-\pi/2 \le \varphi \le \pi/2$ and $0 \le x \le d$. It is apparent that the position of the needle is uniquely determined from the pairs of coordinates (x, φ), where $0 \le x \le d$ and $-\pi/2 \le \varphi \le \pi/2$. It is also clear from figure 2 that the needle will not touch any of the lines L, L' if and only if

$$-\frac{\pi}{2} \le \varphi \le \frac{\pi}{2}, \quad \frac{\ell}{2} \cdot \cos\varphi < x < d - \frac{\ell}{2} \cdot \cos\varphi. \tag{12}$$

Let Ω be the set of pairs (x, φ) satisfying equation (12). Hence, the probability that the needle will not touch any of the parallel lines is

$$\frac{\text{area}(\Omega)}{d \cdot \pi} = \frac{d \cdot \pi - 2 \cdot \ell}{d \cdot \pi} = 1 - \frac{2 \cdot \ell}{d \cdot \pi}, \tag{13}$$

where the area of Ω is computed via

$$\text{area}(\Omega) = \int_{-\pi/2}^{\pi/2} d\varphi (d - \ell \cdot \cos\varphi). \tag{14}$$

It follows from equation (13) that the probability p that the needle will touch one of the lines is

$$p = \frac{2 \cdot \ell}{d \cdot \pi}. \tag{15}$$

Equation (15) and the weak law of large numbers can be used as the basis for an experimental evaluation of π. Indeed, assume for simplicity that $d = 2$ and $\ell = 1$. Then $p = 1/\pi$. Consider an experiment in which the needle is thrown independently n times, and let the random variable X_i be equal to 1 if the needle intersects a line on the i-th throw, and to 0 otherwise. It follows from theorem 3.5 that for any $\epsilon > 0$,

$$Pr\left[\left|\frac{X_1 + \cdots + X_n}{n} - \frac{1}{\pi}\right| \geq \epsilon\right] \leq \frac{1}{4n \cdot \epsilon^2}. \tag{16}$$

Hence, with high probability

$$\pi \approx \frac{n}{X_1 + \cdots + X_n}.$$

(A lower bound $1 - 1/4n\epsilon^2$ on the probability is easily determined from inequality (16).)

Other examples of statistical sampling methods are the probabilistic primality tests of section 2.

In general, a **Monte Carlo method** is a statistical sampling method that can be used to approximate the solution of a certain problem. The computation necessary to find the solution is called a **Monte Carlo computation**. Although a problem might admit more than one Monte Carlo solution, there exist problems for which no Monte Carlo solution is known.

In sections 4, 5, and 6 several Monte Carlo computations are included in the construction of circuits. As described above, these computations are in fact statistical sampling techniques which enable the construction of polynomial size circuits to solve the corresponding problems.

It should also be pointed out that an essential step toward applying the Monte Carlo method in order to solve a specific problem is the ability to do random sampling. However, due to apparent technical limitations it would be unrealistic to hope that one could produce a perfectly random sampling, through an unbiased execution of an experiment. Thus, one is led to replace the notion of random with that of pseudorandom. Details on this last concept will be studied in section 4.

EXERCISES

1: Evaluate the integral in equation (14).

2: Show that both the Solovay - Strassen as well as the Rabin tests are Monte Carlo methods for determining the primality of a given integer.

3.8 Bibliographical Remarks

Probability theory originated with mathematical problems connected to dice throwing. Such problems were mainly concerned with permutations, combinations, and binomial coefficients, and were discussed in letters exchanged between Blaise Pascal and Pierre de Fermat. The measure-theoretic definition of Probability adopted today is due to Kolmogorov (see [K5]). The following books: [G6], [R12] and [K6], give nice introductory accounts of the theory of probability.

All the random variables considered in this section are discrete. However, this restriction would not be necessary if the reader were familiar with the notion of Lebesque integral. For a more general development of the notions of probability theory the reader should consult, e.g., [F1], [G5], [R7], [R8], [R10]. The proof of Bernshtein's law of large numbers given here is partly based on the account given in [R7], pp. 322 - 326, and [R8], page 200.

Buffon's needle problem is due to George Louis Leclerc, Comte de Buffon (better known as Buffon, 1707 - 1788) and is described in his *Essai d'Arithmetique Morale* (see [L3]). The name Monte Carlo method was first used in the article [M6]. For more information on the Monte Carlo method the reader can consult the excellent introductory book [S14]. There are many other useful books and essays on the Monte Carlo method as well. These include [H9], [S12], [B9], [N2] and [H1].

4 PSEUDORANDOM GENERATORS

Il faut donner quelque chose au hasard.
(French Proverb)

4.1 Introduction

According to the *Encyclopedic Dictionary of Mathematics*,[1] a sequence of
random numbers is *a sequence of numbers that can be considered as realiza-
tions of independently and identically distributed random variables*. Such sequences or tables of random numbers are useful in applications of the Monte
Carlo method (e.g. Monte Carlo primality tests), in cryptography, and in
the design of efficient probabilistic algorithms. However, as was mentioned
in section 3, it is impossible to have perfectly random sampling through an
unbiased execution of an experiment (like flips of a coin). In applications
therefore, one is led to use *pseudorandom sequences* of numbers, i.e. finite
sequences of numbers produced by efficient deterministic algorithms, but
which appear to be *sufficiently random*. These finite algorithms, also called
pseudorandom generators, take a short input, called the *seed*, and produce
a longer sequence of numbers. The pseudorandom sequences must have no
apparent regularities and must also pass certain statistical tests (e.g. χ^2,
Kolmogorov - Smirnov), as well as empirical tests on frequency, uniformity,
gaps, permutations and subsequencies (see [K2]).

Of course, *pseudorandomness* can not fully simulate *randomness*. In
particular, given a pseudorandom sequence an exhaustive search could determine the seed from which the sequence was produced. However a search
would be of value only if it were computationally feasible. In this sense
the *Linear Congruence generator* and the $1/p$-*generator* presented in subsections 4.2 and 4.3, respectively, are *predictable*. In fact it is shown that
in each case there exists a polynomial time algorithm, which, given a long
enough sequence of numbers, produced by the generator as input, it will
output the seed which produces this sequence.

Hence, one is led to introduce *polynomial time unpredictability* as a mea-
sure of the randomness of pseudorandom sequences. In particular, it is

---

[1]Mathematical Society of Japan, S. Iyanaga and Y. Kawada, eds., MIT Press, Cambridge
MA, 1954, 2nd edition 1968, english translation and new material, 1977.

shown that the *Quadratic Residue generator* and the *Index generator*, which output bits, are *polynomially unpredictable*, assuming that certain problems in number theory are *polynomially intractable* (see subsections 4.9, 4.11).

Later, as part of the results of section 6, it will be shown that such unpredictable sequences must pass all *polynomial size statistical tests,* i.e. polynomial time unpredictable sequences are indistinguishable from truly random strings of the same length by any polynomial time statistical test. In essence, a polynomial size statistical test checks whether a sequence is random or not and does this in polynomial time. This way it is certain that polynomially unpredictable sequencies must pass *all tests encountered in practice.*

Subsections 4.5 and 4.6 examine questions respectively, relating to factoring and to the periodicity of quadratic residues, and they will be used in the study of the security of the Quadratic Residue generator. The definition of the model of computation to be used in the sequel (the *probabilistic polynomial size circuit*) is given in subsection 4.7.

The reader should notice some of the general notions emerging from the presentation in subsections 4.8, 4.10. These notions, whose study is postponed untill section 6, include the notions of *one to one, one-way function, amplification of advantage,* and *unpredictable pseudorandom generators.* An understanding of the present material will not only provide a good introduction to the general theory, but will also help introduce a number of examples that are essential to clarify the development of the preceding concepts.

4.2   The Linear Congruence Generator

Let a, b, m be given fixed but unknown positive integers such that m is greater than $\max\{a, b\}$. For each nonnegative integer $x < m$, define the infinite sequences

$$x_0, x_1, \ldots, x_i, \ldots, \quad x'_1, x'_2, \ldots, x'_i, \ldots,$$

as follows:

$$x_i \equiv \begin{cases} x & \text{if } i = 0 \\ (a \cdot x_{i-1} + b) \bmod m & \text{if } i > 0, \end{cases}$$

and

$$x'_{i+1} = (x_{i+1} - x_i), \text{ where } i \geq 0.$$

Notice that for all $i \geq 1$,

$$x'_{i+1} \equiv a \cdot x'_i \bmod m.$$

The **linear congruence generator**, abbreviated $LGEN$ accepts as input a quadraple $< x, a, b, m >$ as above; the output $LGEN(x, a, b, m)$ is the infinite sequence $x_0, x_1, \ldots, x_i, \ldots$ defined from x, a, b, m as above.

Example 4.1 $LGEN(3,7,5,12) = 3,2,7,6,11,10,3,2,7,6,11,10,\ldots$.

The problem to be investigated in the sequel is the following:

Question: Is it possible to find an efficient algorithm which, when given as input a sufficiently long initial segment of the infinite sequence $x_0, x_1, \ldots, x_i, \ldots$ will output integers a', b', m' such that for all $i, x_i \equiv (a' \cdot x_{i-1} + b') \bmod m'$?

For each $i \geq 1$, let $g_i = \gcd(x_1', \ldots, x_i')$.

Lemma 4.1

The least $i \geq 1$ such that $g_i | x_{i+1}'$ is $\leq 2 + \lfloor \log_2 m \rfloor$.

Proof: Let $t = $ the least $i \geq 1$ such that $g_i | x_{i+1}'$. Without loss of generality it can be assumed that $t \geq 3$. It is clear that for all i,

$$g_1 = x_1' \text{ and } g_{i+1} = \gcd(g_i, x_{i+1}').$$

However, if g_i does not divide x_{i+1}' then $|g_{i+1}| \leq |g_i|/2$. Consequently,

$$|g_{t-1}| \leq \frac{|g_{t-2}|}{2}, |g_{t-2}| \leq \frac{|g_{t-3}|}{2}, \ldots, |g_2| \leq \frac{|g_1|}{2}.$$

It follows easily that,

$$|g_{t-1}| \leq \frac{|g_1|}{2^{t-2}} = \frac{|x_1'|}{2^{t-2}},$$

and hence,

$$2^{t-2} \leq \frac{|x_1'|}{|g_{t-1}|} < m.$$

This completes the proof of the lemma ●

Using the notation described above the following result can be proved.

Theorem 4.1 (J. Plumstead) *There is an efficient algorithm A which, when given as input the sequence $x_0, x_1, \ldots, x_{t+1}$ (produced by the linear congruence generator $LGEN(x, a, b, m)$), where $t = $ the least $i \geq 1$ such that $g_i | x_{i+1}'$, will output integers a', b' such that for all $i \geq 1$,*

$$x_i \equiv (a' \cdot x_{i-1} + b') \bmod m.$$

The algorithm A runs in time polynomial in $\log_2 m$. Moreover, it is true that $t \leq 2 + \lfloor \log_2 m \rfloor$.

Proof: The upper bound on the size of t is an immediate consequence of lemma 4.1. The algorithm A is defined as follows:

Input: $x_0, x_1, \ldots, x_{t+1}$.

Step 1: Put $x_i' = x_i - x_{i-1}$, where $1 \leq i \leq t+1$.

Step 2: Put $d = \gcd(x_1', \ldots, x_t')$.

Step 3: Compute $u_1, \ldots, u_t$ such that

$$d = \sum_{i=1}^{t} u_i \cdot x_i'.$$

Output:

$$a' = \sum_{i=1}^{t} u_i \cdot \frac{x_{i+1}'}{d}, \quad b' = x_1 - a' \cdot x_0.$$

It will be shown that

Claim: $a' x_i' \equiv x_{i+1}' \bmod m$, for all $i \geq 1$.

Proof of the claim: Let $g = \gcd(m, d)$. Then

$$ad \equiv a \sum_{i=1}^{t} u_i \cdot x_i' \equiv \sum_{i=1}^{t} a \cdot u_i \cdot x_i' \equiv$$

$$\sum_{i=1}^{t} u_i \cdot x_{i+1}' \equiv d \sum_{i=1}^{t} u_i \cdot \frac{x_{i+1}'}{d} \equiv a'd \bmod m.$$

It follows from the definition of g that

$$a \equiv a' \bmod \left(\frac{m}{g}\right).$$

However, for all $i \geq 1$, $g \mid \gcd(x_i', m)$. It follows that for all $i \geq 1$,

$$a \equiv a' \bmod \left(\frac{m}{\gcd(x_i', m)}\right). \tag{1}$$

But a is a solution of the congruence

$$u \cdot x_i' \equiv x_{i+1}' \bmod m. \tag{2}$$

An immediate consequence of the theorem on solving linear congruences (theorem 1.5) is that every solution of (2) is of the form

$$a + \frac{jm}{\gcd(x_i', m)}, \quad j = 0, 1, \ldots, \gcd(x_i', m) - 1.$$

It follows from (1) that a' as well must be a solution of congruence (2). This completes the proof of the claim.

The rest of the proof of the theorem follows from the claim above and the congruences below:

$$a' \cdot x_i + b' - x_{i+1} \equiv a' \cdot x_i + (x_1 - a' \cdot x_0) - x_{i+1} \equiv$$

$$a' \cdot (x_i - x_0) - (x_{i+1} - x_1) \equiv a' \sum_{k=1}^{i} x'_k - \sum_{k=1}^{i} x'_{k+1} \equiv$$

$$\sum_{k=1}^{i} (a' \cdot x'_k - x'_{k+1}) \equiv 0 \bmod m \bullet$$

No small bound on the number of x_i's that will enable one to predict a modulus m' is known, so that the conclusion of theorem 4.1 is valid. In many instances however one can predict such a modulus for sufficiently long finite segments of the sequence $x_0, x_1, \ldots, x_i, \ldots$ produced by $LGEN$ using the following argument. Use the algorithm of theorem 4.1 to compute a', b' such that the conclusion of theorem 4.1 is true (e.g. this can always be done if the given sequence is of length $\geq 2 + \lfloor \log_2 m \rfloor$). For any given modulus M define the following sequence by induction on $i \geq 0$:

$$x_0(M) = x_0, \; x_{i+1}(M) \equiv a' x_i(M) + b' \bmod M.$$

It is not hard to show by induction that for all $i \geq 0$,

$$M^* | M \Rightarrow x_i(M) \equiv x_i(M^*) \bmod M^*. \tag{3}$$

Finally, for each modulus M define

$$k(M) = \text{ least } k \text{ such that } x_{k+1}(M) \not\equiv x_{k+1} \bmod M,$$

$$M^* = \gcd(M, x_{k(M)+1}(M) - x_{k(M)+1}).$$

Since $x_{k(M)+1}(M) \equiv x_{k(M)+1} \bmod M^*$, it follows from (3) that for any modulus M, $k(M^*) \geq k(M) + 1$.

To facilitate the discussion that follows the notation

$$\gcd(a, \infty) = a, \; a \bmod \infty = a,$$

where a is an integer, will be used. The idea in predicting a modulus is the following: given a sequence $x_0, x_1, \ldots, x_s$ produced by $LGEN$, one tries first the modulus $M = \infty$. If $x_k(M) \equiv x_k \bmod M$, for all $k \leq s$, then M is the desired modulus; otherwise update M to M^*. Continue updating the modulus in this way. Clearly, the number of updates necessary is at most $\leq s$.

More formally, given a sequence $x_0, x_1, \ldots, x_s$ produced by $LGEN$ such that $s \geq$ the least $i \geq 1$ such that $g_i | x'_{i+1}$, define the following sequence $m^{(0)}, m^{(1)}, \ldots, m^{(r)}$ of moduli such that the conditions below are met for all $j < r$:

$$m^{(j+1)} = (m^{(j)})^*, k(m^{(j)}) < s \text{ and}$$
$$m^{(0)} = \infty, k(m^{(r)}) \geq s.$$

Put $m' = m^{(r)}$. Since $x_i(m') \equiv x_i \bmod m'$, for all $i \leq k(m')$, it is clear that

$$x_i \equiv a' x_{i-1} + b' \bmod m', \text{ for all } 1 \leq i \leq s. \tag{4}$$

To sum up it has been shown that

Theorem 4.2 (J. Plumstead) *For any sequence $x_0, x_1, \ldots, x_s$ produced by the linear congruence generator $LGEN(x, a, b, m)$, where $s - 1 \geq$ the least $i \geq 1$ such that $g_i | x'_{i+1}$, there is an efficient algorithm A which, when given as input the sequence $x_0, x_1, \ldots, x_s$, will output integers a', b', m' such that for all $s \geq i \geq 1$,*

$$x_i \equiv (a' \cdot x_{i-1} + b') \bmod m'.$$

Moreover, the algorithm A runs in polynomial time in s.

The periodicity of the linear congruence generator, as well as the problem of choosing a modulus to make the generator as secure as possible, are studied in detail in subsection 3.2.1.2. of [K2].

EXERCISES

Throughout the exercises below, the notation of the subsection above will be used. Show that for all $n \geq 1$,

1: $x_n \equiv a^n x_0 + (a^{n-1} + \cdots + a + 1)b \bmod m.$

2: $x'_n \equiv a^{n-1} x'_1 \bmod m.$

Further, assume that $\gcd(a, m) = 1$ and show that

3: $x_n \equiv (x_{n+1} - b)a^{\varphi(m)-1} \bmod m.$

4: If $(a - 1) | b$ then $x_n = x_{\varphi(m)+n}.$ **Hint:** Use exercise 1.

5: $x'_n = x'_{\varphi(m)+n}.$ **Hint:** Use exercise 2.

6: Prove the assertions stated in congruences (3) and (4) of the subsection above.

4.3   The (1/p) - Generator

Throughout the present subsection, p will denote an odd prime number, g a fixed primitive root of Z_p^*, and $|p|$ the length of p in base g, i.e. $|p| = \lceil \log_g p \rceil$. An integer r such that $0 \le r < g$ will also be called a g-**digit.** Given any integer r such that $0 < r < g$, define the infinite sequence $r_0, r_1, \ldots, r_m, \ldots$ as follows:

$$r_m \equiv r \cdot g^m \bmod p, \; m \ge 0. \tag{5}$$

Since g is a primitive root of Z_p^*, it follows from the Euler - Fermat theorem that for any $0 < r < p$, the period of the sequence $r_0, r_1, \ldots, r_m, \ldots$ equals $p - 1$, i.e. $p - 1 = $ the least m such that $r_0 = r_m$. Moreover, $\{r_0, r_1, \ldots, r_{p-2}\} = \{1, 2, \ldots, p - 1\}$.

It is an immediate consequence of the Euclidean algorithm and the definition of r_m that, for each $m \ge 0$, there exists a nonnegative integer $q_{m+1} < g$, such that

$$\frac{r_m}{p} = \frac{q_{m+1}}{g} + \frac{1}{g} \cdot \frac{r_{m+1}}{p}. \tag{6}$$

It follows that for all $m \ge 0$,

$$\frac{r_0}{p} = \frac{q_1}{g} + \frac{q_2}{g^2} + \cdots + \frac{q_m}{g^m} + \frac{1}{g^m} \cdot \frac{r_m}{p}. \tag{7}$$

Multiplying equation (7) by $g^m p$ one obtains

$$r_0 g^m = (q_1 g^{m-1} + q_2 g^{m-2} + \cdots + q_m)p + r_m. \tag{8}$$

For any sequence $x_1, x_2, \ldots, x_m$ of g-digits let the notation

$$x_1 x_2 \ldots x_m, \quad .x_1 x_2 \ldots x_m$$

be used as an abbreviation respectively, of

$$x_1 g^{m-1} + x_2 g^{m-2} + \cdots + x_m, \quad \frac{x_1}{g} + \frac{x_2}{g^2} + \cdots + \frac{x_m}{g^m}.$$

With these abbreviations, equations (7), (8) can be generalized, for each $i \ge 0$, to

$$\frac{r_i}{p} = .q_{i+1} q_{i+2} \cdots q_{i+m} + \frac{1}{g^m} \cdot \frac{r_{i+m}}{p}, \tag{9}$$

$$r_i g^m = (q_{i+1} q_{i+2} \cdots q_{i+m})p + r_{i+m}. \tag{10}$$

An infinite sequence $x_1, x_2, \ldots, x_m, \ldots$ of g-digits is called a **de Bruijn sequence of period** $p-1$ **and base** g if the following three conditions hold:

(1) the sequence $x_1, x_2, \ldots, x_m, \ldots$ of g-digits is periodic with period $p-1$,

(2) every finite sequence of g-digits of length $|p| - 1$ occurs at least once as a segment of $x_1, x_2, \ldots, x_m, \ldots$, and

(3) every finite sequence of g-digits of length $|p|$ occurs at most once as a segment of $x_1, x_2, \ldots, x_m, \ldots$.

Example 4.2 *(1) For $p = 3$ (= 11 in base 2), the sequence $0, 1, 0, 1, \ldots$ is a de Bruijn sequence of period 2 and base 2.*

(2) For $p = 5$ (= 101 in base 2), the sequence $0, 1, 1, 0, 0, 1, 1, 0, \ldots$ is a de Bruijn sequence of period 4 and base 2.

The $1/p$ **generator**, abbreviated by $PGEN$, accepts as input the triple $< p, r, g >$, where p is a prime, $0 < r < g$, and g is a primitive root of Z_p^*; the output $PGEN(p, r, g)$ is the infinite sequence $q_1, q_2, \ldots, q_m, \ldots$ of g-digits which arises when the rational number r/p is represented in base g (see equation (9)).

The notation established above will be used during the proof of the theorems below.

Theorem 4.3 *For any primitive root g modulo p and any g-digit r, the sequence $PGEN(p, r, g)$ is a de Bruijn sequence of period $p-1$ and base g.*

Proof: In view of equation (9) one obtains that for all $k \geq 0$,

$$\frac{r_k}{p} = .q_{k+1} q_{k+2} \cdots = \sum_{i=1}^{\infty} \frac{q_{k+i}}{g^i}. \tag{11}$$

But the sequence $r_0, r_1, \ldots, r_m, \ldots$ is periodic with period $p-1$ and hence for all $i \geq 0$, $r_i = r_{i+p-1}$. It follows from this and equation (11) that

$$.q_{i+1} q_{i+2} \cdots = .q_{i+p} q_{i+p+1} \cdots . \tag{12}$$

Hence, the period of the sequence $q_1, q_2, \ldots, q_m, \ldots$ must be $\leq p-1$. It remains to show that it is exactly equal to $p-1$. Indeed, assume on the contrary that the period is i and $0 < i < p-1$. Then it clear that

$$.q_{i+1} q_{i+2} \cdots = .q_1 q_2 \cdots \tag{13}$$

and hence $r_0/p = r_i/p$, which is a contradiction. It will now be shown that the sequence $q_1, q_2, \ldots$ is a de Bruijn sequence. Let $\overline{d} = d_1, \ldots, d_t$ be an arbitrary finite sequence of g-digits of length $t \geq |p| - 1$. It is then clear that the following statements (14) - (17) are equivalent:

$$\overline{d} \text{ is a segment of the sequence } q_1, q_2, \ldots. \tag{14}$$

$$\text{For some } i \geq 0, \overline{d} \text{ is an initial segment of } q_{i+1}, q_{i+2}, \ldots. \tag{15}$$

$$\text{For some } i \geq 0, \overline{d} \text{ is an initial segment of the expansion of } \frac{r_i}{p}. \tag{16}$$

$$\text{For some } k \geq 0, \overline{d} \text{ is an initial segment of the expansion of } \frac{k}{p}. \tag{17}$$

However, to each finite sequence $\overline{d} = d_1, \ldots, d_t$ of g-digits of length t there corresponds exactly one subinterval

$$\left[\frac{i}{g^t}, \frac{i+1}{g^t} \right), \text{ where } 0 \leq i < g^t,$$

of $[0, 1)$; namely, the subinterval to which the real number $.d_1 \ldots d_t$ belongs. Since, $g^{|p|-1} < p \leq g^{|p|}$, it is clear that

$$\frac{1}{g^{|p|}} \leq \frac{1}{p} < \frac{1}{g^{|p|-1}}. \tag{18}$$

It is now easy to see, using inequality (18) and properties (14) - (17) that for each $i \geq 0$,

$$\text{there is at least one } k < p \text{ such that } \frac{k}{p} \in \left[\frac{i}{g^{|p|-1}}, \frac{i+1}{g^{|p|-1}} \right), and$$

$$\text{there is at most one } k < p \text{ such that } \frac{k}{p} \in \left[\frac{i}{g^{|p|}}, \frac{i+1}{g^{|p|}} \right).$$

This completes the proof of the theorem •

The predictability of the $1/p$ generator follows from the theorem below.

Theorem 4.4 (Blum-Blum-Shub) *Let g be a primitive root modulo a prime p, and let $0 < r < p$. Then there there exists an algorithm A running in polynomial time in $|p|$ such that if $k = \lceil \log_g(2p^2) \rceil$, then for all $m \geq 0$,*

$$A(g, q_{m+1}, q_{m+2}, \ldots, q_{m+k}) = < p, r_m > .$$

Proof: Let $A_1/B_1, A_2/B_2, \ldots$ denote the convergents of the fraction

$$(q_{m+1}q_{m+2}\cdots q_{m+k})/g^k.$$

By assumption, $k = \lceil \log_g(2p^2) \rceil \geq \log_g(2p^2)$, and hence $g^k \geq 2p^2$. It is then clear, using inequality

$$\frac{1}{g^k} \cdot \frac{r_{k+m}}{p} < \frac{1}{g^k}$$

and equation (9) that

$$\left| \frac{(q_{m+1}\cdots q_{m+k})}{g^k} - \frac{r_m}{p} \right| < \frac{1}{g^k} \leq \frac{1}{2p^2}.$$

It follows from results of the subsection on continued fractions that r_m/p is a convergent of $(q_{m+1}q_{m+2}\cdots q_{m+k})/g^k$ and hence,

$$\frac{r_m}{p} = \frac{A_i}{B_i}, \text{ for some } i \geq 0. \tag{19}$$

Since, $\gcd(r_m, p) = \gcd(A_i, B_i) = 1$, it follows that $r_m = A_i$, $p = B_i$. To complete the proof of the theorem it will be shown that A_i/B_i can be obtained by generating the sequence $A_1/B_1, A_2/B_2, \ldots$ of convergents until the j-th fraction A_j/B_j has $q_{m+1}, q_{m+2}, \ldots, q_{m+k}$ as its k first g-digits. Indeed, let j be the first index such that the first k g-digits of the fraction A_j/B_j are $q_{m+1}, q_{m+2}, \ldots, q_{m+k}$. It follows from equation (19) and the minimality of j that $j \leq i$. Assume on the contrary that $A_i/B_i \neq A_j/B_j$. Then it is clear that

$$\frac{1}{B_i B_j} \leq \left| \frac{A_i B_j - A_j B_i}{B_i B_j} \right| = \left| \frac{A_i}{B_i} - \frac{A_j}{B_j} \right| < \frac{1}{g^k}.$$

Since $j \leq i$, it must be true that $B_j \leq B_i$ and hence $2B_i^2 = 2p^2 \leq g^k < B_i B_j \leq B_i^2$, which is a contradiction. Moreover, the amount of steps needed to compute A_i, B_i is polynomial in $|p|$ •

EXERCISES

1: Show that for all $0 < r < p$ and any $i \geq 0$, $r_i = r_{i+p-1}$. Conclude that $\{r_0, r_1, \ldots, r_{p-2}\} = \{1, 2, \ldots, p-1\}$.

2: Show that in the proof of theorem 4.4, both A_i, B_i can be computed in polynomial in $|p|$ many steps. **Hint:** The theory of continued fractions implies that one need only compute A_i, B_i until condition $1/B_i^2 < 1/g^k$ is met.

Let g be a primitive root modulo p, p a prime, $0 < r < p$.

3: There exists an algorithm A_1 running in polynomial time in $|p|$ such that for all m, $A_1(p, g, q_{m+1}, q_{m+2}, \ldots, q_{m+|p|}) = r_m$.

4: There exists an algorithm A_2 running in polynomial time in $|p|$ such that for all m, i, $A_2(p, g, r_m, i) = < r_{m-1}, r_{m+i}, q_m, \ldots, q_{m+i} >$.

5: There exists an algorithm A_3 running in polynomial time in $|p|$ such that for all m, if $r_m g \neq r_{m+1}$ then $A_3(g, r_m, r_{m+1}) = p$. **Hint:** Let S be the set $\{(gr_m - r_{m+1})/i \ : \ i = 0, 1, \ldots, g - 1\}$. By equation (6), $p = (gr_m - r_{m+1})/q_{m+1} \in S$. Show that p is the unique $x \in S$ such that for all $i = 1, \ldots, g$, $\gcd(x, i) = 1$.

4.4   Quadratic Residues in Cryptography

In constructing cryptographic protocols one considers integers $n = pq$, where p, q are two distinct odd primes. For such integers n it is necessary to study the behavior of the Legendre-Jacobi symbol modulo n. **From now on and for the rest of this subsection it will be assumed that $n = pq$, where p, q are two distinct odd primes.**

Let x be a quadratic residue modulo n. Call u a **square root** of x modulo n, if $u^2 \equiv x \bmod n$. The next theorem determines the number of square roots of any given quadratic residue.

Theorem 4.5 *Any quadratic residue has four square roots modulo n.*

Proof: By the Chinese remainder theorem there exist integers a, b such that

$$a \equiv 1 \bmod p \ \text{ and } \ a \equiv -1 \bmod q,$$

$$b \equiv -1 \bmod p \ \text{ and } \ b \equiv 1 \bmod q.$$

Since both p, q are odd it is clear that $a, b, 1, -1$ are distinct modulo n. Moreover, $a^2 \equiv b^2 \equiv 1 \bmod n$. It follows that $1, -1, a, b$ are four distinct modulo n square roots of 1. The rest of the proof follows from exercise 1 of the subsection on the homomorphism theorem (subsection 1.2) •

For the rest of this subsection it will be assumed that $p \equiv q \equiv 3 \bmod 4$, i.e. both $(p - 1)/2$ and $(q - 1)/2$ are odd.

It follows that $(-1|p) = (-1|q) = -1$ and $(-1|n) = (-1|p)(-1|q) = 1$. Hence, for all $x \in Z_n^*$, $(-x|n) = (x|n)$.

Theorem 4.6 *(i) If $x^2 \equiv y^2 \bmod n$, and $x, y, -x, -y$ are distinct modulo n then $(x|n) = -(y|n)$.*

*(ii) The mapping $x \longrightarrow x^2$ modn($x \in QR_n, x^2$ mod$n \in QR_n$) is $1-1$
and onto, i.e. every quadratic residue has a unique square root which is also
a quadratic residue modulo n.*

Proof: (i) Assume that x and y are as above. Then, it is clear that
$n = pq|(x^2 - y^2) = (x - y)(x + y)$. Since $x, -x, y, -y$ are distinct modulo n,
neither $x-y$ nor $x+y$ can be divided by both p, q. Without loss of generality,
assume that $p|(x - y)$, and $q|(x + y)$ (the other case is treated similarly).
Then $x \equiv y$ mod$p$ and $x \equiv -y$ mod$q$. It follows that $(x|p) = (y|p)$ and
$(x|q) = -(y|q)$, and hence the proof of part (i) is complete.

(ii) Let a be any quadratic residue modulo n. By the previous theorem
a has exactly four square roots modulo n, say $x, -x, y, -y$. By part (i),
$(x|n) = -(y|n)$. Let x be the square root of a such that $(x|n) = +1$. It
follows that either $(x|p) = (x|q) = +1$ or $(-x|p) = (-x|q) = +1$. Thus, one
of $x, -x$ must be a quadratic residue modulo n. This completes the proof of
the theorem ●

The theorem above implies that the mapping

$$x \longrightarrow x^2 \text{ mod}n, \text{ where } (x \in QR_n, x^2 \text{ mod}n \in QR_n)$$

is $1-1$ and onto, and hence it has an inverse which will be denoted by

$$x \longrightarrow \sqrt{x} \text{ mod}n, \text{ where } (x \in QR_n, \sqrt{x} \text{ mod}n \in QR_n).$$

It is an immediate consequence of these considerations that every quadratic
residue x has four square roots, x_1, x_2, x_3, x_4, which satisfy:

$$(x_1|p) = (x_1|q) = +1, (x_2|p) = (x_2|q) = -1,$$

$$(x_3|p) = -(x_3|q) = +1, -(x_4|p) = (x_4|q) = +1.$$

Moreover, the square root x_1 is also a quadratic residue modulo n.

EXERCISES

1: Show that $|QR_n| = \varphi(n)/4, |Z_n^*(+1)| = \varphi(n)/2, |Z_n^*(-1)| = \varphi(n)/2$.
2: The mapping $x \longrightarrow x^2$ mod$p$($x \in QR_p, x^2$ mod$p \in QR_p$) is $1-1$ and
onto, i.e. every quadratic residue has a unique square root which is also a
quadratic residue modulo p, where p is a prime with $p \equiv 3$ mod4.
3: Is the result of exercise 2 valid for primes of the form $p \equiv 1$ mod4?

4.5   Factoring and Quadratic Residues

The main theorem of the present subsection is due to Rabin. It shows in effect, that the problems of factoring a composite number, and of solving quadradic congruences modulo a composite number, are equivalent.

Theorem 4.7 *(Rabin) The following statements are equivalent:*

(i) There is an efficient algorithm A such that for all n, if n is the product of two distinct odd primes, both congruent to 3 modulo 4, then $A(n) = p$, where p is a prime factor of n.

(ii) There is an efficient algorithm B such that if n is the product of two distinct odd primes, both congruent to 3 modulo 4, and $x \in QR_n$, then $B(n, x) = \sqrt{x} \bmod n$.

Proof: (ii) $\Rightarrow$ (i)

Assume the algorithm B is given. The algorithm A is defined as follows:

Input: n.

Step 1: Choose a random y such that $(y|n) = -1$.

Step 2: Compute $x \equiv y^2 \bmod n$.

Step 3: Compute $z = B(n, x)$.

Output: $\gcd(y + z, n)$.

It remains to show that this algorithm works. Indeed, it is clear that $x \equiv y^2 \equiv z^2 \bmod n$. Hence, $n|(y^2 - x^2) = (y - z)(y + z)$. Assume that $n = pq$. It follows that $pq|(y - z)(y + z)$. But, $(y|n) = -(z|n) = -1$ and therefore $y \not\equiv z \bmod n$ and $y \not\equiv -z \bmod n$. Consequently, $\gcd(y + z, n)$ must be one of the prime factors of n.

(i) $\Rightarrow$ (ii)

The algorithm B uses the Adelman-Manders-Miller algorithm for computing square roots modulo a prime and is defined as follows:

Input: n, x.

Step 1: Let $p = A(n), q = n/p$.

Step 2: Compute $u \in QR_p$, $v \in QR_q$, such that $x \equiv u^2 \bmod p$, $x \equiv v^2 \bmod q$.

Step 3: Compute a, b such that $1 = ap + bq$.

Step 4: Compute $c = bq$ and $d = ap$.

Output: $cu + dv$.

Let $w = cu + dv$. Since $c \equiv 1 \bmod p$, $d \equiv 1 \bmod q$, it is clear from the above algorithm that $w^2 \equiv x \bmod n$. It remains to show that $w \in QR_n$. Indeed, notice that $c \equiv 0 \bmod q$ and $c \equiv 1 \bmod p$, $d \equiv 0 \bmod p$ and $d \equiv$

1 mod$q$. Hence, $(w|p) = (u|p) = 1$ and $(w|q) = (v|q) = 1$. Thus, $w \in QR_p$ and $w \in QR_q$, and consequently, $w \in QR_n$ •

EXERCISES

1: Show that the following statements are equivalent:

(i) There is an efficient algorithm A such that for all n, if n is the product of two distinct primes, then $A(n) = p$, where p is a prime factor of n.

(ii) There is an efficient algorithm B such that if n is the product of two distinct primes, then $B(n) = \varphi(n)$. **Hint:** To prove (ii) $\Rightarrow$ (i) notice that $p + q = n + 1 - B(n)$, $p - q = \sqrt{(p+q)^2 - 4n}$.

4.6   Periodicity of Quadratic Residues

For each n and each x in Z_n^*, the **order** of x with respect to n, abbreviated order$_n(x)$, is the least nonnegative exponent e such that $x^e \equiv 1$ mod$n$. Throughout this subsection $n = pq$, where p, q are two distinct odd primes such that $p \equiv q \equiv 3$ mod4. For each quadratic residue $x \in QR_n$, define the infinite sequence of quadratic residues,

$$\ldots, x_{n,-2}, x_{n,-1}, x_{n,0} = x, x_{n,1}, x_{n,2}, \ldots$$

as follows:

$$x_{n,i} \equiv \begin{cases} x^{2^i} \bmod n & \text{if } i \geq 0 \\ \sqrt{x_{n,i+1}} & \text{if } i < 0. \end{cases}$$

The modulus n used as a subscript in $x_{n,i}$ will usually be omitted, but this will cause no confusion because n will be easily understood from the context.

Call the **period** of x, abbreviated $\overline{\pi}(x)$, the least positive integer i such that $x_i = x$. The purpose of the theorems below is to determine the size of $\overline{\pi}(x)$.

Theorem 4.8 (Blum-Blum-Shub) *For all $x \in Z_n^*$,*

$$\text{order}_n(x) = \lambda(n)/2 \text{ and order}_{\lambda(n)/2}(2) = \lambda(\lambda(n)) \Rightarrow \lambda(\lambda(n)) = \overline{\pi}(x).$$

Proof: Put $\overline{\pi} = \overline{\pi}(x)$. By assumption $\lambda(n)/2$ is the least exponent e such that $x^e \equiv 1$ mod$n$. But $x_{\overline{\pi}} \equiv x \equiv x^{2^{\overline{\pi}}}$ mod$n$. It follows that $x^{2^{\overline{\pi}}-1} \equiv 1$ mod$n$, and consequently $\lambda(n)/2|(2^{\overline{\pi}} - 1)$. Thus, $2^{\overline{\pi}} \equiv 1 \bmod(\lambda(n)/2)$. Using the hypothesis that order$_{\lambda(n)/2}(2) = \lambda(\lambda(n))$, one obtains that $\lambda(\lambda(n)) = $ the least exponent e such that $2^e \equiv 1 \bmod(\lambda(n)/2)$. It follows that $\lambda(\lambda(n))|\overline{\pi}$.

Hence, the theorem will follow from the following

Claim: $\overline{\pi}|\lambda(\lambda(n))$.

Proof of the Claim: First notice that the congruence $a \equiv b^2 \bmod n$ implies that $\text{order}_n(a)|\text{order}_n(b)$. Indeed, set $e = \text{order}_n(b)$. Then $b^e \equiv 1 \bmod n$. Hence, $a^e \equiv b^{2e} \equiv 1 \bmod n$. Thus, $\text{order}_n(a)|\text{order}_n(b) = e$. It follows from the preceding observation that for all i, $\text{order}_n(x_{i+1})|\text{order}_n(x_i)$. However $x_0 = x_{\overline{\pi}}$. It is therefore clear that for all i, $\text{order}_n(x_i) = \text{order}_n(x_0)$. Further, it can be proved that $\text{order}_n(x)$ is odd. Indeed, assume on the contrary that $\text{order}_n(x) = 2^e m$, where m is odd, $e > 0$. Then $x^{2^e m} \equiv x_1^{2^{e-1}m} \equiv 1 \bmod n$, which contradicts $\text{order}_n(x_1) = \text{order}_n(x_0)$.

It is immediate from the definition of $\overline{\pi}(x) = \overline{\pi}$ that $\overline{\pi}$ equals the least exponent e such that $2^e \equiv 1 \bmod(\text{order}_n(x))$. Since $\gcd(2, \text{order}_n(x)) = 1$, it follows from Carmichael's theorem that $\overline{\pi}|\lambda(\text{order}_n(x))$. But $od_n(x)|\lambda(n)$, and consequently $\lambda(od_n(x))|\lambda(\lambda(n))$. This is enough to complete the proof of the claim, and hence of the theorem •

Clearly, the theorem above supplies the necessary hypotheses which imply that $\lambda(\lambda(n)) = \overline{\pi}(x)$. Next it will be determined for which integers these conditions are satisfied. A prime number p is called **special** if there exist prime numbers p_1, p_2 such that $p = 2p_1 + 1$, $p_1 = 2p_2 + 1$, and $p_2 > 2$. The number $n = pq$ is called **special** if both primes p and q are special and $p \neq q$.

Remark: It is not known if there exist infinitely many special primes. Some examples of special primes are obtained for $q = 11, 23, 83$, in which case $p = 2q+1$ is a special prime. For a detailed discussion of this conjecture, as well as for a table of bigger special primes, see [S3] (pp. 28 - 30).

Theorem 4.9 *(Blum-Blum-Shub) Let $n = pq$ be special, such that $p = 2p_1 + 1$, $p_1 = 2p_2 + 1$, $q = 2q_1 + 1$, $q_1 = 2q_2 + 1$, and p_1, p_2, q_1, q_2 are primes. If 2 is a quadratic residue modulo at most one of p_1, q_1 then*

$$\text{order}_{\lambda(n)/2}(2) = \lambda(\lambda(n)).$$

Proof: It is a consequence of the definition of the Carmichael function that $\lambda(n) = 2p_1q_1$, $\lambda(n)/2 = p_1q_1$, $\lambda(\lambda(n)) = 2p_2q_2$, $\lambda(\lambda(n)/2) = 2p_2q_2$. It follows from Carmichael's theorem that $\text{order}_{\lambda(n)/2}(2)|\lambda(\lambda(n)/2) = 2p_2q_2$. Assume on the contrary that $\text{order}_{\lambda(n)/2}(2) \neq 2p_2q_2$. In each of the three cases below a contradiction will be derived.

Case 1: $od_{\lambda(n)/2}(2)|2p_2$.

It is clear that $2^{2p_2} \equiv 1 \bmod(p_1q_1)$. Hence, $2^{2p_2} \equiv 1 \bmod q_1$. By the Euler-Fermat theorem it is true that $2^{2q_2} \equiv 1 \bmod q_1$. It follows that

$2^{\gcd(2p_2,2q_2)} \equiv 1 \bmod q_1$, and hence $2^2 \equiv 1 \bmod q_1$, since $\gcd(2p_2,2q_2) = 2$. But this contradicts the fact that $q_1 > 3$.

Case 2: $od_{\lambda(n)/2}(2)|2q_2$.
This is similar to case 1.

Case 3: $od_{\lambda(n)/2}(2)|p_2q_2$.
It is clear that $2^{p_2q_2} \equiv 1 \bmod(p_1q_1)$. Hence, $2^{p_2q_2} \equiv 1 \bmod q_1$. Since p_2 is an odd prime, the last congruence implies that $2^{q_2} \not\equiv -1 \bmod q_1$. By Euler's criterion, and since $q_2 = (q_1 - 1)/2$, $2^{q_2} \equiv (2|q_1) \bmod q_1$. It follows that $(2|q_1) \equiv 1$, and hence $2 \in QR_{q_1}$. Similarly $2 \in QR_{p_1}$. But it is clear that this is a contradiction ●

Theorem 4.9 provides integers n satisfying $order_{\lambda(n)/2}(x) = \lambda(\lambda(n))$. It turns out that integers n satisfying $order_n(x) = \lambda(n)/2$ are much easier to locate.

Theorem 4.10 $|\{x \in QR_n : od_n(x) = \lambda(n)/2\}| = \Omega(n/(\log\log n)^2)$.

Proof: By assumption $n = pq$ is a product of two primes. Z_p^* (respectively Z_q^*) has exactly $\varphi(\varphi(p))$ (respectively $\varphi(\varphi(q))$) generators or primitive roots. Let $g \in Z_p^*$ (respectively $h \in Z_q^*$) be a generator of Z_p^* (respectively Z_q^*). By the Chinese remainder theorem there exists a unique modulo n integer a such that $a \equiv g \bmod p$ and $a \equiv h \bmod q$. It follows that $order_n(a) = \lambda(n) = \text{lcm}(p - 1, q - 1)$. Consequently, there exist at least $\varphi(\varphi(p)) \cdot \varphi(\varphi(q))$ elements in Z_n^* of order $\lambda(n)$. It follows from a theorem of E. Landau that for all $x > 2$,

$$\frac{x}{\varphi(x)} < 6 \log\log x.$$

To complete the proof of the theorem notice that

$$\varphi(\varphi(p)) \cdot \varphi(\varphi(q)) = \varphi(p - 1) \cdot \varphi(q - 1) \geq$$

$$\frac{p - 1}{6\log\log(p - 1)} \cdot \frac{q - 1}{6\log\log(q - 1)} \geq \frac{n - p - q - 1}{(6\log\log n)^2} \geq \frac{n/2}{(6\log\log n)^2}.$$

But the mapping $x \longrightarrow x^2 \bmod n (x \in Z_n^*, x^2 \bmod n \in QR_n)$ is $4 - 1$. Moreover, if $x \in Z_n^*$ is of order $\lambda(n)$, then $x^2 \bmod n \in QR_n$ is of order $\lambda(n)/2$. Using this observation one can complete the proof of the theorem easily ●

The next theorem establishes the connection between computing the period of quadratic residues and the factoring problem.

Theorem 4.11 *(Blum-Blum-Shub) Assume that there exist efficient algorithms A, A' such that for all n, which are the product of two distinct odd primes, for all $x \in QR_n$ and for all $i \geq 0$,*

$$A(n,x) = \overline{\pi}(x) \quad \text{and} \quad A'(n,x,i) = x_i.$$

Then there exists an efficient algorithm which when given as input an integer n that is the product of two distinct odd primes, will output a prime factor of n .

Proof: The factoring algorithm is defined as follows:
Input: n.
Step 1: Choose a random y such that $(y|n) = -1$.
Step 2: Compute $x \equiv y^2 \bmod n$.
Step 3: Compute $\overline{\pi} = A(n,x)$.
Step 4: Compute $z = A'(n,x,\overline{\pi} - 1)$.
Output: $\gcd(z - y, n)$.
The proof that this algorithm works is similar to the proof of theorem 4.7 and uses the fact that in the algorithm, $x \equiv y^2 \equiv z^2 \bmod n$. Details are left to the reader as an exercise •

EXERCISES

1: Prove results similar to those of theorems 4.8, 4.9, 4.10 for quadratic residues modulo p, where p is prime; to be more specific show that for $x \in QR_p$, the following statements hold:
(i) If $\text{order}_p(x) = \lambda(p)/2$ and $\text{order}_{\lambda(p)/2}(2) = \lambda(\lambda(p))$ then $\lambda(\lambda(p)) = \overline{\pi}(x)$.
(ii) If p is special and $2 \in QNR_{(p-1)/2}$, then $\text{order}_{\lambda(p)/2}(2) = \lambda(\lambda(p))$.
(iii)$|\{x \in QR_p : \text{order}_p(x) = \lambda(p)/2\}| = \Omega(p/\log\log p)$.
2: Complete the details of the proof of theorem 4.11.

4.7   The Circuit as a Model of Computation

An (n,t) **circuit** is an **acyclic, labeled, digraph** (i.e. a graph with no cycles, with labeled nodes, and with directed edges) consisting of
(1) a list of n distinguished **input** nodes each of which has indegree 0 (i.e. no entering edges) and outdegree 1 (i.e. exactly one exiting edge),
(2) **internal** nodes, each of which has outdegree 1 and is labeled with one of the symbols $\oplus, \otimes$,

(3) a list of t distinguished **output** nodes, each of which has outdegree 0 and is labeled with one of the symbols $\oplus, \otimes$.

The nodes of the circuit are also called **gates**. Each gate of the circuit can hold one of the two boolean values 0 or 1. An **assignment** of the input nodes of an (n, t) circuit is an n-tuple $(x_1, \ldots, x_n) \in \{0, 1\}^n$ such that the i-th input node is assigned the value x_i. If an internal $\oplus$ (respectively $\otimes$) gate has indegree k, then the output of this gate, on input $(u_1, \ldots, u_k) \in \{0, 1\}^k$, is $u_1 \oplus \cdots \oplus u_k$ (respectively $u_1 \otimes \cdots \otimes u_k$). The **value** of the circuit on the input assignment $(x_1, \ldots, x_n) \in \{0, 1\}^n$ is the value of the circuit obtained at the t output gates when one evaluates the output of each of the internal gates in topological order along the circuit.

Thus, every (n, t) circuit C determines a function,

$$f_C : \{0, 1\}^n \longrightarrow \{0, 1\}^t,$$

called the **circuit function**, such that $f_C(x_1, \ldots, x_n) = (y_1, \ldots, y_t)$, where $(y_1, \ldots, y_t)$ is the t - tuple of the values of the t output gates of the circuit C when the input assignment is $(x_1, \ldots, x_n)$.

Example 4.3 *The circuit in figure 1 computes the function*

$$f(x_1, \ldots, x_9) = [(x_1 \oplus x_2 \oplus x_3) \oplus (x_4 \otimes x_5)] \oplus [(x_6 \otimes x_7) \otimes (x_8 \oplus x_9)].$$

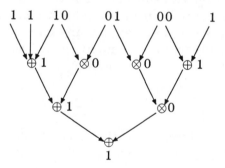

Figure 1: A Deterministic Circuit

The **size** $|C|$ of the circuit C is the total number of its gates and the **depth** $d(C)$ of the circuit is the length of its longest path.

An (n, m, t) **probabilistic circuit** C is an $(n + m, t)$ circuit with two distinct types of input gates:

(1) a list of n distinguished input gates called **deterministic gates**,

(2) a list of m distinguished input gates called **random gates**.

Let C be an (n, m, t) probabilistic circuit. To evaluate the value of C on the input assignment $(x_1, \ldots, x_n)$, one assigns the deterministic input gates the values $(x_1, \ldots, x_n)$, the random gates the values $(y_1, \ldots, y_m)$ each with probability $1/2$, and then computes the output of the circuit C on the input assignment

$$(x_1, \ldots, x_n, y_1, \ldots, y_m).$$

A **polynomial size family of probabilistic circuits** (or **probabilistic circut**, for short) is a family $C = \{C_n : n \geq 1\}$ of probabilistic circuits such that

(1) there exists a polynomial P with positive integer coefficients of degree ≥ 1 such that for all $n \geq 1$, each circuit C_n has $P(n)$ many deterministic input gates, and

(2) there exists a polynomial P' with positive integer coefficients of degree ≥ 1 such that $|C_n| \leq P'(n)$, for all $n \geq 1$.

The polynomials P, P' usually will not be mentioned. **From now on and for the rest of the book all the circuits considered will be probabilistic, unless otherwise specified. For that reason, the term circuit, whenever used, will mean probabilistic circuit. In addition, in order to simplify the notation, for any circuit C considered, its random gates usually will not be mentioned.** Thus, if C is an $(n, m, 1)$ probabilistic circuit and $\epsilon > 0$, then the symbol

$$Pr[C(x) = 0] \geq \epsilon$$

will mean that with probability $\geq \epsilon$, the circuit C will output 0 on input x, where the probability space is the set $\{0, 1\}^m$.

The probabilistic polynomial size circuit will be used in the sequel as the main model of computation. To be sure, all the theorems mentioned below could have been proved using probabilistic polynomial time Turing machines. However, there is a slight advantage in using circuits. The theorems can be formulated, without having to specify each time a lower bound on the number of steps the Turing machine will have to run in order to obtain optimal security. For more on this, see [G8], page 297.

4.8   The Quadratic Residue Generator

Throughout the present subsection, n will range over integers which are the product of two distinct odd primes p, q such that $p \equiv q \equiv 3 \bmod 4$. $N = \{N_k : k \in I\}$ will denote a family of **nonempty** sets N_k of nonnegative integers such that I is an infinite set of indices; and for all $n \in N_k$ the integer n has binary length exactly k. By theorem 4.6 the squaring mapping $x \longrightarrow x^2 \bmod n$ $(x \in QR_n, x^2 \bmod n \in QR_n)$ is $1 - 1$ and onto, and hence it has an inverse which will be denoted by $x \longrightarrow \sqrt{x} \bmod n$ $(x \in QR_n, \sqrt{x} \bmod n \in QR_n)$.

From now on and for the rest of this section the upper case Roman letters P, Q with subscripts or superscripts will range over nonzero polynomials with positive coefficients, one indeterminate, and degree ≥ 1, and the lowercase Greek letters ϵ, δ with subscripts or superscripts will range over positive real numbers.

Also the **parity function** will be used frequently in the sequel:

$$\mathrm{par}(x) = \begin{cases} 0 & \text{if } x \text{ is even} \\ 1 & \text{if } x \text{ is odd.} \end{cases}$$

Definition 4.1 *A polynomial size circuit $C = \{C_k : k \geq 1\}$ has a $1/P$-advantage for computing the parity function for the family N (and this will be abbreviated by $APAR(C, N, 1/2 + 1/P)$), if, for all but a finite number of indices $k \in I$, the following property holds for all $n \in N_k$,*

$$Pr[x \in QR_n : C_k(n, x) = \mathrm{par}(\sqrt{x} \bmod n)] \geq \frac{1}{2} + \frac{1}{P(k)}.$$

Definition 4.2 *A polynomial size circuit $C = \{C_k : k \geq 1\}$ has a $1/P$-advantage for determining quadratic residuosity for the family N (and this will be abbreviated by $AQR(C, N, 1/2 + 1/P)$), if, for all but a finite number of indices $k \in I$, the following property holds for all $n \in N_k$,*

$$\frac{1}{2}(Pr[C_k(n, x) = 1 \mid x \in QR_n] + Pr[C_k(n, x) = 0 \mid x \notin QR_n]) \geq \frac{1}{2} + \frac{1}{P(k)},$$

where for each $n \in N_k$, x ranges over $Z_n^*(+1)$.

Theorem 4.12 *For all polynomials P,*

$$(\exists C)APAR(C, N, 1/2 + 1/P) \Rightarrow (\exists C)AQR(C, N, 1/2 + 1/P).$$

Proof: The proof is based on the following

Claim: For all $x \in Z_n^*(+1)$, $x \in QR_n \Leftrightarrow \mathrm{par}(x) = \mathrm{par}(\sqrt{x^2} \bmod n)$.

Proof of the claim: ($\Rightarrow$) Assume $x \in QR_n$. Then x is the unique square root modulo n of $x^2 \bmod n$. Hence, $x = \sqrt{x^2} \bmod n$. Conversely, ($\Leftarrow$) suppose that $x \notin QR_n$ and put $x_0 = \sqrt{x^2} \bmod n$. Let $n = p \cdot q$. By assumption, $(x|n) = 1$ and $x \notin QR_n$. Since both x, x_0 are square roots of $x^2 \bmod n$, it follows that $(x|p) = (x|q) = -1$ and $x = -x_0$. Thus, $\mathrm{par}(x) \neq \mathrm{par}(\sqrt{x^2} \bmod n)$, which is a contradiction.

Based on the claim, one can give the proof of the theorem. Let C be a circuit such that $APAR(C, N, 1/2 + 1/P)$. It remains to find a circuit $C' = \{C_k' : k \geq 1\}$ such that $AQR(C', N, 1/2 + 1/P)$. Put:

$$C_k'(n, x) = C_k(n, x^2 \bmod n) \oplus \mathrm{par}(x) \oplus 1. \qquad (20)$$

It is clear from the definitions that

$$C_k'(n, x) = 1 \Leftrightarrow C_k(n, x^2 \bmod n) = \mathrm{par}(x). \qquad (21)$$

Consider the sets

$$A_n = \{x \in QR_n : C_k(n, x) = \mathrm{parity}(\sqrt{x} \bmod n)\},$$

$$X_n = \{x \in QR_n : x^2 \bmod n \in A_n\},$$

$$Y_n = \{x \in Z_n^*(+1) - QR_n : x^2 \bmod n \in A_n\},$$

$$W_n = \{x \in Z_n^*(+1) : x^2 \bmod n \in A_n\}.$$

It is then clear that $W_n = X_n \cup Y_n$ and $|X_n| = |A_n| = |Y_n|$. It follows that

$$Pr[x \in Z_n^*(+1) : x \in W_n] = \frac{|W_n|}{|Z_n^*(+1)|} =$$

$$\frac{|X_n| + |Y_n|}{2|QR_n|} = \frac{|A_n|}{|QR_n|} = Pr[x \in QR_n : x \in A_n]. \qquad (22)$$

As a consequence of equations (22), definition 4.1, and the claim above one obtains easily that

$$\frac{1}{2}\left(Pr[C_k'(n, x) = 1 \mid x \in QR_n] + Pr[C_k'(n, x) = 0 \mid x \notin QR_n]\right) =$$

$$Pr[x \in Z_n^*(+1) : x \in X_n] + Pr[x \in Z_n^*(+1) : x \in Y_n] =$$

$$Pr[x \in QR_n : x \in A_n] \geq \frac{1}{2} + \frac{1}{P(k)}.$$

This completes the proof of the theorem $\bullet$

Definition 4.2 is strengthened in the following:

Definition 4.3 *A polynomial size circuit $C = \{C_k : k \geq 1\}$ has a $(1/2 - 1/P)$-advantage for determining quadratic residuosity for the family N (and this will be abbreviated by $AQR(C, N, 1-1/P)$), if, for all but a finite number of indices $k \in I$, the following property holds for all $n \in N_k$:*

$$\frac{1}{2}(Pr[C_k(n,x) = 1 \mid x \in QR_n] + Pr[C_k(n,x) = 0 \mid x \notin QR_n]) \geq 1 - \frac{1}{P(k)},$$

where for each $n \in N_k$, x ranges over $Z_n^*(+1)$.

Theorem 4.13 *(Goldwasser-Micali)*

$$(\exists C)(\exists P)AQR(C, N, 1/2 + 1/P) \Rightarrow (\forall Q)(\exists C)AQR(C, N, 1 - 1/Q)$$

Proof: Assume that C is a polynomial size circuit and P is a polynomial such that the inequality of definition 4.2 holds. Put:

$$p_n = Pr[C_k(n,x) = 1 \mid x \in QR_n] \text{ and } q_n = Pr[C_k(n,x) = 1 \mid x \notin QR_n].$$

Then it is clear that for all but a finite number of indices $k \in I$,

$$\frac{p_n + (1 - q_n)}{2} \geq \frac{1}{2} + \frac{1}{P(k)},$$

and therefore

$$\frac{p_n}{2} - \frac{q_n}{2} \geq \frac{1}{P(k)}. \tag{23}$$

The aim of the construction below, which is based on the weak law of large numbers, is to construct for every polynomial Q a new circuit C' that will satisfy the conclusion of the theorem. Indeed, let Q be given and define the circuit C' as follows:

Input: $k \geq 1$, $n \in N_k$, $x \in Z_n^*(+1)$.
Step 1: Put $m = 16 \cdot Q(k) \cdot P(k)^2$.
Step 2: Select m random quadratic residues

$$s_1^2 \bmod n, \ldots, s_m^2 \bmod n \in QR_n.$$

Step 3: Compute the following two integers:

$$R_n = |\{1 \leq i \leq m \ : \ C_k(n, s_i^2 \bmod n) = 1\}| \text{ and}$$

$$\overline{R}_{n,x} = |\{1 \leq i \leq m \ : \ C_k(n, x \cdot s_i^2 \bmod n) = 1\}|.$$

Step 4: Compute $d_{n,x} = |R_n - \overline{R}_{n,x}|/m$.
Output :

$$C'_k(n, x) = \begin{cases} 1 & \text{if } d_{n,x} \leq \frac{1}{P(k)} \\ \\ 0 & \text{if } d_{n,x} > \frac{1}{P(k)}. \end{cases}$$

It remains to show that the foregoing polynomial size circuit C' satisfies property $AQR(C', N, 1 - 1/Q)$. First notice (see exercise 5 at the end of this subsection) that if $x \in QR_n$ (respectively $x \notin QR_n$), then

$$xs_1^2 \bmod n, \ldots, xs_m^2 \bmod n$$

is a sequence of m random quadratic residues (respectively nonresidues). Recall that the notation $Pr_A[E]$ abbreviates the conditional probability $Pr[E|A]$ of the event E under the condition that the event A holds. Next, the weak law of large numbers implies that

$$Pr_{QR_n}\left[x \in Z_n^*(+1) : \left|p_n - \frac{R_n}{m}\right| > \frac{1}{2P(k)}\right] < \frac{1}{4Q(k)},$$

$$Pr_{QR_n}\left[x \in Z_n^*(+1) : \left|p_n - \frac{\overline{R}_{n,x}}{m}\right| > \frac{1}{2P(k)}\right] < \frac{1}{4Q(k)},$$

$$Pr_{QNR_n}\left[x \in Z_n^*(+1) : \left|p_n - \frac{R_n}{m}\right| > \frac{1}{2P(k)}\right] < \frac{1}{4Q(k)}, \qquad (24)$$

$$Pr_{QNR_n}\left[x \in Z_n^*(+1) : \left|q_n - \frac{\overline{R}_{n,x}}{m}\right| > \frac{1}{2P(k)}\right] < \frac{1}{4Q(k)}. \qquad (25)$$

Now the following two claims will be proved. (In the proofs below x ranges over $Z_n^*(+1)$.)

Claim 1: $Pr_{QR_n}[|R_n/m - \overline{R}_{n,x}/m| \leq 1/P(k)] > 1 - 1/Q(k)$.
Indeed,

$$Pr_{QR_n}\left[\left|\frac{R_n}{m} - \frac{\overline{R}_{n,x}}{m}\right| \leq \frac{1}{P(k)}\right] =$$

$$Pr_{QR_n}\left[\left|\frac{R_n}{m} - p_n - \left(\frac{\overline{R}_{n,x}}{m} - p_n\right)\right| \leq \frac{1}{P(k)}\right] \geq$$

$$Pr_{QR_n}\left[\left|\frac{R_n}{m} - p_n\right| \leq \frac{1}{2P(k)} \text{ and } \left|\frac{\overline{R}_{n,x}}{m} - p_n)\right| \leq \frac{1}{2P(k)}\right] =$$

$$Pr_{QR_n}\left[\left|\frac{R_n}{m}-p_n\right|\le\frac{1}{2P(k)}\right]\cdot Pr_{QR_n}\left[\left|\frac{\overline{R}_{n,x}}{m}-p_n\right|\le\frac{1}{2P(k)}\right]\ge$$

$$\left(1-\frac{1}{4Q(k)}\right)\cdot\left(1-\frac{1}{4Q(k)}\right)>1-\frac{1}{Q(k)}.$$

Claim 2: $Pr_{QNR_n}[|R_n/m-\overline{R}_{n,x}/m|>1/P(k)]>1-1/Q(k)$.
By the assumption in inequality (23),

$$p_n-q_n\ge\frac{2}{P(k)}.$$

Using inequalities (24) and (25) it follows that with probability $\ge 1-1/(4Q(k))$, R_n/m must lie outside the closed interval

$$\left[q_n+\frac{1}{2P(k)},p_n-\frac{1}{2P(k)}\right].$$

For the same reason, $\overline{R}_{n,x}/m$ must lie outside the same closed interval. It follows that

$$Pr_{QNR_n}\left[\left|\frac{R_n}{m}-\frac{\overline{R}_{n,x}}{m}\right|>\frac{1}{P(k)}\right]\ge\left(1-\frac{1}{4Q(k)}\right)^2>1-\frac{1}{Q(k)}.$$

This completes the proof of the theorem •

Recall that to each $x\in QR_n$, an infinite sequence of quadratic residues

$$\ldots,x_{n,-2},x_{n,-1},x_{n,0}=x,x_{n,1},x_{n,2},\ldots$$

was associated, as follows:

$$x_{n,i}\equiv\begin{cases}x^{2^i}\bmod n & \text{if } i\ge 0\\ \sqrt{x_{n,i+1}} & \text{if } i<0.\end{cases}$$

For each $x\in QR_n$ and each integer i, define the bits

$$b_{n,i}(x)=\mathrm{par}(x_{n,i}).$$

The Quadratic Residue Generator, abbreviated $QRGEN$, accepts as input a pair $<x,n>$, where $x\in QR_n$; the output is the infinite sequence of bits $\ldots,b_{n,i-1}(x),b_{n,i}(x),b_{n,i+1}(x),\ldots$.

Remark 1: The sequence $\ldots,b_{n,i-1}(x),b_{n,i}(x),b_{n,i+1}(x),\ldots$, can also be defined as follows. Given an integer n as above define the function

$$f_n:QR_n\longrightarrow QR_n:x\longrightarrow f_n(x)=x^2\bmod n,$$

and its inverse

$$f_n^{-1} \ : \ QR_n \longrightarrow QR_n : x \longrightarrow f_n^{-1}(x) = \sqrt{x} \bmod n$$

Further, let the functions f_n^i be defined as follows:

$$f_n^i(x) = \begin{cases} x & \text{if } i = 0 \\ f_n(f_n^{i-1}(x)) & \text{if } i > 0 \\ f_n^{-1}(f_n^{i+1}(x)) & \text{if } i < 0. \end{cases}$$

For each n, and each $x \in QR_n$ define the bits

$$b'_{n,i}(x) = B_n(f_n^i(x)),$$

where, for $x \in QR_n$,

$$B_n(x) = \mathrm{par}(x).$$

It is easy to show that for all n, x, as above,

$$b'_{n,i}(x) = b_{n,i}(x).$$

Definition 4.4 *A polynomial size circuit $C = \{C_k : k \geq 1\}$ has a $1/P$-advantage for predicting correctly from sequences of bits of length $Q(k)$ produced by the generator $QRGEN$ (for the family N) (and this is abbreviated by $APR(C, N, Q, 1/2 + 1/P)$), if, for all but a finite number of indices $k \in I$ the following property holds for all $n \in N_k$,*

$$Pr[C_k(b_{n,0}(x), \ldots, b_{n,Q(k)-1}(x)) = b_{n,-1}(x)] \geq \frac{1}{2} + \frac{1}{P(k)}, \qquad (26)$$

where for each $n \in N_k$, x ranges over QR_n.

Theorem 4.14 *For all polynomials P,*

$$(\exists C)(\exists Q) APR(C, N, Q, 1/2 + 1/P) \Rightarrow (\exists C) APAR(C, N, 1/2 + 1/P).$$

Proof: Let P, Q be polynomials and C a polynomial size circuit such that inequality (26) holds. Define a new polynomial size circuit via the equation below:

$$C'_k(x) = \mathrm{par}(C_k(b_{n,0}(x), \ldots, b_{n,Q(k)-1}(x))). \qquad (27)$$

Notice that

$$C_k(b_{n,0}(x), \ldots, b_{n,Q(k)-1}(x)) = b_{n,-1}(x) \Rightarrow C'_k(x) = \mathrm{par}(\sqrt{x} \bmod n).$$

One can then verify easily that the circuit C' satisfies the inequality in definition (4.1) •

Remark 2: Theorem 4.14 will be further improved in section 5.

EXERCISES

In the exercises below, the notation of subsection 4.8 is used.

1: The **location function**, denoted by loc_n, is defined by:

$$\mathrm{loc}_n(x) = \begin{cases} 0 & \text{if } x < n/2 \\ 1 & \text{if } x > n/2. \end{cases}$$

Show that for all $x \in Z_n^*$, $x < n/2 \Leftrightarrow 2x \bmod n$ is even. Moreover, for all $x \in QR_n$, $\mathrm{par}(2\sqrt{x} \bmod n) = \mathrm{loc}_n(\sqrt{x} \bmod n)$.

2: A polynomial size circuit $C = \{C_k : k \geq 1\}$ has a $1/P$-advantage for computing the location function of the family N (and this will be abbreviated by $ALOC(C, N, 1/2 + 1/P)$), if, for all but a finite number of indices $k \in I$, the following property holds for all $n \in N_k$:

$$Pr[x \in QR_n : C_k(n, x) = \mathrm{loc}_n(\sqrt{x} \bmod n)] \geq \frac{1}{2} + \frac{1}{P(k)}.$$

Show that for all polynomials P,

$$(\exists C)ALOC(C, N, 1/2 + 1/P) \Rightarrow (\exists C)APAR(C, N, 1/2 + 1/P)$$

Hint: Let $C = \{C_k : k \geq 1\}$ be a polynomial size circuit such that the hypothesis above, $ALOC(C, N, 1/2 + 1/P)$, is true. It is required to find a circuit $C' = \{C'_k : k \geq 1\}$ such that $APAR(C', N, 1/2 + 1/P)$ is true. Use exercise 1 to show that the circuit $C'_k(n, x) = C_k(n, 4^{-1}x \bmod n)$ satisfies the requirements of the conclusion.

3: Define the following notions, by analogy with the definitions of the previously defined predicates:

$ALOC(C, N, 1/2 + \epsilon)$, $APAR(C, N, 1/2 + \epsilon)$, $AQR(C, N, 1/2 + \epsilon)$,
$AQR(C, N, 1 - \epsilon)$, $APR(C, N, Q, 1/2 + \epsilon)$,

where $\epsilon > 0$ is a constant. Show that for all circuits C,

(1) $(\exists \epsilon)ALOCR(C, N, 1/2 + \epsilon) \Rightarrow (\forall P)ALOCR(C, N, 1/2 + 1/P)$,
(2) $(\exists \epsilon)APAR(C, N, 1/2 + \epsilon) \Rightarrow (\forall P)APAR(C, N, 1/2 + 1/P)$,
(3) $(\exists \epsilon)AQR(C, N, 1/2 + \epsilon) \Rightarrow (\forall P)AQR(C, N, 1/2 + 1/P)$,
(4) $(\exists P)AQR(C, N, 1 - 1/P) \Rightarrow (\forall \epsilon)AQR(C, N, 1 - \epsilon)$,
(5) $(\exists \epsilon)APR(C, N, Q, 1/2 + \epsilon) \Rightarrow (\forall P)APR(C, N, Q, 1/2 + 1/P)$.

(6) Prove corresponding versions of theorems 4.12, 4.13, 4.14 for the notions of advantage defined above.

4: Show that for any family N, the following statements are equivalent:

(1) $(\exists C)(\exists \epsilon) AQR(C, N, 1/2 + \epsilon)$.

(2) $(\exists C)(\exists \epsilon) AQR(C, N, 1 - \epsilon)$.

(3) $(\exists C)(\exists P) AQR(C, N, 1/2 + 1/P)$.

(4) $(\exists C)(\exists P) AQR(C, N, 1 - 1/P)$.

(5) $(\forall P)(\exists C) AQR(C, N, 1 - 1/P)$.

(6) $(\forall \epsilon)(\exists C) AQR(C, N, 1 - \epsilon)$.

5: Let $x \in Z_n^*(+1)$ be fixed. Show that:

(1) If $x \in QR_n$, then $QR_n = \{xs^2 \bmod n : s \in Z_n^*\}$.

(2) If $x \in QNR_n$, then $QNR_n = \{xs^2 \bmod n : s \in Z_n^*\}$.

4.9   The Quadratic Residuosity Assumption

As in subsection 4.8, throughout the present subsection, n will range over integers which are the product of two distinct odd primes p, q such that $p \equiv q \equiv 3 \bmod 4$; $N = \{N_k : k \in I\}$ will denote a family of **nonempty** sets N_k of nonnegative integers such that I is an infinite set of indices and for all $n \in N_k$ the integer n has binary length exactly k.

The notions of advantage defined in subsection 4.8 will now be altered in order to reflect the fact that this advantage is valid only for a certain fraction of the $n \in N_k$. The generalization is as follows.

Definition 4.5 *A polynomial size circuit* $C = \{C_k : k \geq 1\}$ *has a* $1/P$-*advantage for computing the parity function for a fraction* $1/P'$ *of the integers in* N_k *(and this will be abbreviated by* $\overline{APAR}(C, N, 1/P', 1/2 + 1/P)$*), if, for all but a finite number of indices* $k \in I$ *the set*

$$\left\{ n \in N_k : Pr[x \in QR_n : C_k(n, x) = \text{par}(\sqrt{x} \bmod n)] \geq \frac{1}{2} + \frac{1}{P(k)} \right\}$$

has size $\geq |N_k|/P'(k)$.

The remaining overlined versions (i.e. generalizations) of the previously defined notions of advantage can be defined as above. In addition, one can prove the following theorem exactly as before.

Theorem 4.15 *For all polynomials P, P', the following statements hold:*

(1) $(\exists C)\overline{APAR}(C, N, 1/P', 1/2 + 1/P) \Rightarrow$
   $(\exists C)\overline{AQR}(C, N, 1/P', 1/2 + 1/P)$.

(2) $(\exists C, P)\overline{AQR}(C, N, 1/P', 1/2 + 1/P) \Rightarrow$
   $(\forall Q)(\exists C)\overline{AQR}(C, N, 1/P', 1 - 1/Q)$.

(3) $(\exists C, Q)\overline{APR}(C, N, Q, 1/P', 1/2 + 1/P) \Rightarrow$
   $(\exists C)\overline{APAR}(C, N, 1/P', 1/2 + 1/P)$ •

If n is prime, the problem of deciding whether a given $x \in Z_n^*$ is a quadratic residue or not is easy, because it reduces to evaluating $(x|n)$. However, if n is composite the problem is no longer simple. In fact, for composite n, it is an open problem to find an efficient algorithm that will decide if a given $x \in Z_n^*(+1)$ is a quadratic residue or not, assuming the factorization of n is not known. The formal statement of this problem, also known as the **Quadratic Residuosity Problem**, will be formalized and used in the sequel.

Given a circuit C, an integer $n \in N_k$, and an $x \in Z_n^*(+1)$, $C_k(n, x)$ **decides correctly if a given** x **is in** QR_n if and only if $C_k(n, x) = 1$, assuming that $x \in QR_n$, and $C_k(n, x) = 0$ assuming that $x \notin QR_n$. Recall that from definition 4.2,

$$\frac{1}{2}(Pr[C_k(n, x) = 1 \mid x \in QR_n] + Pr[C_k(n, x) = 0 \mid x \notin QR_n]) =$$

$$= Pr[C_k(n, x) \text{ decides correctly } x \in QR_n].$$

Definition 4.6 *The Quadratic Residuosity Assumption for the family* $N = \{N_k : k \in I\}$, *abbreviated* $QRA(N)$, *is the following statement: if* $C = \{C_k : k \geq 1\}$ *is a polynomial size, 0, 1-valued circuit, and* P, P' *are polynomials with positive integer coefficients, then, for all but a finite number of indices* $k \in I$, *the set*

$$\left\{ n \in N_k \ : \ Pr[C_k(n, x) \text{ decides correctly } x \in QR_n] \geq 1 - \frac{1}{P(k)} \right\}$$

has size $\leq |N_k|/P'(k)$.

Theorem 4.16

$$QRA(N) \Leftrightarrow \neg(\exists P, P', Q, C)\overline{APR}(C, N, Q, 1/P', 1/2 + 1/P)$$

Proof: Assume that the hypothesis $QRA(N)$ is true, but that the conclusion $\neg(\exists P, P', Q, C)\overline{APR}(C, N, Q, 1/P', 1/2 + 1/P)$ fails. By theorem 4.15 there exist polynomials P, P' with positive coefficients, and a polynomial size circuit C such that $\overline{AQR}(C, N, 1/P', 1 - 1/P)$. Consider the polynomial $P''(k) = P'(k) + 1$. On the one hand, the definition of $\overline{AQR}(C, N, 1/P', 1 - 1/P)$ implies that, for all but a finite number of indices $k \in I$, the set

$$\left\{ n \in N_k : Pr[C_k(n, x)\text{decides correctly } x \in QR_n] \geq 1 - \frac{1}{P(k)} \right\}$$

has size $\geq |N_k|/P'(k)$. On the other hand, $QRA(N)$ implies that, for all but a finite number of indices $k \in I$, the set

$$\left\{ n \in N_k : Pr[C_k(n, x) \text{ decides correctly } x \in QR_n] \geq 1 - \frac{1}{P(k)} \right\}$$

has size $\leq |N_k|/P''(k)$. But this is a contradiction, because $N_k \neq \emptyset$. The proof in the other direction is similar •

Remark 1: A typical example of a family N to which the preceding results apply is defined as follows: let N_k be the set of all integers n of length k such that n is a product of two primes p, q such that $p \equiv q \equiv 3 \bmod 4$ and $||p| - |q|| \leq 1$, where $|p|$ (respectively $|q|$) is the binary length of p (respectively q). The quadratic residuosity assumption for this family is abbreviated by QRA.

Finally, using the predicate $\overline{APR}$ to define unpredictability of the generator, it can be shown easily that

Theorem 4.17 *(Assume QRA) The quadratic residue generator is unpredictable* •

EXERCISES

1: Give the details of the proof of theorem 4.15.

2: Explicitly define the remaining overlined notions of advantage and show that each of them is implied by its corresponding nonoverlined counterpart.

3: (Blum-Blum-Shub) The location loc_n function defined in exercise 1 of subsection 4.8 gives rise to a pseudorandom generator. Define this generator and use QRA to show that it is unpredictable.

4.10   The Index Generator

Let g be a primitive root modulo the odd prime number p. Let $x \in QR_p$ be an arbitrary quadratic residue modulo p. It is known that $\text{index}_{p,g}(x) = 2t$, for some integer $t < (p-1)/2$ (see also exercise 4 in the subsection on indices). The **principal square root** of x with respect to p, g, abbreviated $PQR(p,g,x)$, is the integer $g^t \bmod p$; the **nonprincipal square root** of x with respect to p, g, abbreviated $NPQR(p,g,x)$, is the integer $g^{t+(p-1)/2} \bmod p$. For each p, g as above define, the predicate $B_{p,g}$ as follows:

$$B_{p,g}(x) = \begin{cases} 1 & \text{if } x = PQR(p,g,x^2 \bmod p) \\ 0 & \text{if } x = NPQR(p,g,x^2 \bmod p). \end{cases}$$

It is now easy to see that

$$B_{p,g}(g^t \bmod p) = \begin{cases} 1 & \text{if } t < (p-1)/2 \\ 0 & \text{if } t \geq (p-1)/2. \end{cases}$$

A very significant observation is that the existence of an efficient algorithm to compute the function $B_{p,g}$, leads to an efficient algorithm to compute the function $\text{index}_{p,g}$ (see exercise 4 below). Theorem 4.18 below shows that the existence of an efficient algorithm to compute PQR leads to the existence of an efficient algorithm to compute the function $\text{index}_{p,g}$, a result that will be used in the sequel. For each p, let $|p|$ denote the binary length of p.

Theorem 4.18 *Suppose there exists an algorithm A running in polynomial time in $|p|$ such that for any odd prime p, any primitive root $g \in Z_p^*$, and any $x \in QR_p$,*

$$A(p,g,x) = PQR(p,g,x).$$

Then there exists an algorithm A' running in polynomial time in $|p|$ such that for any odd prime p, any primitive root $g \in Z_p^*$, and any $x \in Z_p^*$,

$$A'(p,g,x) = \text{index}_{p,g}(x).$$

Proof: For any sequence of bits u and any bit b let ub be the sequence of bits obtained from u by adjoining the bit b at its rightmost end. Recall that testing $x \in QR_p$ is easy; one need only compute the Langrange symbol $(x|p)$. Assume that A is an algorithm that satisfies the hypothesis of the theorem. On input p, g, x the algorithm A', using the integer c as a counter, outputs the sequence d of bits, which constitutes the binary representation of $\text{index}_{p,g}(x)$ and is defined as follows:

Input: p prime, g primitive root modulo p, $x \in Z_p^*$.

Step 1: Put $d = \emptyset$, $c = 0$.

Step 2: Test if $x \in QR_p$.

Step 3: Put $d = db(x)$, $c = c + 1$, where

$$b(x) = \begin{cases} 0 & \text{if } x \in QR_p \\ 1 & \text{if } x \notin QR_p. \end{cases}$$

Step 4: Put

$$x = \begin{cases} x & \text{if } x \in QR_p \\ xg^{-1} \bmod p & \text{if } x \notin QR_p. \end{cases}$$

Step 5: Put $x = A(p, g, x)$.

Output: If $c < |p| - 1$ **then goto** Step 2 with this new x; **else:** output d and **stop**.

The proof that this algorithm works is easy •

Throughout the rest of this subsection, p will range over odd primes. $N = \{N_k : k \in I\}$ will denote a family of **nonempty** sets N_k such that I is an infinite set of positive integers and for all $n \in N_k$, the integer n is an odd prime of binary length exactly k.

Definition 4.7 *A polynomial size circuit* $C = \{C_k : k \geq 1\}$ *has a* $1/P$-*advantage for determining the indices (for the family N, and this will be abbreviated by* $AIND(C, N, 1/2 + 1/P)$*), if, for all but a finite number of indices $k \in I$, the following property holds for all $p \in N_k$ and all primitive roots g modulo p:*

$$Pr[x \in Z_p^* : C_k(p, g, x) = \text{index}_{p,g}(x)] \geq \frac{1}{2} + \frac{1}{P(k)}.$$

Similarly, one can define the notion $AIND(C, N, 1 - 1/P)$.

Definition 4.8 *A polynomial size circuit* $C = \{C_k : k \geq 1\}$ *has a* $(1/2 - 1/P)$-*advantage for determining indices (for the family N, and this will be abbreviated by* $AIND(C, N, 1 - 1/P)$*), if, for all but a finite number of indices $k \in I$, the following property holds for all $p \in N_k$, and all primitive roots g modulo p:*

$$Pr[x \in Z_p^* : C_k(p, g, x) = \text{index}_{p,g}(x)] \geq 1 - \frac{1}{P(k)}.$$

For technical reasons, that will become apparent in the proofs below, the following notion will also be used

Definition 4.9 *For any polynomial Q, let $E(p,g,Q)$ denote the event:*

$$\text{index}_{p,g}(x) \in \left[0, \frac{p-1}{Q(k)}\right].$$

Definition 4.10 *A polynomial size circuit $C = \{C_k : k \geq 1\}$ computes the indices which lie in the closed interval $[1, (p-1)/Q(k)]$ for primes p which belong to N_k with $1/P$-advantage (and this will be abbreviated by $IND(C, N, 1/Q, 1/P)$), if, for all but a finite number of indices $k \in I$ the following property holds for all $p \in N_k$, and all primitive roots g modulo p,*

$$Pr_{E(p,g,Q)}\left[x \in Z_p^* : C_k(p,g,x) = \text{index}_{p,g}(x)\right] \geq \frac{1}{2} + \frac{1}{P(k)}.$$

Theorem 4.19 *(Blum-Micali)*

$$(\exists C, P, Q)IND(C, N, 1/Q, 1/P) \Rightarrow (\forall P)(\exists C)AIND(C, N, 1 - 1/P).$$

Proof: Assume that P, Q are polynomials, and that C is a polynomial size circuit such that the inequality of definition 4.10 holds. The circuit C' is defined as follows:

Input: $p \in N_k$, g primitive root modulo p, $x \in Z_p^*$.
Step 1: Guess an integer $0 \leq i < Q(k)$ such that

$$\text{index}_{p,g}(x) \in \left[\frac{i(p-1)}{Q(k)}, \frac{(i+1)(p-1)}{Q(k)}\right].$$

Step 2: Compute $x_i = xg^{-i(p-1)/Q(k)} \bmod p$.
Step 3: Compute $d = C_k(p, g, x_i)$.
Output: If $x \equiv g^{d+i(p-1)/Q(k)} \bmod p$, **then** output

$$\text{index}_{p,g}(x_i) + i(p-1)/Q(k).$$

If $i \geq Q(k)$ then put $i = 0$ and **goto** Step 2;
else: put $i = i + 1$ and **goto** Step 2.
Since the probability that the circuit C_k will give the wrong answer is $\leq 1/2 - 1/P(k)$, the probability that the circuit C_k' will give the wrong answer is $\leq (1/2 - 1/P(k))^{Q(k)}$. This completes the proof of the theorem ●

Definition 4.11 *A polynomial size circuit* $C = \{C_k : k \geq 1\}$ *has a* $1/P$-*advantage for computing the function* $B_{p,g}$ *for the family* N *(and this will be abbreviated by* $AB(C, N, 1/2 + 1/P)$*), if, for all but a finite number of indices* $k \in I$*, the following property holds for all* $p \in N_k$ *and all primitive roots* g *modulo* p:

$$Pr[x \in QR_p \;:\; C_k(p, g, x) = B_{p,g}(x)] \geq \frac{1}{2} + \frac{1}{P(k)}.$$

Definition 4.12 *A polynomial size circuit* $C = \{C_k : k \geq 1\}$ *has a* $1/P$-*advantage in computing the function* PQR *for the family* N *(and this will be abbreviated as* $APQR(C, N, 1/2 + 1/P)$*), if, for all but a finite number of indices* $k \in I$*, the following property holds for all* $p \in N_k$ *and all primitive roots* g *modulo* p:

$$Pr[x \in QR_p \;:\; C_k(p, g, x) = PQR(p, x, g)] \geq \frac{1}{2} + \frac{1}{P(k)}.$$

Definition 4.13 *A polynomial size circuit* $C = \{C_k : k \geq 1\}$ *has a* $1/P$-*advantage for computing the function* PQR *only for indices which lie in the interval* $[1, (p-1)/Q(k)]$ *(for the family* N*, abbreviated as* $APQR(C, N, 1/Q,$ $1/2 + 1/P)$*), if, for all but a finite number of indices* $k \in I$*, the following property holds for all* $p \in N_k$ *and all primitive roots* g *modulo* p:

$$Pr_{E(p,g,Q)}[x \in QR_p : C_k(p, g, x) = PQR(p, x, g)] \geq \frac{1}{2} + \frac{1}{P(k)}.$$

The main result of the present subsection is the following

Theorem 4.20 *(Blum-Micali)*

$$(\exists C, P)AB(C, N, 1/2 + 1/P) \Rightarrow (\forall Q)(\exists C, P')APQR(C, N, 1/P', 1 - 1/Q).$$

Proof: Let C be a polynomial size circuit which computes the function $B_{p,g}$ with a $1/P$-advantage. For each $e \in QR_p$, let e', e'' denote the two square roots of e modulo the prime p. The function PQR^C computes the *principal square root* with the aid of the circuit C and is defined as follows:

$$PQR^C(p, g, e) = \begin{cases} e' & \text{if } C_k(p, g, e') > C_k(p, g, e'') \\ e'' & \text{if } C_k(p, g, e') < C_k(p, g, e'') \\ \text{random}\{e', e''\} & \text{if } C_k(p, g, e') = C_k(p, g, e''). \end{cases}$$

Let Q be any polynomial, and let the polynomial P' be defined by $P'(k) = 4 \cdot P(k) \cdot Q(k)^2$. It will be shown that there exists a polynomial size circuit C' such that property $APQR(C', N, 1/P', 1 - 1/Q)$ holds, i.e. for all but a finite number of $k \in I$, and all primitive roots g modulo p,

$$Pr_{E(p,g,Q)}\left[x \in QR_p : C'_k(p,g,x) = PQR(p,g,x)\right] \geq 1 - \frac{1}{Q(k)}.$$

The circuit C' is defined as follows:

Input: $p \in N_k$, g primitive root modulo p, $e \in QR_p$ such that

$$\text{index}_{p,g}(e) \leq (p - 1)/P'(k).$$

Step 1: Compute the two square roots e', e'' of e modulo p.

Step 2: Put $m = P'(k)$.

Step 3: Select m random integers $r_1, \ldots, r_m$ such that $2r_1, \ldots, 2r_m \leq p - 1$.

Step 4: Compute $e_i \equiv eg^{2r_i} \bmod p$, where $i = 1, \ldots, m$.

Step 5: Compute $e'_i \equiv e'g^{r_i} \bmod p$, and $e''_i \equiv e''g^{r_i} \bmod p$, where $i = 1, \ldots, m$.

Step 6: Compute the following two integers:

$$L'(p,g,e) = |\{1 \leq i \leq m \; : \; PQR^C(p,g,e_i) = e'_i\}|$$

$$L''(p,g,e) = |\{1 \leq i \leq m \; : \; PQR^C(p,g,e_i) = e''_i\}|.$$

Output:

$$C'_k(e,p,g) = \begin{cases} e' & \text{if } L'(p,g,e) > L''(p,g,e) \\ e'' & \text{if } L'(p,g,e) < L''(p,g,e). \end{cases}$$

It remains to show that the circuit C' actually works. Let $2s = \text{index}_{p,g}(e)$, $T = \{1 \leq i \leq m \; : \; 2s + 2r_i \leq p - 1\}$, and $t = |T|$. It follows from exercise 3 that there exist at least t many i's such that

$$2r_i \in \left[\frac{(m-1)(p-1)}{m}, p - 1\right].$$

However, the closed interval above is the rightmost subinterval of the partition

$$\left\{\left[\frac{i(p-1)}{m}, \frac{(i+1)(p-1)}{m}\right] \; : \; i \leq m\right\}$$

of the closed interval $[(p-1)/m, p-1]$, into closed subintervals each of length $(p-1)/m$. Since the integers $2r_1, \ldots, 2r_m$ are randomly chosen from the closed interval $[1, p-1]$, it follows that t must be small. Moreover, for all $i \in T$ if y is a square root of e, then by exercise 2,

$$yg^{r_i} \bmod p = PQR(p, g, e_i) \Leftrightarrow y = PQR(p, g, e).$$

Next, the following two cases can be considered.

Case 1: If $e' = PQR(p, g, e)$.

In this case, using the fact that the circuit C has a $1/P$ advantage for computing the function $B_{p,g}$, the expected value of $L'(p, g, e)$ is $m/2 + m/P(k)$. Similarly, the expected value of $L''(p, g, e)$ is $m/2 - m/P(k)$. Thus, using the weak law of large numbers, with probability $\geq 1 - 1/Q(k)$, $L'(p, g, e) > L''(p, g, e)$.

Case 2: If $e'' = PQR(p, g, e)$.

In this case, using the fact that the circuit C has a $1/P$ advantage for computing the function $B_{p,g}$, the expected value of $L'(p, g, e)$ is $m/2 - m/P(k)$. Similarly, the expected value of $L''(p, g, e)$ is $m/2 + m/P(k)$. Thus, using the weak law of large numbers, with probability $\geq 1 - 1/Q(k)$, $L''(p, g, e) > L'(p, g, e)$.

This completes the proof of the theorem •

As an application of theorems 4.18 and 4.20 one obtains the following:

Theorem 4.21 *(Blum-Micali)*

$$(\exists C, P) AB(C, N, 1/2 + 1/P) \Rightarrow (\exists C, P, Q) AIND(C, N, 1/Q, 1/2 + 1/P).$$

Proof: Apply the result of theorem 4.20 to the polynomial $Q(k) = 2k$ to find a polynomial $P'(k)$ and a polynomial size circuit C' such that

$$Pr_{E(p,g,Q)} \left[x \in QR_p : C'_k(p, g, x) = PQR(p, g, x) \right] \geq 1 - \frac{1}{2k}.$$

Next, apply the algorithm of theorem 4.18, but use the circuit C'_k instead of the algorithm A used there. Call C'' the resulting circuit. As before, the circuit C'_k will be applied $|p| = k$ times. Each time C'_k will supply the correct answer with probability $\geq (1 - 1/2k)$. Thus, C''_k will supply the correct answer with probability

$$\geq \left(1 - \frac{1}{2k} \right)^k \approx \exp\left(\frac{-1}{2} \right).$$

It follows that there exists a polynomial $P(k)$ such that

$$\left(1 - \frac{1}{2k}\right)^k \geq \frac{1}{2} + \frac{1}{P(k)}.$$

This completes the proof of the theorem •

Given an odd prime p and a primitive root modulo p consider the function

$$f_{p,g} : Z_p^* \longrightarrow Z_p^* : x \longrightarrow f_{p,g}(x) = g^x \bmod p$$

and its inverse

$$f_{p,g}^{-1} : Z_p^* \longrightarrow Z_p^* : x \longrightarrow f_{p,g}^{-1}(x) = \text{index}_{p,g}(x).$$

Further, let the functions $f_{p,g}^i$ be defined as follows:

$$f_{p,g}^i(x) = \begin{cases} x & \text{if } i = 0 \\ f_{p,g}(f_{p,g}^{i-1}(x)) & \text{if } i > 0 \\ f_{p,g}^{-1}(f_{p,g}^{i+1}(x)) & \text{if } i < 0. \end{cases}$$

For each odd prime p, for each primitive root g modulo p, and each $x \in Z_p^*$ define the bits

$$b_{p,g,i}(x) = B_{p,g}(f_{p,g}^i(x)).$$

The **index generator**, abbreviated INDGEN, accepts as inputs the triples $< p, g, x >$, where p is an odd prime, g is a primitive root modulo p and $x \in Z_p^*$; the output is the infinite sequence $b_{p,g,0}(x), b_{p,g,1}(x), \ldots, b_{p,g,i}(x), \ldots$.

Definition 4.14 *A polynomial size circuit $C = \{C_k : k \geq 1\}$ has a $1/P$-advantage for predicting correctly from sequences of bits of length $Q(k)$ produced by $INDGEN$ (for the family N, and this will be abbreviated by $APR(C, N, Q, 1/2 + 1/P)$), if, for all but a finite number of indices $k \in I$ the following property holds for all $p \in N_k$, and all primitive roots g modulo p:*

$$Pr[C_k(b_{p,g,1}(x), \ldots, b_{p,g,Q(k)-1}(x)) = b_{p,g,0}(x)] \geq \frac{1}{2} + \frac{1}{P(k)}. \qquad (28)$$

Theorem 4.22 *For all polynomials P,*

$$(\exists C)(\exists Q)APR(C, N, Q, 1/2 + 1/P) \Rightarrow (\exists C)AB(C, N, 1/2 + 1/P).$$

Proof: Let Q be a polynomial and let C be a polynomial size circuit such the inequality in definition 4.14 holds. Define a new circuit C' as follows:

$$C'_k(x) = C_k(b_{p,g,1}(x), \ldots, b_{p,g,Q(k)-1}(x)).$$

It is now easy to see that the circuit C' must satisfy the inequality of definition 4.11 •

Remark: Theorem 4.22 will be further improved in section 5.

EXERCISES

1: Complete the details of the proof of theorem 4.19.

2: Assume that $x \in QR_p$ and $2r + \mathrm{index}_{p,g}(x) < p - 1$. Show that for any square root of y of x modulo p,

$$yg^r \bmod p = PQR(p,g,xg^{2r}) \Leftrightarrow y = PQR(p,g,x).$$

3: If $\mathrm{index}_{p,g}(x) \leq (p-1)/m$ and $2 \leq 2r \leq p - 1$, then

$$2r + \mathrm{index}_{p,g}(x) \geq p - 1 \Rightarrow 2r \geq \frac{(m-1)(p-1)}{m}.$$

4:(Blum-Micali) Repeat the proof of theorem 4.18 to show that if there exists an algorithm A running in polynomial time in $|p|$ such that for any odd prime p, any primitive root $g \in Z_p^*$, and any $x \in QR_p$,

$$A(p,g,x) = B_{p,g}(x),$$

then there exists an algorithm A' running in polynomial time in $|p|$ such that for all p,g,x as above,

$$A'(p,g,x) = \mathrm{index}_{p,g}(x).$$

Hint: Steps 1 - 4 remain exactly the same. The new step 5 is the following:

Step 5: Use the Adelman-Manders-Miller algorithm to compute the two square roots of x modulo p, say x', x''.

The new step 6 to replace the old step 5 is the following:

Step 6: Put

$$x = \begin{cases} x' & \text{if } A(p,g,x') = 1 \\ x'' & \text{if } A(p,g,x') = 0. \end{cases}$$

4.11   The Discrete Logarithm Assumption

As in subsection 4.10, throughout the present subsection p will range over odd primes. $N = \{N_k : k \in I\}$ will denote a family of **nonempty** sets N_k of nonnegative integers such that I is an infinite set of positive integers, and for all $n \in N_k$ the integer n is an odd prime of length exactly k.

From the notions of advantage defined in subsection 4.10 one can define overlined notions, just like in subsection 4.9, as follows:

Definition 4.15 *A polynomial size circuit* $C = \{C_k : k \geq 1\}$ *has a* $1/P$-*advantage for computing the function* $B_{p,g}$ *for a fraction* $1/P'$ *of the primes in* N_k *(abbreviated as* $\overline{AB}(C, N, 1/P', 1/2 + 1/P)$*), if, for all but a finite number of indices* $k \in I$*, for all* $p \in N_k$*, and all primitive roots* g *modulo* p*, the set*

$$\left\{ p \in N_k : Pr[x \in Z_p^* : C_k(p,g,x) = B_{p,g}(x)] \geq \frac{1}{2} + \frac{1}{P(k)} \right\}$$

has size $\geq |N_k|/P'(k)$.

The remaining overlined versions of the previously defined notions of advantage can be defined as above. In addition, one can prove the following theorem exactly as before:

Theorem 4.23 *For all polynomials* P, P', *the following statements hold:*

(1) $(\exists C, P, Q)\overline{IND}(C, N, 1/Q, 1/P', 1/2 + 1/P) \Rightarrow$
    $(\forall P)(\exists C)\overline{AIND}(C, N, 1/P', 1 - 1/P)$.

(2) $(\exists C, P)\, \overline{AB}(C, N, 1/P', 1/2 + 1/P) \Rightarrow$
    $(\forall Q)(\exists C, R)\overline{APQR}(C, N, 1/P', 1/R, 1 - 1/Q)$.

(3) $(\exists C, P)\, \overline{AB}(C, N, 1/P', 1/2 + 1/P) \Rightarrow$
    $(\exists C, P, Q)\overline{IND}(C, N, 1/Q, 1/P', 1/2 + 1/P)$.

(4) $(\exists C, Q)\overline{APR}(C, N, Q, 1/P', 1/2 + 1/P) \Rightarrow$
    $(\exists C)\overline{AB}(C, N, 1/P', 1/2 + 1/P)$ •

Definition 4.16 *The Discrete Logarithm Assumption for the family* $N = \{N_k : k \in I\}$ *(abbreviated* $DLA(N)$*) is the following statement: if* $C = \{C_k : k \geq 1\}$ *is a polynomial size, 0, 1-valued circuit, and* P, P' *are polynomials*

with positive integer coefficients, then for all but a finite number of indices
$k \in I$, *the set*

$$\left\{ p \in N_k : (\forall g) \left(Pr[C_k(p, g, x) = \text{index}_{p,g}(x)] \geq 1 - \frac{1}{P(k)} \right) \right\},$$

where g ranges over primitive roots modulo p, has size $\leq |N_k|/P'(k)$.

Now, it is not difficult to show that

Theorem 4.24

$$DLA(N) \Leftrightarrow \neg(\exists P, P', Q, C)\overline{APR}(C, N, Q, 1/P', 1/2 + 1/P) \bullet$$

Remark 1: A typical example of a family N to which the foregoing results apply is defined as follows: let N_k be the set of all primes such that $|p| = k$, where $|p|$ is the binary length of p. The Discrete Logarithm Assumption for this family is abbreviated by DLA.

Remark 2: The DLA is related to the Pohlig-Hellman algorithm given in section 1. Intuitively, the Pohlig-Hellman algorithm says that if the prime factors of $p - 1$ are small relative to the binary length of p, then it is easy to compute discrete logarithms.

To sum up it has been shown that

Theorem 4.25 *(Assume DLA) The index generator is unpredictable* •

EXERCISES

1: Give the proof of theorems 4.23, 4.24.

2: Explicitly define the remaining overlined notions of advantage and show that each of them is implied by its corresponding nonoverlined counterpart.

4.12   Bibliographical Remarks

The linear congruence generator, $LGEN$, defined in subsection 4.2, is one of the most popular pseudo-random generators in use today, and is based on a scheme first devised by D. H. Lehmer in 1949. The general theorem 4.1 on the predictability of the linear congruence generator is the main result in [P4], which also gives a different proof of theorem 4.1. Additional information on the linear congruence generator can be found in [K2] (pp.

1 - 37) as well as in [N2]. Recent work in [F3] shows that the sequence produced by a linear congruence generator is predictable even if only a constant proportion α of the leading bits of the first few numbers generated is given, where $\alpha > 2/5$.

The $1/p$-generator is due to Blum, Blum, and Shub. The predictability of the $1/p$ generator proved in theorem 4.4, and exercises 3, 4 and 5 at the end of this subsection, are from [B5].

Another useful pseudo random generator, also called the **Middle Square generator**, was proposed by Von Neumann: square an n - digit integer and keep the middle n digits of the resulting integer as the next term (see [K2], subsection 3.2.2).

The equivalence of factoring and computing square roots modulo a composite number (theorem 4.7) was first discovered by Rabin (see [R1]). The periodicity of $x^2 \bmod n$ is useful in the study of the security of the $x^2 \bmod n$ generator. The results of subsection 4.6 appear in [B5].

The definition of the probabilistic polynomial size circuit given in subsection 4.7 is based partly on the definition given in [A6].

A study of the security of the $x^2 \bmod n$ generator, as well as the reduction of its unpredictability to the Quadratic Residuosity Assumption, can be found in [B5]. Theorem 4.13 on amplifying the advantage of predicting quadratic residues is extracted from [G8]. The security of the index$_{p,g}$ generator, as well as the reduction of its unpredictability to the Discrete Logarithm Assumption can be found in [B6].

It is interesting that the origins of both the Discrete Logarithm Assumption as well as the Quadratic Residuosity Assumption go back to Gauss (see [G3], Art. 107, 58). A similar assumption, called the **Factoring Assumption**, has been used in [G10] for the construction of strong signature schemes.

Moreover, a parallel algorithm for pseudorandom bit generators can be found in [R6].

5   PUBLIC KEY CRYPTOSYSTEMS

Secret de deux, secret de Dieu,
secret de trois, secret de tous.
(French Proverb)

5.1   Introduction

It was only recently that public key cryptography developed into a precise mathematical subject, mainly as a response to the growing need for secure transmission of information via the electronic media. The main new idea was to base the security of cryptosystems on the intractability of number theory problems.

Subsections 5.2 and 5.3 set the ground by giving all the definitions and terminology necessary to understand the development of public key cryptosystems. The cryptosystems presented in this section have been chosen so as to illuminate how the intractability of number theory problems can be used to prove the security of specially defined cryptosystems.

The RSA (subsection 5.4) and Rabin systems (subsection 5.6) are similar in the sense that they are based on the selection of a trapdoor function f; encryption of a given (plaintext) message P is simply based on the evaluation of $f(P)$. However, as pointed out in [G8], the following questions raise serious doubts about their security:

- Can one compute P from $f(P)$ when P is of a special form?

- Can one compute some partial information about P from $f(P)$?

The Quadratic Residue System, which is based on probabilistic encryption, is meant to rectify this problematic situation and is presented in subsection 5.10.

The Merkle-Hellman system, given in subsection 5.8, is based on the **NP** - complete knapsack problem. The single iteration Merkle-Hellman system is not secure; an outline of Shamir's cryptanalytic attack is presented in subsection 5.9.

In addition, the security of the RSA and Rabin systems is studied relative to the security of single RSA and Rabin bits respctively (see subsections 5.5 and 5.7).

5.2   The Setup of a Nonpublic Key Cryptosystem

Suppose that user S, called a **sender**, wants to transmit a given message P to another user R, called a **receiver**, via a certain communication channel in such a way that it will be very difficult for any unauthorized user to read the message P. To accomplish this task the sender resorts to **encryption** or **enciphering** of the message P, i.e. he scrambles the original message P, also called the **plaintext**, and transmits the resulting scrambled text, say C. The scrambled text C thus obtained from the plaintext P is also called the **ciphertext**.

The receiver must now convert the ciphertext C back into the original plaintext P. This conversion process is also called **decryption** or **deciphering**. In addition, the encryption and decryption processes mentioned above are in fact efficient algorithms, called the **encryption algorithm** and the **decryption algorithm** respectively, transforming a given message into another one. The function E (respectively D) determined by the encryption (respectively decryption) algorithm is called the **encryption** (respectively **decryption**) **function**.

An **interceptor** is a user other than the sender or the receiver who gets hold of the transmitted ciphertext C. An interceptor who tries to reconstruct the original plaintext P from the inercepted ciphertext C is called a **cryptanalyst**, and the deciphering analysis he applies is called **cryptanalysis** (see figure 1).

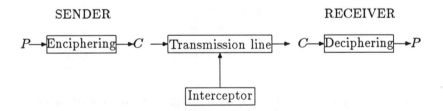

Figure 1: Message Transmission

In order to make the cryptanalysis even more difficult, the encryption and decryption functions depend on a set K of parameters, also called the **set of keys**; each $k \in K$ is called a **key**.

Thus, a **nonpublic** or **private key** cryptosystem, abbreviated $NPKC$, consists of two families, $\{E_k : k \in K\}, \{D_k : k \in K\}$, of, respectively, encryption and decryption functions such that:

1. For all $k \in K$, E_k is the inverse of D_k.

2. For all $k \in K$, E_k (respectively D_k) is known only to the sender (respectively receiver).

3. For all $k \in K$, the algorithms E_k, D_k are efficient.

4. It is difficult to compute the plaintext P from the ciphertext $E_k(P)$ alone without prior knowledge of the decryption function D_k used.

To transmit messages the sender and the receiver agree in advance on a key, say k, chosen from the set K of keys; the sender transmits the ciphertext $E_k(P)$ to the receiver; the receiver uses $D_k(E_k(P)) = P$ in order to obtain the plaintext P (see figure 2).

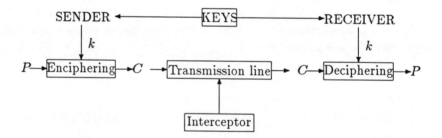

Figure 2: Nonpublic key cryptosystem

The following is an example of a widely used (but rather wasteful) system in nonpublic key cryptography.

Example 5.1 The Vernam System: *Let both plaintexts and keys be represented by sequences of bits. Let $k = (k_0, \ldots, k_n)$ be the key agreed upon by the sender and the receiver. Let $\oplus$ represent modulo 2 addition between bits. In this system $E_k = D_k$ and for any plaintext $P = (P_0, \ldots, P_n)$,*

$$E_k(P) = (k_0 \oplus P_0, \ldots, k_n \oplus P_n).$$

*Clearly, the Vernam system requires a key whose length is at least as long
as the message transmitted. This is accomplished by providing the key in a
sufficiently long tape; once used, each section of the tape is then discarded
(for that reason it is also called* one-time-pad*).*

5.3   The Setup of a Public Key Cryptosystem

As was noted above, a nonpublic key cryptosystem requires the exchange,
in advance, of a key between the sender and the receiver. However, such
a limitation is indeed impractical for today's electronic communication requirements. A public key cryptosystem, abbreviated PKC, overcomes this
limitation by allowing for the existence of a private file as well as a public
file (see figure 3). Thus, for each user U, the (**public**) file of U is made

USER	PUBLIC FILE	PRIVATE FILE
A	E_A	D_A
B	E_B	D_B
C	E_C	D_C
...	...	...
...	...	...
...	...	...

Figure 3: The Files in a PKC

available to all potential users, and it includes the encryption function E_U.
However, the (**private**) file of U is known only to U itself and consists of
the decryption function D_U. Moreover, the construction of the encryption
and decryption functions is based on the notion of a **trapdoor function**.
Loosely speaking, a trapdoor function is a function f such that the following
properties hold:

1. f is easy to compute.

2. f^{-1} is difficult to compute.

3. f^{-1} is easy to compute when a **trapdoor** (i.e. a secret string of
   information associated with the function) becomes available.

A function f satisfying only (1), (2) above is also called $\mathbf{1-1}$ **one-way**, or
simply **one-way**.

Consequently, a PKC consists of two families $\{E_U\}, \{D_U\}$ (where U ranges over the set of all potential users) of encryption and decryption functions such that

1. For all U, E_U is the inverse of D_U.

2. For all U, E_U is in the public file but D_U is known only to U.

3. For all U, E_U is a trapdoor function.

To transmit a plaintext P, the sender S transmits the ciphertext $E_R(P)$ to the receiver, where E_R is the public encryption function of the receiver R. The receiver uses $D_R(E_R(P)) = P$ in order to obtain the plaintext P (see also figure 4).

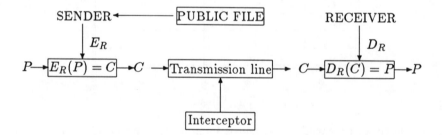

Figure 4: Public key cryptosystem

5.4   The RSA System

The first system to be examined is called RSA (after the initials of the last names of its three inventors: Rivest, Shamir and Adleman). In the RSA system, two distinct odd primes p, q are selected and kept secret; their product $N = p \cdot q$ is made known. Further, each user chooses integers $e, d < \varphi(N)$ such that

$$\gcd(e, \varphi(N)) = 1, \ e \cdot d \equiv 1 \ \mathrm{mod} \varphi(N);$$

e is made known, but d is kept secret. The encryption and decryption functions, respectively, are

$$E(x) = x^e \bmod N, \ D(x) = x^d \bmod N.$$

Figure 5 describes the RSA system.

USER	PUBLIC FILE	PRIVATE FILE
1	$e_1, N_1 = p_1 \cdot q_1$	d_1
2	$e_2, N_2 = p_2 \cdot q_2$	d_2
3	$e_3, N_3 = p_3 \cdot q_3$	d_3
...	...	...
...	...	...
...	...	...

Figure 5: The RSA System

Since N is the product of the two primes p, q, $\varphi(N) = (p-1) \cdot (q-1)$. Thus, any prime $e > \max(p, q)$ will be relatively prime to $\varphi(N)$. Using the Euclidean algorithm one can now determine an integer d such that $e \cdot d \equiv 1 \bmod N$. Hence it is easy to find integers e, d as above. It follows from results of section 1 that both RSA encryption and RSA decryption are easy (see the subsection on modular exponentiation). It remains to show that the functions E, D are the inverse of each other, i.e. to show that for all $1 \le x < N$,

$$E(D(x)) = x, \ D(E(x)) = x. \tag{1}$$

To prove (1) notice that

$$E(D(x)) = E(x^d \bmod N) = x^{e \cdot d} \bmod N.$$

However, $e \cdot d \equiv 1 \bmod \varphi(N)$. Hence, there exists an integer k (easily computed via the Euclidean algorithm) such that

$$e \cdot d = 1 + k \cdot \varphi(N).$$

It follows that for $x \in Z_N^*$,

$$E(D(x)) = x^{e \cdot d} \bmod N \equiv x^{1 + k \cdot \varphi(N)} \bmod N$$

$$\equiv x \cdot x^{k \cdot \varphi(N)} \bmod N \equiv x \cdot (x^{\varphi(N)})^k \bmod N \equiv x \bmod N,$$

using the Euler-Fermat theorem (see exercise 1 for the case $x \notin Z_N^*$).

The rest of this subsection will be devoted to some security consider-ations arising from the study of RSA and related to the factoring of the integer N.

Let $N = p \cdot q, e$ be a given instance of RSA. If $\varphi(N)$ is known, then one can factor N easily (see exercise 2 below).

Now assume that an arbitrary integer $d < \varphi(N)$ is known such that $ed \equiv 1 \bmod \varphi(N)$. It is then clear that $s = ed - 1$ is a factor of $\varphi(N)$ and hence

$$\forall a \in Z_N^* (a^s \equiv 1 \bmod N). \tag{2}$$

Write $s = 2^t u$, where u is odd and consider the set $A_N = Z_N^* - B_N$, where B_N is defined by

$$B_N = \{a \in Z_N^* : a^u \equiv 1 \bmod N \text{ or } \exists j < t (a^{2^j u} \equiv -1 \bmod N)\}.$$

For any element $a \in A_N$ choose k minimal with $a^{2^k u} \equiv 1 \bmod N$. Since $a \in A_N$, $k \geq 1$. Put $b \equiv a^{2^{k-1} u} \bmod N$. Then

$$b \not\equiv^\pm 1 \bmod N \text{ and } b^2 \equiv 1 \bmod N.$$

It follows that $\gcd(b - 1, N)$ is a proper factor of N.

Next, write $p - 1 = 2^{\nu_1} u_1$, $q - 1 = 2^{\nu_2} u_2$, with u_1, u_2 odd, and put $\nu = \min\{\nu_1, \nu_2\}$. Let $K = \gcd(u, u_1) \cdot \gcd(u, u_2)$. A repetition of the proof of Monier's theorem (see section 2, subsection on Rabin's test) shows that

$$|B_N| = \left(1 + \frac{4^\nu - 1}{3}\right) \cdot K \leq \frac{\varphi(N)}{2} = 2^{\nu_1 + \nu_2 - 1} \cdot u_1 \cdot u_2. \tag{3}$$

It follows that

$$Pr[a \in Z_N^* : a \in A_N] \geq \frac{1}{2}.$$

Hence, with probability $\geq 1/2$, a random element $a \in Z_N^*$ is also a member of A_N, and consequently, by the result in the previous paragraph, it can be used to factor N. To sum up, it has been shown that

Theorem 5.1 *Given any instance N, e of RSA and an arbitrary d such that $ed \equiv 1 \bmod \varphi(N)$, there exists an efficient probabilistic algorithm for factoring the integer N* •

EXERCISES

1: Show that (1) holds for $x \in Z_N^*$ as well. **Hint:** By Fermat's theorem the following congruences hold for all $i < q, j < p$:

$$(p \cdot i)^{q-1} \equiv 1 \bmod q, \quad (q \cdot j)^{p-1} \equiv 1 \bmod p.$$

2: Use the identity $\varphi(N) = N - p - q - 1$ to show that if $\varphi(N)$ is known, then N can easily be factored (do not use theorem 5.1!).

3: Prove inequality (3) in detail.

4: Show that the probability that a random plaintext message $x < N$ factors $N = pq$ is $< (1/p) + (1/q)$.

5: If the factorization of N is known, then the RSA function $x^e \bmod N$ is easy to invert. **Hint:** Compute a d such that $ed \equiv 1 \bmod \varphi(N)$.

6: For each $k \geq 1$, let RSA_k be the following generalization of RSA: the encryption key is a k - tuple $e_1, \ldots, e_k < \varphi(N)$, $N = pq$ is the product of distinct odd primes, and $\gcd(\varphi(N), e_1, \ldots, e_k) = 1$; the decryption key is a k - tuple $d_1, \ldots, d_k < \varphi(N)$ such that $e_1 d_1 + \cdots + e_k c_k \equiv 1 \bmod \varphi(N)$. The encryption algorithm is: $E(x) = (x^{e_1} \bmod N, \ldots, x^{e_k} \bmod N)$. The decryption algorithm is: $D(x_1, \ldots, x_k) = x_1^{d_1} \cdots x_k^{d_k} \bmod N$. Show that for each $k \geq 1$, RSA and RSA_k are equivalent in the following sense: if there is an efficient algorithm inverting the RSA function, then there is an efficient algorithm inverting the RSA_k function, and vice versa (for more details see [K11]).

5.5   RSA Bits

In studying the security of RSA it is reasonable to examine specific bits of the transmitted message. One might hope it would be easy to devise an algorithm that would output a specific bit of the original message, given the encrypted message. To be more specific, the present subsection is motivated by the following

Question: Suppose a cryptanalyst knows an efficient algorithm which, when given as input an RSA message $x^e \bmod N$ (of a certain instance of RSA), will output a certain bit of the original message x. Can he then devise an efficient algorithm which, when given as input an RSA message $x^e \bmod N$ (of the same instance of RSA) will output the whole message x?

Nevertheless, it might come as a surprise that, in certain cases (to be studied below) devising an algorithm to output a specific bit of the original message, given the encrypted message, is just as difficult as devising an algorithm that will output the entire original message (given the encrypted message).

If the representation of the integer N in the binary system is

$$N = \sum_{i=0}^{n-1} N_i \cdot 2^i,$$

then let $\text{bit}(N)$ denote the sequence $N_{n-1} \ldots N_0$. Conversely, given a sequence $S = N_{n-1} \ldots N_0$ of bits let the **representation** of S, abbreviated $\text{rep}(S)$, be

$$\text{rep}(S) = \sum_{i=0}^{n-1} N_i \cdot 2^i.$$

For any instance N, e of RSA, define the following bit functions:
Location Function:

$$\text{loc}_{N,e}(x^e \bmod N) = \begin{cases} 0 & \text{if } x < N/2 \\ 1 & \text{if } x > N/2, \end{cases}$$

s-th Bit Function:

$$\text{bit}_{N,e}^s(x^e \bmod N) = x_s,$$

where $\text{bit}(x) = x_{n-1} \ldots x_s \ldots x_0$.

As a special case one obtains the
Last Bit Function:

$$\text{bit}_{N,e}^0(x^e \bmod N) = x_0 = \begin{cases} 0 & \text{if } x \text{ is even} \\ 1 & \text{if } x \text{ is odd.} \end{cases}$$

For any odd integer N such that $\text{bit}(N) = N_{n-1} \ldots N_0$, it makes sense to define the **significant position** of N, abbreviated $s(N)$, by

$$s(N) = \text{ the largest } k \text{ such that } N_{k+1} = 0 < N_k = \cdots = N_0 = 1.$$

Notice that since N is odd, $s(N) \geq 1$.

The following result formalizes and answers the question stated above.

Theorem 5.2 *(Goldwasser-Micali-Tong) For any instance N, e of RSA and any $0 \leq s \leq s(N)$, the following statements are equivalent:*

(1) There is an efficient algorithm A such that
   $A(x^e \bmod N) = x$, *for all $x \in Z_N^*$.*

(2) There is an efficient algorithm computing the function $\text{bit}_{N,e}^0$.

(3) There is an efficient algorithm computing the function $\text{loc}_{N,e}$.

(4) There is an efficient algorithm computing the function $\text{bit}_{N,e}^s$.

Proof: Fix any $0 \leq s \leq s(N)$. It is obvious that (1) implies each of the statements (2), (3) and (4). Since N is odd N, 2^e are relativily prime; hence there exists an integer I such that $I \cdot 2^e \equiv 1 \bmod N$ (such an I can be computed using the Euclidean algorithm).

Proof of (2) $\Leftrightarrow$ (3): It is clear that for all $x \in Z_N^*$,

$$x < \frac{N}{2} \Leftrightarrow 2x \bmod N \text{ is even}. \tag{4}$$

It follows from (4) that

$$\text{loc}_{N,e}(x) = \text{bit}_{N,e}^0(2^e \cdot x \bmod N), \tag{5}$$

$$\text{bit}_{N,e}^0(x) = \text{loc}_{N,e}(I \cdot x \bmod N) \tag{6}$$

(see exercise 1). Now the proof of (2) $\Leftrightarrow$ (3) can be completed easily.

The rest of the proof requires the following simple lemma, whose proof is left as an exercise (see exercise 2).

Lemma 5.1 *For I, N, e as above, the following statements hold:*

(1) $N - x^e \equiv (N - x)^e \bmod N$.

(2) If x is even, then $I \cdot x^e \equiv (\frac{x}{2})^e \bmod N$.

(3) If x is odd, then $I \cdot (N - x^e) \equiv (\frac{N-x}{2})^e \bmod N$.

From now on and for the rest of this proof the subscripts of $\text{bit}_{N,e}^s$ will be omitted. For any sequence $u = u_{n-1}, \ldots, u_0$ of bits let $\ell(u) = n$ denote the length of u, and let $u \uparrow i$ denote the sequence $u_{n-1}, \ldots, u_{n-i}$, i.e. the sequence consisting of the first i bits of u. Hence, if $i \geq \ell(u)$, then $u \uparrow i = u$. For any sequences of bits u, u' let $u \triangle u'$ denote the last $\ell(u')$ bits in the binary representation of the number $\text{rep}(u) - \text{rep}(u')$, where $\text{rep}(u) \geq \text{rep}(u')$; further, let $u \frown u'$ denote the concatenation of u, u', i.e. the sequence obtained from u by adjoining at the end the bits of u'. It is then easy to prove (see exercise 3) that

Claim 1: For any $x < N/2$ there exists a sequence of bits w such that

$$\text{bit}(N - 2x) = w \frown [\text{bit}(N) \triangle (\text{bit}(x) \frown 0)].$$

Proof of (2) $\Rightarrow$ (1):

Let A be the efficient algorithm computing the last bit function bit^0. The idea of the proof is based on repeating the following algorithm $\ell(\text{bit}(N))$ times:

Input: $x^e \bmod N$.
Step 1: Compute $b = A(x^e \bmod N)$.
Step 2:
(1) If $b = 0$, then compute $I \cdot x^e \bmod N = (\frac{x}{2})^e \bmod N$.
(2) If $b = 1$, then compute $I \cdot (N - x^e) \bmod N = (\frac{N-x}{2})^e \bmod N$.
Step 3: Use the number computed in Step 2 as new input and repeat the process. (This number is either $(x/2)^e \bmod N$ or $((N - x)/2)^e \bmod N$.)

The sequence of bits given in successive applications of Step 1 constitutes the binary representation of x. The formal aspects of the proof are given in the sequel. Let $n = \ell(\,\mathrm{bit}(N))$. Define r_i, a_i, t_i (where $i = 1, \ldots, n$) as follows, by induction:

$$r_1 = x^e \bmod N; a_i = \mathrm{bit}^0(r_i),$$

$$r_i = \begin{cases} I \cdot r_{i-1} \bmod N & \text{if } a_{i-1} = 0 \\ I \cdot (N - r_{i-1}) \bmod N & \text{if } a_{i-1} = 1. \end{cases}$$

Also, define, by reverse induction, $t_n = a_n$ and

$$t_{i-1} = \begin{cases} t_i \frown 0 & \text{if } a_i = 0 \\ \mathrm{bit}(N) \Delta [t_i \frown 0] & \text{if } a_i = 1. \end{cases}$$

Clearly, for all i, $\ell(t_i) = n - i + 1$. Also, for each i there exists a unique integer u_i such that $u_i^e \equiv r_i \bmod N$. Put $v_i = \mathrm{bit}(u_i)$. Then one can prove by reverse induction on i that for all i there exists a sequence w_i such that
Claim 2: $v_i = w_i \frown t_i$.

Indeed, the case $i = n$ is immediate from the definitions. Assume that the claim is true for i, and let w_i be a sequence such that $v_i = w_i \frown t_i$. It remains to find a w_{i-1} such that $v_{i-1} = w_{i-1} \frown t_{i-1}$. If, on the one hand, $a_{i-1} = 0$, then $r_i = I \cdot r_{i-1} \bmod N$. Thus,

$$u_{i-1}^e \equiv r_{i-1} \equiv 2^e \cdot r_i \equiv 2^e \cdot u_i^e \equiv (2 \cdot u_i)^e \bmod N.$$

Consequently, $2 \cdot u_i = u_{i-1}$. It follows from the induction hypothesis that

$$v_{i-1} = \mathrm{bit}(u_{i-1}) = \mathrm{bit}(u_i) \frown 0 = w_i \frown t_i \frown 0.$$

If, on the other hand, $a_{i-1} = 1$, then $r_i = I \cdot (N - r_{i-1}) \bmod N$. Thus,

$$u_{i-1}^e \equiv r_{i-1} \equiv N - 2^e \cdot r_i \equiv N - 2^e \cdot u_i^e \equiv$$

$$N - (2 \cdot u_i)^e \equiv (N - 2 \cdot u_i)^e \bmod N.$$

Consequently, $N - 2 \cdot u_i = u_{i-1}$. It follows from claim 1 that there exists a sequence w'_{i-1} such that

$$v_{i-1} = \mathrm{bit}(u_{i-1}) = \mathrm{bit}(N - 2 \cdot u_i) = w'_{i-1} \frown [\, \mathrm{bit}(N)\Delta(v_i \frown 0)].$$

Hence, the result follows easily from the induction hypothesis.

Finally, claim 2 implies that $w_1 = \emptyset$ and hence $v_1 = \mathrm{bit}(x) = t_1$.

Proof of (4) $\Rightarrow$ (1):

Define $r_i, a_i, f_{i,s}, \ldots, f_{i,0}$ (where $i = 1, \ldots, n$) by induction on i:

$$f_{i,s} = \mathrm{bit}^s(r_i), \quad f_{1,s-1} = \cdots = f_{1,0} = 0,$$

$$r_1 = x^e \bmod N, \quad a_i = f_{i,0}.$$

r_i is now defined exactly as before, i.e.

$$r_i = \begin{cases} I \cdot r_{i-1} \bmod N & \text{if } a_{i-1} = 0 \\ I \cdot (N - r_{i-1}) \bmod N & \text{if } a_{i-1} = 1. \end{cases}$$

Further, put:

$$f_{i,s-1} \cdots f_{i,0} = \begin{cases} f_{i-1,s} \cdots f_{i-1,1} & \text{if } a_{i-1} = 0 \\ (1 - f_{i-1,s}) \cdots (1 - f_{i-1,1}) & \text{if } a_{i-1} = 1. \end{cases}$$

The sequence t_i is defined by reverse induction; one sets $t_n = f_{n,s} \cdots f_{n,0}$, and for $i \geq s + 1$ one puts

$$t_{i-1} = \begin{cases} t_i \frown 0 & \text{if } a_{i-1} = 0 \\ \mathrm{bit}(N)\Delta[t_i \frown 0] & \text{if } a_{i-1} = 1. \end{cases}$$

Clearly, for all $1 \leq i \leq n - s$, $\ell(t_{n+1-i}) = s + i$. Hence, $\ell(t_{s+1}) = n$. As before, let u_i be such that $u_i^e \equiv r_i \bmod N$. It will be shown by induction on $s + 1 \geq i \geq 1$ that

Claim 3: $[f_{i,s} \cdots f_{i,0}] \uparrow i = [\text{last } s + 1 \text{ bits of } \mathrm{bit}(u_i)] \uparrow i$.

Proof of Claim 3: The case $i = 1$ is trivial. Assume the claim is true for i. It will be shown that the claim is true for $i + 1$. On the one hand, if $a_i = 0$ then

$$[f_{i+1,s} \cdots f_{i+1,0}] \uparrow (i + 1) = f_{i+1,s} f_{i,s} f_{i,s-1} \cdots f_{i,s-i+1} =$$

$$\mathrm{bit}^s(r_{i+1}) f_{i,s} f_{i,s-1} \cdots f_{i,s-i+1} =$$

$$[(s + 1) - \text{st bit from the end of } \mathrm{bit}(u_{i+1})] f_{i,s} f_{i,s-1} \cdots f_{i,s-i+1}.$$

The claim now follows from the fact that $f_{i,0} = 0$, $u_i = 2u_{i+1}$ (see claim 1). On the other hand, if $a_i = 1$, then

$$[f_{i+1,s} \cdots f_{i+1,0}] \uparrow (i+1) =$$

$$[(s+1) - st \text{ bit from the end of } \text{bit}(u_{i+1})](1 - f_{i,s}) \cdots (1 - f_{i,s-i+1}).$$

The claim now follows from the fact that $f_{i,0} = 1$, $u_i = N - 2u_{i+1}$ (see claim 1).

Next, one can show, as in claim 2 above, that for all $i \geq s+1$ there exists a sequence w_i such that $v_i = w_i \frown t_i$. In particular, $v_{s+1} = t_{s+1}$ and hence, $u_{s+1} = \text{bit}(t_{s+1})$. It follows from the definition of u_i that for all i,

$$2 \cdot u_{i+1} \equiv u_i \bmod N \text{ or } 2 \cdot u_{i+1} \equiv -u_i \bmod N.$$

In particular, since $x = u_1$,

$$2^s \cdot u_{s+1} \equiv x \bmod N \text{ or } 2^s \cdot u_{s+1} \equiv -x \bmod N.$$

It is now clear that if one puts $y \equiv 2^s \cdot \text{rep}(t_{s+1}) \bmod N$, then

$$x = \begin{cases} y & \text{if } y^e \equiv x^e \bmod N \\ N - y & \text{if } y^e \not\equiv x^e \bmod N. \end{cases}$$

The foregoing recursive construction can easily be converted into an efficient algorithm for computing x from $x^e \bmod N$ •

EXERCISES

1: Give the proof of equations (5) and (6).

2: Give the proof of lemma 5.1. **Hint:** Use the fact that e is odd and that $I \cdot 2^e \equiv 1 \bmod N$.

3: Give the proof of Claim 1.

4: Give in detail the algorithms described in the proof of $(2) \Rightarrow (1)$ and $(4) \Rightarrow (1)$ of theorem 5.2.

5: Prove the analogue of theorem 5.2 for the RSA_k system, which was defined in exercise 6 of subsection 5.4.

5.6   The Rabin System

The main strength of RSA is based on the (supposed) difficulty of factoring. Thus, if a cryptanalyst knows how to factor efficiently, he will also be able to break RSA (see exercise 5 in subsection 5.4). However, it is not known if the converse of this last statement is true. In fact, the following question seems to be open:

Question: Assume there exists an efficient algorithm for inverting the RSA function, i.e. so that given an instance $e, N, x^e \bmod N$ of RSA as input, the algorithm will output x. Is there an efficient algorithm for factoring?

Rabin, in an attempt to resolve this intricate situation has proposed a public key cryptosystem (to be defined below) for which the problem of factoring is equivalent to that of breaking the system.

In the Rabin system each user selects a pair p, q of distinct odd primes, to be kept secret, and then publicizes $N = p \cdot q$; further, each user chooses an integer $b < N$. The **encryption** function is

$$E_{N,b}(x) = x \cdot (x + b) \bmod N.$$

The **decryption** function $D_{N,b}$ supplies, for each given encoded message m, a solution u (there are four possible solutions) of the quadratic equation $x \cdot (x + b) \equiv m \bmod N$. Figure 6 describes the Rabin system.

USER	PUBLIC FILE	PRIVATE FILE
1	$b_1, N_1 = p_1 \cdot q_1$	p_1, q_1
2	$b_2, N_2 = p_2 \cdot q_2$	p_2, q_2
3	$b_3, N_3 = p_3 \cdot q_3$	p_3, q_3
...	...	...
...	...	...
...	...	...

Figure 6: The Rabin System

It is clear that the encryption $E_{N,b}(x) \equiv x \cdot (x + b) \bmod N$ requires one addition, one multiplication, and one division by N. Decryption is also easy if the factorization $N = p \cdot q$ of N is known. Indeed, given an encrypted message m (such that p, q do not divide m), use the Adleman, Manders, and Miller algorithm to compute the roots r, s of the congruences $x \cdot (x + b) \equiv m \bmod p$ and $x \cdot (x + b) \equiv m \bmod q$, respectively. Next, use the Euclidean algorithm to compute integers k, l such that $k \cdot p + l \cdot q = 1$. It is now easy to see that $lqr + kps$ is a solution of the congruence $x \cdot (x + b) \equiv m \bmod N$.

Further, it is easy to show that the functions $E_{N,b}, D_{N,b}$ are the inverse of each other.

It will simplify the remaining proofs if one notices that the congruence $x \cdot (x + b) \equiv m \bmod N$ has a solution if and only if the congruence $y^2 \equiv m + \frac{b^2}{4} \bmod N$ has a solution. To see this last claim, one merely has to complete the squares in the congruence $x^2 + x \cdot b \equiv m \bmod N$; this can be done since N is odd; one merely has to define $4^{-1} \bmod N$, the inverse of 4 modulo N. Thus, from now on only congruences of the form $x^2 \equiv m \bmod N$ will be considered.

As promised, it remains to show that decryption is equivalent to factorization. This is proved in the theorem below.

Theorem 5.3 *(Rabin's Factorization Theorem) Let N be the product of two odd primes. Then the following statetements are equivalent:*
(1) There is an efficient algorithm A such that for all $m \in QR_N$, $A(N, m)$ is a random solution of the congruence $x^2 \equiv m \bmod N$.
(2) There is an efficient algorithm for factoring N.

Proof: The proof of $(2) \Rightarrow (1)$ was given in the discussion above (see also exercise 1). Thus, it remains to prove $(1) \Rightarrow (2)$. Choose at random an integer a such that $\gcd(a, N) = 1$ and let $m \equiv a^2 \bmod N$. If $u = A(N, m)$, then both a, u are solutions of the congruence $x^2 \equiv m \bmod N$. So, on the one hand, if $u \notin \{a, N - a\}$, then $\gcd(N, u + a)$ is a prime factor of N; on the other hand, if $u \in \{a, N - a\}$, then choose another a and repeat the foregoing procedure. Since, with probability $\geq 1/2$, $u \notin \{a, N - a\}$, it is expected that after two trials one will be able to factor N •

A closer examination of the proof of the previous theorem can also show the following:

Theorem 5.4 *(Rabin) Let A be an efficient algorithm such that for any N which is the product of two odd primes, and any $m \in QR_N$, $A(N, m)$ outputs, in $F(N)$ steps a random solution of the congruence $x^2 \equiv m \bmod N$ with probability at least $\frac{1}{e(N)}$. Then there exists an efficient algorithm B such that for any positive integer N which is the product of two odd primes, the algorithm $B(N)$ will output the factors of N in at most $2 \cdot e(N) \cdot F(N) + 2 \cdot \log_2 N$ steps •*

EXERCISES

1: Show that if r (respectively s) is a solution of the congruence $x(x+b) \equiv m \bmod p$ (respectively $x(x+b) \equiv m \bmod q$) and $kp + \ell q = 1$, then $kps + \ell qr$ is a solution of the congruence $x(x+b) \equiv m \bmod N$.

2: Prove theorem 5.4 using an argument similar to that of theorem 5.3.

5.7 Rabin Bits

Just as in the case of the RSA system, it is reasonable to examine the secutity of specific bits of messages transmitted via the Rabin system. To be more specific, the present subsection is motivated by the following

Question: Suppose a cryptanalyst knows an efficient algorithm which, when given as input a Rabin message $x^2 \bmod N$ (of a certain instance of Rabin's system), will output a certain bit of the original message x. Can he then devise an efficient algorithm which, when given as input a Rabin message $x^2 \bmod N$ (of the same instance of Rabin's system) will output the whole message x?

The notation of subsection 5.5 will be used also in the present subsection.

Each $x \in QR_N$ has exactly four square roots; let x^+ (respectively x^-) denote the square root of x which is $< N/2$ and such that the Legendre - Jacobi symbol of x^+ (respectively of x^-) with respect to N is $+1$ (respectively -1). For any instance N of Rabin's system, define the following bit functions whose domain is the set QR_N of quadratic residues modulo N:

Residue Parity Function:

$$RPar_N(x) = \mathrm{par}(x^+),$$

Parity Comparison Function:

$$CPar_N(x) = \begin{cases} 0 & \text{if } \mathrm{par}(x^+) = \mathrm{par}(x^-) \\ 1 & \text{if } \mathrm{par}(x^+) \neq \mathrm{par}(x^-). \end{cases}$$

The following result formalizes and answers the question stated above.

Theorem 5.5 *(Goldwasser-Micali-Tong) Given any integer N which is the product of two distinct odd primes p, q such that $N \equiv 1 \bmod 8$, the following statements are equivalent:*

(1) There is an efficient algorithm for factoring N.

(2) There is an efficient algorithm computing the function $RPar_N$.

(3) There is an efficient algorithm computing the function $CPar_N$.

Proof: Fix N as in the hypothesis of the theorem. It is obvious that (1) implies each of the statements (2) and (3). Since N is odd $N, 4$ are relativily prime; hence there exists an integer I such that $I \cdot 4 \equiv 1 \bmod N$ (such an I can be computed using the Euclidean algorithm).

Proof of (2) $\Rightarrow$ (1): The proof is similar to that of theorem 5.2. The following algorithm factors N:

Input: N.
Step 1: Choose $a < N/2$ at random such that $(a|N) = -1$.
Step 2: Compute $r_1 \equiv a^2 \bmod N, a_1 = RPar_N(r_1)$.
Step 3: Compute the length $n = \ell(\text{bit}(N))$ of N.
Step 4: For $i = 1$ **to** n **compute:**

$$r_i \equiv I \cdot r_{i-1} \bmod N, \quad a_i = RPar_N(r_i).$$

Step 5: Compute $t_n = a_n$.
Step 6: For $i = n$ **down to 2 compute:**

$$t_{i-1} = \begin{cases} t_i \frown 0 & \text{if } a_{i-1} = 0 \\ \text{bit}(N) \triangle [t_i \frown 0] & \text{if } a_{i-1} = 1. \end{cases}$$

Output: $\gcd(a + \text{rep}(t_1), N)$.

For each i let u_i be the unique root of $x^2 \equiv r_i \bmod N$ such that $u_i < N/2$, $(u_i|N) = +1$. However, recall the following properties of the Legendre - Jacobi symbol:

$$(-1|N) = (-1)^{(N-1)/2}, \quad (2|N) = (-1)^{(N^2-1)/8}.$$

Hence, for the N considered in the present theorem, $(-1|N) = (2|N) = +1$. Using this and arguing as in the proof of theorem 5.2 one can show that

$$a_{i-1} = 0 \Rightarrow u_{i-1} = 2 \cdot u_i,$$

$$a_{i-1} = 1 \Rightarrow u_{i-1} = N - 2 \cdot u_i.$$

For each i let $v_i = \text{rep}(u_i)$. As in the proof of theorem 5.2 it can be shown that for all i there exists a w_i such that $v_i = w_i \frown t_i$. In particular, $v_1 = t_1$. It follws that $\gcd(a + u_1, N)$ is a prime factor of N.

The proof of (3) $\Rightarrow$ (1) is left as an exercise to the reader $\bullet$

EXERCISES

1: Complete the details of the proof of (2) $\Rightarrow$ (1) in theorem 5.5.
2: Give the proof of (3) $\Rightarrow$ (1) in theorem 5.5. Hint: The algorithm is similar to that given in the proof of (2) $\Rightarrow$ (1).

5.8   The Merkle - Hellman System

In the Merkle-Hellman system each user selects a pair w, m of positive integers, to be kept in a private file, such that $\gcd(w, m) = 1$; w is called the **multiplier** and m is called the **modulus**. In addition, each user keeps in a private file a **superincreasing** sequence $a' = (a'_1, \ldots, a'_n)$ of positive integers, i.e. a sequence that satisfies

$$a'_i > \sum_{j=1}^{i-1} a'_j, \text{ for all } i \geq 1, \text{ and } m > \sum_{j=1}^{n} a'_j.$$

The user makes known the sequence $a = (a_1, \ldots, a_n)$ which is defined by

$$a_i \equiv w \cdot a'_i \bmod m \text{ for all } i \geq 1.$$

A message $x = (x_1, \ldots, x_n)$ (which is a sequence of $0, 1$ bits) is encrypted via the **encryption** function

$$E(x) = \sum_{i=1}^{n} x_i \cdot a_i.$$

The **decryption** function D supplies, for each given encoded message S, a solution $u = (u_1, \ldots, u_n)$ of the equation

$$S = \sum_{i=1}^{n} u_i \cdot a_i. \tag{7}$$

Figure 7 describes the Merkle-Hellman system.

USER	PUBLIC FILE	PRIVATE FILE
1	$a_1 = (a_{1,1}, \ldots, a_{1,n_1})$	$w_1, m_1, a'_1 = (a'_{1,1}, \ldots, a'_{1,n_1})$
2	$a_2 = (a_{2,1}, \ldots, a_{2,n_2})$	$w_2, m_2, a'_2 = (a'_{2,1}, \ldots, a'_{2,n_2})$
3	$a_3 = (a_{3,1}, \ldots, a_{3,n_3})$	$w_3, m_3, a'_3 = (a'_{3,1}, \ldots, a'_{3,n_3})$
...	...	...
...	...	...
...	...	...

Figure 7: The Merkle-Hellman System

Equation (7) is based on a knapsack problem and is in general difficult to solve (recall that the knapsack problem is **NP** complete). However, the following lemma indicates how one can efficiently solve knapsack problems for superincreasing sequences.

Theorem 5.6 *Let $a' = (a'_1, \ldots, a'_n)$ be a superincreasing sequence of positive integers and let $S' > 0$. Then the following equation has at most one solution $x = (x_1, \ldots, x_n) \in \{0, 1\}^n$ which satisfies*

$$S' = \sum_{i=1}^{n} x_i \cdot a'_i. \tag{8}$$

In fact, if equation (8) has a solution then

$$S' \leq \sum_{i=1}^{n} a'_i.$$

Proof: The proof is straightforward. One merely needs to observe that any solution of (8) must satisfy

$$x_i = 1 \Leftrightarrow S' \geq a'_i + \sum_{j=i+1}^{n} x_j \cdot a'_j,$$

for all $i = 1, \ldots, n$. Indeed, ($\Rightarrow$) is an immediate consequence of (8), and to prove ($\Leftarrow$) it is enough to prove the contrapositive. Let $x_i = 0$. Then

$$S' = \sum_{j=1}^{i-1} x_j a'_j + \sum_{j=i+1}^{n} x_j a'_j < a'_i + \sum_{j=i+1}^{n} x_j a'_j \bullet$$

It remains to show that encryption is easy. Indeed, when the user receives the encrypted message S he is supposed to solve equation (7) to obtain the original message $x = (x_1, \ldots, x_n)$. Instead, he computes w^{-1}, the inverse of w modulo m, and solves the equivalent knapsack problem

$$w^{-1} \cdot S \equiv \sum_{i=1}^{n} x_i \cdot a'_i \mod m. \tag{9}$$

Since the sequence $a' = (a'_1, \ldots, a'_n)$ is superincreasing, equation (9) can be solved easily using theorem 5.6.

An obvious generalization of the above system is the **iterated** Merkle-Hellman system, also considered by Merkle and Hellman. In such a system one successively applies pairs w^k, m^k of multipliers and moduli respectively (such that $\gcd(w^k, m^k) = 1$, where $k = 1, \ldots, r - 1$) to the original vector a to obtain a sequence $a = a^0, a^1, \ldots, a^r$ of vectors satisfying, componentwise,

$$a^k \equiv w^{k+1} * a^{k+1} \bmod m^{k+1}, \text{ for } k = 0, \ldots, r - 1.$$

(Here, the symbol $*$ is used to indicate multiplication of a scalar with a vector.) The last vector a^r is chosen in advance to constitute a superincreasing sequence. For more details the reader should consult [M5].

EXERCISES

1: For each n construct a superincreasing sequence of length n.

5.9 Security of the Merkle - Hellman System (Outline)

Let $w, m, a' = (a'_1, \ldots, a'_n)$, $a = (a_1, \ldots, a_n)$ be an instance of the Merkle Hellman system. A cryptanalyst is in possession of the sequence a, but not of w, m, a'. In order to analyze this instance, the cryptanalyst might try to compute a **trapdoor** pair for the sequence a, i.e. a pair $\overline{w}, \overline{m}$ of integers such that the sequnce $\overline{a} = (\overline{a}_1, \ldots, \overline{a}_n)$, defined by

$$\overline{a}_i \equiv a_i \cdot \overline{w} \bmod \overline{m}, \tag{10}$$

is superincreasing and satisfies

$$\sum_{i=1}^{n} \overline{a}_i < \overline{m}. \tag{11}$$

It is clear from the argument in subsection 5.8 that any trapdoor pair could be used to decrypt easily any transmitted message of the foregoing instance of the Merkle-Hellman system.

Dividing congruences (10), (11) by $\overline{m}$ one obtains that

$$\frac{\overline{a}_i}{\overline{m}} \equiv \left(a_i \cdot \frac{\overline{w}}{\overline{m}} \right) \bmod 1, \tag{12}$$

$$\sum_{i=1}^{n} a_i \cdot \overline{r} \bmod 1 < 1, \tag{13}$$

where $\overline{r} = \frac{\overline{w}}{\overline{m}}$. The function $(a_i \cdot \overline{r}) \bmod 1$, for real numbers $\overline{r}$, is represented in figure 8. (Notice that for convenience the unit length in the horizontal axis is bigger than the unit length in the vertical axis.)

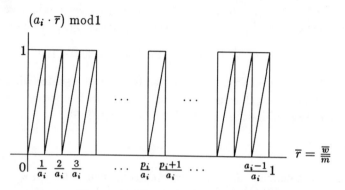

Figure 8: The i-th sawtooth function

In order to compute such a trapdoor pair one first determines a point $\bar{r}_0$ on the $\bar{r}$- axis such that inequality (13) is valid (such a point is guaranteed to exist because this is required in the construction of the Merkle-Hellman system). Hence, an interval $[r_1, r_2]$ must also exist such that for all points $\bar{r} \in [r_1, r_2]$, inequality (13) is valid. If one thinks of the sawtooth curves superimposed one upon the other, then what is desired is to determine accumulation points of minima of all these sawtooth curves. In fact such accumulation points will occur at intervals $[r_1, r_2]$, as before.

Let $p_i =$ the p_i-th minimum of the i-th sawtooth curve. One obtains the following two systems of inequalities with the integral unknowns $p_1, \ldots, p_n$.

$$
\begin{array}{ll}
1 \leq p_1 \leq a_1 - 1, & -\epsilon_2 \leq p_1/a_1 - p_2/a_2 \leq \epsilon'_2 \\
1 \leq p_2 \leq a_2 - 1, & -\epsilon_3 \leq p_1/a_1 - p_3/a_3 \leq \epsilon'_3 \\
\quad \vdots & \quad \vdots \\
1 \leq p_n \leq a_n - 1, & -\epsilon_n \leq p_1/a_1 - p_n/a_n \leq \epsilon'_n,
\end{array}
\tag{14}
$$

where ϵ_i, ϵ'_i are the acceptable deviations of the differences $p_1/a_1 - p_i/a_i$, respectively, for $i = 1, \ldots, n$. The deviations should be chosen small enough to be able to determine accumulation points. Usually it will be enough to consider a constant number of inequalities in (14) that are independent of n. System (14) can be solved using Lenstra's integer programming algorithm (see [L11]).

Let p_1 be one of the values determined by the procedure above and let $\bar{r}_1, \ldots, \bar{r}_k$ be a list of all discontinuity points of all the sawtooth curves such that

$$\bar{r}_1, \ldots, \bar{r}_k \in \left[\frac{p_1}{a_1}, \frac{p_1 + 1}{a_1} \right),$$

arranged in increasing order. Between any two such discontinuity points each sawtooth curve looks like a line segment; moreover, the linear segment corresponding to the i-th sawtooth curve is represented by the formula

$$\bar{r} \cdot a_i - q_i^t, \ \bar{r}_t \leq \bar{r} < \bar{r},$$

where $q_i^t = $ the number of minima of the i-th sawtooth curve which lie in the interval $(0, \bar{r}_t)$. Thus, for each $1 \leq t \leq k$ conditions (12), (13) can now be formulated as the following system of linear inequalities with unknown $\bar{r}$, such that $\bar{r}_t \leq \bar{r} < \bar{r}_{t+1}$:

$$\sum_{i=1}^{n} (\bar{r} \cdot a_i - q_i^t) < 1, \tag{15}$$

$$(\bar{r} \cdot a_i - q_i^t) > \sum_{j=1}^{i-1} (\bar{r} \cdot a_j - q_j^t), \ \text{for } i = 1, \ldots, n. \tag{16}$$

The solution of the foregoing system provides a subinterval of $[\bar{r}_t, \bar{r}_{t+1})$. Any $\bar{r} = \bar{w}/\bar{m}$ lying in this subinterval gives a trapdoor pair $\bar{w}, \bar{m}$. For more details the reader should consult [S10].

5.10   The Quadratic Residue System

The quadratic residue system, abbreviated QRS, to be described below, replaces the notion of trapdoor function with the notion of probabilistic encryption, i.e. to encrypt a given message the user will use the result of a sequence of coin tosses.

Suppose that a sender S wants to send a binary message $M = (m_1 \cdots m_r)$ to receiver R. S obtains the numbers n, y, where $y \notin QR_n$, corresponding to R from the public file; n is the product of two odd primes p, q known only to R such that $p \equiv q \equiv 3 \bmod 4$ (see figure 9). S encrypts the message M by choosing a random sequence $x = (x_1, \ldots, x_r)$ of r elements of Z_n^* and setting

$$E_n(x; M) = (y^{m_1} \cdot x_1^2 \bmod n, \ldots, y^{m_r} \cdot x_r^2 \bmod n).$$

Given $(e_1, \ldots, e_r)$ the receiver who knows the factorization of n, reconstructs the message $M = D_n(e_1, \ldots, e_r) = (m_1, \ldots, m_r)$ via

$$m_i = \begin{cases} 1 & \text{if } e_i \in QR_n \\ 0 & \text{if } e_i \notin QR_n, \end{cases}$$

where $i = 1, \ldots, r$.

USER	PUBLIC FILE	PRIVATE FILE
1	$y_1 \notin QR_{n_1}, n_1 = p_1 \cdot q_1$	p_1, q_1
2	$y_2, \notin QR_{n_2}, n_2 = p_2 \cdot q_2$	p_2, q_2
3	$y_3, \notin QR_{n_3}, n_3 = p_3 \cdot q_3$	p_3, q_3
...	...	...
...	...	...
...	...	...

Figure 9: The Quadratic Residue System

The following definitions will be needed in the study of the security of the QRS. The **signature** of an integer $x \in Z_n^*$ is defined by

$$\sigma_n(x) = \begin{cases} 1 & \text{if } x \in QR_n \\ 0 & \text{if } x \notin QR_n. \end{cases}$$

Thus, the preceding definition of the decryption function D_n implies that

$$D_n(e_1, \ldots, e_r) = (\sigma_n(e_1), \ldots, \sigma_n(e_r)).$$

The r-**signature** of the r- tuple $x = (x_1, \ldots, x_r)$, where each $x_i \in Z_n^*$, is defined by

$$\sigma_{n,r}(x_1, \ldots, x_r) = (\sigma_n(x_1), \ldots, \sigma_n(x_r)).$$

If $\ell = (\ell_1, \ldots, \ell_r)$ is a given sequence of bits let

$$\Omega_{r,n,\ell} = \{(x_1, \ldots, x_r) \in (Z_n^*)^r : \sigma_{n,r}(x_1, \ldots, x_r) = \ell\}.$$

Given two sequences of bits $a = (a_1, \ldots, a_r), b = (b_1, \ldots, b_r)$ the (**Hamming**) **distance** between a, b, abbreviated dis(a, b), is the number of indices $1 \le i \le r$ such that $a_i \ne b_i$; a, b are called **adjacent** if their distance is equal to 1.

Recall the notation of the subsection on the Quadratic Residue Generator. $N = \{N_k : k \in I\}$ will denote a family of **nonempty** sets N_k of nonnegative integers such that I is an infinite set of indices, and for all $n \in N_k$ the integer n has binary length exactly k; throughout the present subsection n will range over integers which are the product of two distinct odd primes p, q such that $p \equiv q \equiv 3 \bmod 4$. The uppercase Roman letters P, Q, R with subscripts or superscripts will range over nonzero polynomials with positive coefficients, one indeterminate, and degree ≥ 1, and the lowercase Greek letters ϵ, δ with subscripts or superscripts will range over positive real numbers.

A **decision function** is any family $d = \{d_n : n \in N_k, k \in I\}$ of functions $d_n : (Z_n^*)^{P(k)} \longrightarrow \{0, 1\}$, where P is a polynomial. For any decision function d, any sequence $\ell(n)$ of $P(k)$ bits, and any $n \in N_k$, let

$$P_{d,n}(\ell(n)) = Pr[d_n(x) = 1 | x \in \Omega_{P(k),n,\ell(n)}].$$

For technical reasons, to become apparent below, the definition of advantage for determining quadratic residuosity will be extended to the definition of advantage for determining quadratic residuosity assuming a quadratic nonresidue is known.

Definition 5.1 *A polynomial size circuit $C = \{C_k : k \geq 1\}$ has a $(1/2 - 1/P)$-advantage for determining quadratic residuosity (for the family N), assuming a quadratic nonresidue is known (and this will be abbreviated by $AQR^+(C, N, 1 - 1/P)$), if, for all but a finite number of indices $k \in I$, the following property holds for all $n \in N_k$:*

$$\frac{1}{2}Pr[C_k(n, x, y) = 1 \mid x \in QR_n \text{ and } y \notin QR_n]+$$

$$\frac{1}{2}Pr[C_k(n, x, y) = 0 \mid x \notin QR_n \text{ and } y \notin QR_n] \geq 1 - \frac{1}{P(k)},$$

where for each $n \in N_k$, x, y range over $Z_n^*(+1)$.

The following two lemmas will be used in the study of QRS.

Lemma 5.2 *(Goldwasser-Micali)*

$$(\exists C)(\exists P)AQR^+(C, N, 1 - 1/P) \Rightarrow (\forall Q)(\exists C)AQR(C, N, 1 - 1/Q).$$

Proof: (Outline) Let $C = \{C_k : k \in I\}$ be a polynomial size circuit and P a polynomial as in definition 5.1. Let $n \in N_k$ and let Q be any given fixed polynomial. Put $m = 4 \cdot Q(k) \cdot P(k)^2$ and select at random m quadratic residues

$$s_1^2 \bmod n, \ldots, s_m^2 \bmod n.$$

Further, select at random m elements

$$y_1, \ldots, y_m \in Z_n^*(+1),$$

and put $Y = \{y_1, \ldots, y_m\}$. The idea is now the following: one of the elements of Y is a quadratic nonreridue with high probability (in fact the probability is $1 - 2^{-m}$); it is natural to search for such an element, say $z \in Y$, and then to use the circuit C' defined by

$$C_k'(n, x) = C_k(n, x, z), \text{ where } x \in Z_n^*(+1). \tag{17}$$

To search for an element $z \in Y$ it is enough to check the performance of the circuit C.

Thus, **for** $t = 1, \ldots, m$ **do:**
Step 1: Compute the integers:

$$R_{n,t} = |\{1 \le i \le m \ : \ C_k(n, s_i^2 \bmod n, y_t) = 1\}|,$$

$$R_{n,t,j} = |\{1 \le i \le m \ : \ C_k(n, y_j \cdot s_i^2 \bmod n, y_t) = 1\}|.$$

Step 2: Compute

$$d_{n,t,j} = \frac{|R_{n,t} - R_{n,t,j}|}{m}$$

until for some $j = 1, \ldots, m$, the following holds:

$$d_{n,t,j} > \frac{1}{P(k)}. \tag{18}$$

If a j can be found such that (18), is true then define the circuit C' as in (17) with $z = y_t$. The rest of the proof is an application of the weak law of large numbers and will be left as an exercise (see exercise 2) •

Lemma 5.3 *(Goldwasser-Micali) Let P, R be polynomials and let d be an easily computed decision function such that the following statement holds for all but a finite number of $k \in I$: for all $n \in N_k$ one can efficiently compute $u, u' \in \{0,1\}^{P(k)}$ such that*

$$|P_{d,n}(u) - P_{d,n}(u')| > \frac{1}{R(k)}. \tag{19}$$

Then one can prove that

$$(\forall Q)(\exists C)AQR^{+}(C, N, 1 - 1/Q).$$

Proof: Without loss of generality it can be assumed that u, u' in (19) are adjacent. To see this, let $n \in N_k$ and let u, u' witness the validity of (19). If $\Delta = \text{dis}(u, u')$ then there exists a sequence $u_0 = u, u_1, \ldots, u_\Delta = u' \in \{0, 1\}^{P(k)}$ such that for all $1 \leq i \leq \Delta$, u_{i-1}, u_i are adjacent. It follows that

$$\sum_{i=1}^{\Delta} |P_{d,n}(u_{i-1}) - P_{d,n}(u_i)| \geq |P_{d,n}(u) - P_{d,n}(u')| > \frac{1}{R(k)}.$$

Hence, there exists an $1 \leq i \leq \Delta$ such that

$$|P_{d,n}(u_{i-1}) - P_{d,n}(u_i)| > \frac{1}{\Delta \cdot R(k)} \geq \frac{1}{R'(k)},$$

where $R'(k) = R(k) \cdot P(k)$ (here one uses the fact that $\Delta \leq P(k)$).

Next, let Q be an arbitrary but fixed polynomial and define the circuit C as follows:

Input: $n \in N_k, x \in Z_n^*(+1), y \in Z_n^*(+1) - QR_n$.
Step 1: Put $m = 16 \cdot Q(k) \cdot R(k)^2$.
Step 2: Choose at random m quadratic residues

$$s_1^2 \bmod n, \ldots, s_m^2 \bmod n \in QR_n,$$

and put:

$$y_1 \equiv x \cdot s_1^2 \bmod n, \ldots, y_m \equiv x \cdot s_m^2 \bmod n.$$

Step 3: Compute $u = (u_1, \ldots, u_{P(k)}), u' = (u_1', \ldots, u_{P(k)}')$ adjacent, witnessing the validity of (19); let r be such that $u_r \neq u_r'$ (without loss of generality assume $u_r = 1, u_r' = 0$).
Step 4: Choose at random m elements $w_1, \ldots, w_m \in \Omega_{P(k),n,u}$ and m elements $w_1', \ldots, w_m' \in \Omega_{P(k),n,u'}$.
Step 5: For $i = 1, \ldots, r - 1, r + 1, \ldots, P(k)$ **do:**
For $j = 1, \ldots, m$ draw $z_j \in Z_n^*(+1)$ at random and put

$$y_{j,i} \equiv y^{u_i \oplus 1} \cdot z_j^2 \bmod n.$$

Moreover, put

$$y_{j,r} = y_j, \quad \text{for } j = 1, \ldots, m.$$

Step 6: For each $j = 1, \ldots, m$ put

$$x_j = (y_{j,1}, \ldots, y_{j,r-1}, y_j, y_{j,r+1}, \ldots, y_{j,P(k)}).$$

Step 7: Compute

$$d_{x,y} = \left| \frac{d(x_1) + \cdots + d(x_m)}{m} - \frac{d(w_1) + \cdots + d(w_m)}{m} \right|,$$

$$d'_{x,y} = \left| \frac{d(x_1) + \cdots + d(x_m)}{m} - \frac{d(w'_1) + \cdots + d(w'_m)}{m} \right|.$$

Output:

$$C_k(n, x, y) = \begin{cases} 1 & \text{if } d_{x,y} < \frac{1}{R(k)} \\ \\ 0 & \text{if } d'_{x,y} < \frac{1}{R(k)}. \end{cases}$$

To show that this circuit works notice that for all $j = 1, \ldots, m$,

$$\sigma_n(y_{i,j}) = \begin{cases} u_i & \text{if } i \neq r \\ \sigma_n(y_j) & \text{if } i = r. \end{cases}$$

However, by definition, either all the y_j are quadratic residues or else they are all quadratic nonresidues. It follows that either $\{x_1, \ldots, x_m\} \subseteq \Omega_{P(k),n,u}$ or $\{x_1, \ldots, x_m\} \subseteq \Omega_{P(k),n,u'}$ depending on whether x is a quadratic residue or not (recall that $u_r = 1$ and $u'_r = 0$). The rest of the proof is an application of the weak law of large numbers. Indeed, let $A_n = \{(x, y) : x \in QR_n, y \notin QR_n\}$ and $B_n = \{(x, y) : x \notin QR_n, y \notin QR_n\}$. Then it is true that

$$Pr_{A_n} \left[\left| \frac{d(x_1) + \cdots + d(x_m)}{m} - P_{d,P(k),u} \right| > \frac{1}{2R(k)} \right] < \frac{1}{Q(k)},$$

$$Pr_{B_n} \left[\left| \frac{d(x_1) + \cdots + d(x_m)}{m} - P_{d,P(k),u'} \right| > \frac{1}{2R(k)} \right] < \frac{1}{Q(k)}.$$

Hence the result follows from the foregoing inequalities as well as

$$Pr \left[\left| \frac{d(w_1) + \cdots + d(w_m)}{m} - P_{d,P(k),u} \right| > \frac{1}{2R(k)} \right] < \frac{1}{Q(k)},$$

$$Pr \left[\left| \frac{d(w'_1) + \cdots + d(w'_m)}{m} - P_{d,P(k),u'} \right| > \frac{1}{2R(k)} \right] < \frac{1}{Q(k)} \bullet$$

Let P be a fixed polynomial, $n \in N_k$. For each integer k let $\Theta_{P(k)}$ be the set of all messages of length $P(k)$. For any message $M \in \Theta_{P(k)}$, let $M^{(e)}$ be the set of all encodings of M, i.e.

$$M^{(e)} = \{E_n(x; M) : x = (x_1, \ldots, x_{P(k)}) \in (Z_n^*)^{P(k)}\}.$$

It is easy to see that for any two messages $M, \overline{M} \in \Theta_{P(k)}$, $|M^{(e)}| = |\overline{M}^{(e)}|$ (see exercise 3).

A **predicate** S on the family of messages $\{\Theta_{P(k)} : k \in I\}$ is a family $S = \{S_k : k \in I\}$ of functions such that for all $k \in I$, $S_k : \Theta_{P(k)} \longrightarrow \{0, 1\}$.

Theorem 5.7 *(Goldwasser-Micali) Let P, Q be polynomials, S an easily computed predicate on the family $\{\Theta_{P(k)} : k \in I\}$, and $C = \{C_k : k \in I\}$ a polynomial size circuit such that C_k has $k \cdot P(k)$ input gates and one output gate. Further, assume that for all but a finite number of $k \in I$, and all $n \in N_k$,*

$$Pr[C_k(n, E_n(x; M)) = S_k(M)] \geq Pr[S_k(M) = 1] + \frac{1}{Q(k)}. \qquad (20)$$

Then there exists a polynomial R and an easily computed decision function $d = \{d_n : n \in N_k, k \in I\}$, where $d_n : (Z_n^*)^{P(k)} \longrightarrow \{0, 1\}$, such that for all but a finite number of $k \in I$, and for all $n \in N_k$ one can efficiently compute $u, u' \in \{0, 1\}^{P(k)}$ such that

$$|P_{d,n}(u) - P_{d,n}(u')| > \frac{1}{R(k)}. \qquad (21)$$

Proof: Let $k \in I, n \in N_k$ be fixed and let χ be the common value of $|M^{(e)}|$, where $M \in \Theta_{P(k)}$. Further, put $\Theta = \Theta_{P(k)}$ and $\theta = |\Theta|$. For any $M \in \Theta$, and any $i \in \{0, 1\}$, let $G^i(M)$ be the number of encodings e of M such that $C_k(n, e) = i$, i.e.

$$G^i(M) = |\{E_n(x; M) : C_k(n, E_n(x; M)) = i\}|.$$

Finally, let

$$G(M) = \begin{cases} G^1(M) & \text{if } S_k(M) = 1 \\ G^0(M) & \text{if } S_k(M) = 0. \end{cases}$$

It is then clear that

$$Pr[C_k(n, E_n(x; M)) = S_k(M)] = \frac{1}{\chi \cdot \theta} \sum_{M \in \Theta} G(M). \qquad (22)$$

Partition the set Θ into $R(k) = 10 \cdot Q(k)$ sets $\{\Theta(t) : t = 1, \ldots, R(k)\}$ defined by

$$M \in \Theta(t) \Leftrightarrow \frac{t-1}{R(k)} \leq \frac{G^1(M)}{\chi} < \frac{t}{R(k)}. \tag{23}$$

Since,

$$\theta = \sum_{t=1}^{R(k)} |\Theta(t)|, \tag{24}$$

it follows that there exists $1 \leq t \leq R(k)$ such that

$$|\Theta(t)| > \frac{\theta}{R(k)^2}. \tag{25}$$

The main part of the proof of the theorem consists of proving the following

Claim: There exist $1 < s + 1 < t \leq R(k)$ such that (25) holds for both s and t.

Proof of the Claim: Assume on the contrary that there are no $1 < s + 1 < t \leq R(k)$ such that (25) holds for both s and t. Then one of the following two cases can occur:

1. There exists exactly one t such that (25) holds for t.

2. There exists exactly one t such that (25) holds for both $t - 1$ and t.

Put $p_k = Pr[S_k(M) = 1]$. In case 1, $\sum_{M \in \Theta(i)} G(M)$ is maximum when $i = R(k)$ and $(\forall M)(S_k(M) = 1 \Rightarrow M \in \Theta(R(k)))$; thus, using (20) and (22) one can show that

$$p_k + \frac{1}{Q(k)} \leq \frac{1}{\chi \cdot \theta} \left[\sum_{M \in \Theta(R(k))} G(M) + \sum_{M \in \Theta(i), i < R(k)} G(M) \right]$$

$$\leq \frac{1}{\chi \cdot \theta} \left[\theta \chi p_k + \frac{\theta}{R(k)^2} R(k) \chi \right] = p_k + \frac{1}{R(k)},$$

which is a contradiction. In case 2, $\sum_{M \in \Theta(i-1)} G(M) + \sum_{M \in \Theta(i)} G(M)$ is maximum when $i = R(k)$ and $(\forall M)(S_k(M) = 1 \Rightarrow M \in \Theta(R(k)))$ and $(\forall M)(S_k(M) = 0 \Rightarrow M \in \Theta(R(k) - 1))$; thus, using (20) one can show that

$$p_k + \frac{1}{Q(k)} \leq$$

$$\frac{1}{\chi \cdot \theta} \left[\sum_{M \in \Theta(R(k)-1)} G(M) + \sum_{M \in \Theta(R(k))} G(M) + \sum_{M \in \Theta(i), i < R(k)-1} G(M) \right]$$

$$\leq \frac{1}{\chi \cdot \theta} \left[\theta \chi p_k + 2(1 - p_k) \frac{\theta \chi}{R(k)} + \frac{\theta \chi}{R(k)} \right] < p_k + \frac{1}{2Q(k)},$$

which is a contradiction. This completes the proof of the claim.

To define the decision function d, for each $k \in I, n \in N_k$ let

$$d_n(x) = C_k(n, x), \text{ where } x \in (Z_n^*)^{P(k)}.$$

Let $1 < s + 1 < t \leq R(k)$ be such that (25) holds for s and t. Then it is clear that for all $u \in \Theta(s), u' \in \Theta(t)$,

$$\left| \frac{G^1(u)}{\chi} - \frac{G^1(u')}{\chi} \right| > \frac{1}{R(k)}. \tag{26}$$

Using a Monte Carlo computation one can easily compute $u \in \Theta(s), u' \in \Theta(t)$. However,

$$P_{d,n}(u) = \frac{G^1(u)}{\chi}, P_{d,n}(u') = \frac{G^1(u')}{\chi}.$$

Thus, the theorem follows from the equations above and inequality (26) •

The following interpretation of the hypothesis of theorem 5.7 is useful. Let $S = \{S_k : k \in I\}$ be an easily computed predicate on the family $\{\Theta_{P(k)} : k \in I\}$ of sets of messages. Call S_k true of the message M, where $M \in \Theta_{P(k)}$, if $S_k(M) = 1$, and false otherwise. Then $Pr[S_k(M) = 1]$ is the probability that $S_k(M)$ is true on a random message $M \in \Theta_{P(k)}$. Let $C = \{C_k : k \in I\}$ be a polynomial size circuit such that C_k has $k \cdot P(k)$ input gates and one output gate. Then the quantity

$$Pr[C_k(n, E_n(x; M)) = S_k(M)],$$

is the probability that the polynomial size circuit C guesses correctly the value of $S_k(M)$ assuming only knowledge of the encoded message $E_n(x; M)$. The hypothesis of the theorem now states:

There exists a polynomial Q, an easily computed predicate S, and a polynomial size circuit C such that for all but a finite number of k, C_k guesses the correct value of $S_k(M)$ from a random encoding $E_n(x; M)$ of M with a $1/Q(k)$ advantage.

If one, first recalls that $QRA(N)$ is an abbreviation of the Quadratic Residuosity Assumption for the family N; second, takes into account the results in the subsection on the Quadradic Residue Generator; and third, combines them with lemmas 5.2, 5.3 and theorem 5.7, then it is immediate that

Theorem 5.8 *(Assume $QRA(N)$) There is no polynomial Q, no easily computed predicate S, and no polynomial size circuit C such that for all but a finite number of k, C_k guesses the correct value of $S_k(M)$ from a random encoding $E_n(x; M)$ of M with a $1/Q(k)$ advantage* •

EXERCISES

1: Show that for each r-tuple $x = (x_1, \ldots, x_r)$ of r elements of Z_n^* the encryption and decryption functions $E_n(x; \cdot), D_n(\cdot)$ of QRS are inverses of each other.

2: Complete the details of the proof of lemma 5.2.

3: Show that for any two messages $M, \overline{M} \in \Theta_{P(k)}$, $|M^{(e)}| = |\overline{M}^{(e)}|$. **Hint:** Show that the mapping $E_n(x; M) \longrightarrow E_n(x; \overline{M})$ is one to one and onto.

4: Prove equation (22) above.

5: Show that for all messages M, $G^0(M) + G^1(M) = |M^{(e)}|$.

5.11   Bibliographical Remarks

A well researched, *cryptography centered* view of history is given by David Kahn.[1] A history of Alan Turing and the Enigma machine is given by Andrew Hodges.[2]

The recent rapid development of public key cryptosystems followed immediately after the publication of Diffie and Hellman in [D6]. Before this the security of cryptosystems was based on absolute security criteria (see [S11] and [K8]). For further general remarks on cryptosystems the reader should consult [P1], [L8], [B4]. Some recent works which include material on public key cryptosystems are [K8], [D4], [D3], [S1], and [M4]. This last reference also includes an analysis of DES, the Data Encryption Scheme.

---

[1] *The Codebreakers: The Story of Secret Writing*, Macmillan Publ. Co. Inc., New York 1967.

[2] *Alan Turing: The Enigma*, Simon and Schuster, New York 1983.

The RSA system described in subsection 5.4 was developed in [R9], and the Rabin system described in subsection 5.6 in [R1]. The proof of theorem 5.1 is in [D2]. It is clear, however, that the idea of its proof goes back to Miller's paper [M9]. The security of RSA bits and Rabin bits studied in subsections 5.5 and 5.7, respectively is from [G9]. In fact, [G9] includes the proof of a slightly stronger result: if there is an efficient algorithm A such that

$$Pr[A(x^e \bmod N) = \operatorname{bit}^0_{N,e}(x^e \bmod N)] \geq 1 - \frac{1}{\log_2 N}, \qquad (27)$$

then there is an efficient algorithm for inverting the RSA function. Recently it has been shown that the RSA function can be inverted even if one assumes that the right side of inequality (27) is $1/2 + 1/P(\log_2 N)$, for some polynomial P (see [A7]).

The Merkle Hellman system is based on knapsacks and was developed in [M5]. The presentation of the security of the Merkle Hellman system in subsection 5.9 is based partly on [S10] and [E1]. Recent work of Adleman (see [A3]), Lagarias, Odlyzko and Brickel (see [S7]) shows that the iterated Merkle - Hellman Public Key Cryptosystem is not secure. There is also a generalization of the Merkle - Hellman Public Key Cryptosystem using Galois fields (see [C4]).

Under the influence of the Merkle Hellman system, the reader might get the false impression that the construction of secure public key cryptosystems could be based on **NP** complete problems. That this is not the case can be seen from [L8], which describes an easily breakable cryptosystem such that computing its secret key is an **NP** complete problem.

The presentation of the Quadratic Residue System, given in subsection 5.10, is a continuation of the presentation of the Quadratic Residue generator and comes from [G8].

A development of security for public key cryptosystems, which has less emphasis on number theory, can be found in the unpublished [R3] and [R4]. In addition, the survey article [A9] can be useful. An annotated bibliography on Public Key Cryptography can be found in [F2].

6   TOWARDS A GENERAL THEORY

Die Theorie träumt,
die Praxis belehrt.
(Karl von Holtei)

6.1   Introduction

A closer look at the proofs in subsections 4.8 and 4.10 will reveal the basic principles needed to construct secure pseudo randomgenerators. Starting from a *one way function* $f : X \longrightarrow X$, an *unapproximable predicate* $B : X \longrightarrow \{0,1\}$, and a seed $x \in X$, one defines the sequence of bits $b_0(x), \ldots, b_i(x), \ldots$ by:

$$b_i(x) = B(f^i(x))$$

(e.g. one can use $f(x) = x^2 \bmod n, B(x) = \mathrm{par}(\sqrt{x} \bmod n)$, where $n = p \cdot q$, with $p \equiv q \equiv 3 \bmod 4$, and the factorization of n is unknown). It is shown in subsection 6.2 that the security of these sequences of bits is *theoretically ideal*. In fact, it is shown, assuming the quadratic residuosity assumption, that not only do they pass the *Blum-Micali* (or *next bit*) test, but they also pass all *polynomial size statistical tests*. Hence, they are indistinguishable from truly random strings of the same length by polynomial size statistical tests. An extension of these results to *pseudorandom functions* is presented in subsection 6.3.

The motivation of the notion of XOR, presented in subsection 6.4, is rather simple. Given a *magic box* (i.e. a device which outputs bits $0, 1$, but whose internal structure is unknown) $B : X \longrightarrow \{0,1\}$ one is interested to predict (with his polynomial size resources) the output $B(x)$ of B, on input $x \in X$, without any prior knowledge of how the magic box B executes the computation of $B(x)$. Clearly, by flipping a fair coin he could predict the output $B(x)$ correctly for at least half the inputs $x \in X$. Hence, it is more interesting to ask if one could predict correctly the output $B(x)$ for more than half, say $1/2 + \epsilon$, of the $x \in X$, where $0 < \epsilon < 1/2$ is sufficiently small. Consider the following XOR magic box $B' = B \oplus B$ defined by: $B'(x, x') = B(x) \oplus B(x')$, where $x, x' \in X$. The XOR lemma, presented in subsection 6.4 and formally proved in subsection 6.5, asserts the following: if, for a magic box B, one could predict correctly (with his polynomial size circuit) the output $B(x) \oplus B(x')$ for at least a ratio $1/2 + \epsilon$ of the given $x, x' \in X$, then he could also predict the output $B(x)$ correctly (with another polynomial size circuit) for at least a ratio $1/2 + 4\epsilon^2$ of the given $x \in X$. Hence, the magic box $B \oplus B$ appears to be more difficult to predict than B itself. The formal proof of the XOR lemma is not necessary to understand the rest of the material. The reader may decide to skip the proof at first reading.

Repeated *xoring* leads to generalizations of the XOR lemma, namely the XOR and multiple XOR theorems. The two subsections following deal with three applications of the XOR theorem: to *unapproximable predicates*, to *pseudorandom generators*, and to *one way functions*. In particular, in subsection 6.7 it is shown how to construct *unapproximable predicates* and their *friendship functions*, as well as pseudorandom generators that pass the *next bit test*, using only one way functions.

Assuming the existence of a pseudorandom generator which passes all polynomial size statistical tests, it is natural to attempt to replace flips of a fair coin by bits produced from this pseudorandom generator. The significant impact of this observation on sets computable in *random polynomial time* is studied in subsection 6.8.

6.2   Security Tests

As usual, the uppercase Roman letters P, Q with or without subscripts and superscripts will range over polynomials of degree ≥ 1 with positive coefficients. Further, recall that all the circuits considered are probabilistic.

Let $S_m = \{0,1\}^m$ be the set of sequences of bits of length exactly m. Let $X = \{X_m : m \geq 0\}$ denote a family of nonempty sets such that for some polynomial Q each X_m is a subset of $S_{Q(m)}$, let $f = \{f_m : m \geq 0\}$ be a family of polynomial time computable functions such that each f_m is a permutation of X_m, and let $B = \{B_m : m \geq 0\}$ be a family functions such that each $B_m : X_m \longrightarrow \{0,1\}$ is a 0,1-valued function with domain X_m. Any such family $\{B_m : m \geq 0\}$ of functions is called a **predicate** on $\{X_m : m \geq 0\}$.

Definition 6.1 *A polynomial size circuit* $C = \{C_m : m \geq 0\}$ P **predicts** *the predicate* $B = \{B_m : m \geq 0\}$ *if the following statement holds for in-*

finitely many m,

$$Pr\left[x \in X_m : B_m(x) = C_m(x)\right] \geq \frac{1}{2} + \frac{1}{P(m)}.$$

Definition 6.2 *The predicate* $B = \{B_m : m \geq 0\}$ *is* **unapproximable** *if*

$$(\forall P, C)(C \text{ does not } P - \text{predict } B).$$

Definition 6.3 *The family* $f = \{f_m : m \geq 0\}$ *of functions is a* **friendship function** *for the unapproximable predicate* $B = \{B_m : m \geq 0\}$ *if both of the following two functions are computable in polynomial time in* m,
(1) $< m, x > \longrightarrow f_m(x)$,
(2) $< m, x > \longrightarrow B_m(f_m(x))$.

   Remark: Notice that the function $< m, x > \longrightarrow B_m(x)$ in definition 6.3 need not be computable in polynomial time in m.

Example 6.1 *For any two primes* p, q *satisfying* $p \equiv q \equiv 3 \bmod 4$ *consider the following function and predicate:*
(1) $f_n : QR_n \longrightarrow QR_n : x \longrightarrow x^2 \bmod n$,
(2) $B_n : QR_n \longrightarrow \{0, 1\} : x \longrightarrow B_n(x) = \mathrm{par}(\sqrt{x} \bmod n)$,
where $n = pq$. *Assuming the Quadratic Residuosity Assumption it is easy to see that the above family satisfies the requirements of definition 6.3.*

Example 6.2 *For any prime* p *and any generator* $g \in Z_p^*$ *consider the following function and predicate:*
(1) $f_{p,g} : Z_p^* \longrightarrow Z_p^* : x \longrightarrow g^x \bmod p$,
(2) $B_{p,g} : Z_p^* \longrightarrow \{0, 1\} : x \longrightarrow B_{p,g}(x)$, *where*

$$B_{p,g}(x) = \begin{cases} 1 & \text{if } x = PQR(p, g, x^2 \bmod p) \\ 0 & \text{if } x = NPQR(p, g, x^2 \bmod p), \end{cases}$$

and $PQR(p, g, x^2 \bmod p), NPQR(p, g, x^2 \bmod p)$ *respectively denote the principal, nonprincipal square root of* $x^2 \bmod p$. *Assuming the Discrete Logarithm Assumption, it is easy to see that the above family satisfies the requirements of definition 6.3.*

Definition 6.4 *A family* $G = \{G_m : m \geq 0\}$ *of functions is a* **(pseudo-random) generator**, *if there exists a polynomial* Q *such that*
(1) For all m, $G_m : X_m \longrightarrow S_{Q(m)}$ *and*
(2) $< m, x > \longrightarrow G_m(x)$ *is computable in polynomial time in* m.

The elements $x \in X_m$ which produce the sequences $G_m(x)$ of bits are called **seeds**. To any pseudorandom generator G as in definition 6.4 associate the sequence $b_{m,0}^G(x), \ldots, b_{m,Q(m)-1}^G(x)$ of bits generated by G, where for each index m, $b_{m,i}^G(x)$ is the i-th bit of $G_m(x)$.

Definition 6.5 *(**Blum-Micali***) A polynomial size circuit $C = \{C_m : m \geq 0\}$ P **predicts** the pseudorandom generator $G = \{G_m : m \geq 0\}$, if for infinitely many m, there exists an $i < Q(m)$ such that*

$$Pr\left[x \in X_m : C_m(b_{m,0}^G(x), \ldots, b_{m,i-1}^G(x)) = b_{m,i}(x)\right] \geq \frac{1}{2} + \frac{1}{P(m)}.$$

Definition 6.6 *A pseudorandom generator $G = \{G_m : m \geq 0\}$ **passess the Blum-Micali test**, and the test will be abbreviated BMT, if the following statement holds:*

$$(\forall C, P)(C \text{ does not } P \text{ predict } G).$$

For any function $h : Y \longrightarrow Y$ and any integer $i \geq 0$ recall that $h^i : Y \longrightarrow Y$ stands for the function defined by induction as follows:

$$h^i(x) = \begin{cases} x & \text{if } i = 0 \\ h(h^{i-1}(x)) & \text{if } i > 0. \end{cases}$$

The following theorem is very important, because it provides a technique for constructing pseudorandom generators that pass the Blum-Micali test from an unapproximable predicate $B = \{B_m : m \geq 0\}$, and a friendship function $f = \{f_m : m \geq 0\}$ for B.

Theorem 6.1 *(**The Blum-Micali Generator Theorem***) For any polynomial Q, any unapproximable predicate $B = \{B_m : m \geq 0\}$, and any friendship function $f = \{f_m : m \geq 0\}$ for B, the pseudorandom generator $G^{B,f,Q} = \{G_m^{B,f,Q} : m \geq 0\}$ defined for $x \in X_m$ by*

$$G_m^{B,f,Q}(x) = < B_m(f_m^{Q(m)}(x)), \ldots, B_m(f_m^{Q(m)-j}(x)), \ldots, B_m(f_m(x)) >,$$

passes the BMT.

Proof: Consider the abbreviation

$$b_{m,j}^G(x) = B_m(f_m^{Q(m)-j}(x)), \text{ for } 0 \leq j < Q(m),$$

and assume on the contrary that the pseudorandom generator $G^{B,f,Q}$ does not pass the Blum-Micali test. It follows that there exists a polynomial size circuit $C = \{C_m : m \geq 0\}$ and a polynomial P such that the circuit C, P predicts the generator $G^{B,f,Q}$. It follows from the definition of $G^{B,f,Q}$ that for infinitely many m, there exists an $i < Q(m)$ such that

$$Pr\left[x \in X_m : C_m(b^G_{m,0}(x), \ldots, b^G_{m,i-1}(x)) = b^G_{m,i}(x)\right] \geq \frac{1}{2} + \frac{1}{P(m)}. \quad (1)$$

Let M be the set of indices m which satisfy inequality (1). Clearly, for each $m \in M$ there exists an integer $i_m < Q(m)$ such that

$$Pr\left[x \in X_m : C_m(b^G_{m,0}(x), \ldots, b^G_{m,i_m-1}(x)) = b^G_{m,i_m}(x)\right] \geq \frac{1}{2} + \frac{1}{P(m)}. \quad (2)$$

For $x \in X_m$, define the following new circuit $C' = \{C'_m : m \geq 0\}$:

$$C'_m(x) = C_m(B_m(f^{i_m}_m(x)), B_m(f^{i_m-1}_m(x)), \ldots, B_m(f_m(x))).$$

One can then prove that the following claim holds:

Claim: For all $m \in M$,

$$Pr\left[x \in X_m : C'_m(x) = B_m(x)\right] \geq \frac{1}{2} + \frac{1}{P(m)}.$$

Proof of Claim: Fix an arbitrary $m \in M$ and put $i = i_m$, $j = i - Q(m)$, $x' = f^j(x)$, where x ranges over X_m. Then the following statements are equivalent for each $x \in X_m$,

$$C'_m(x) = B_m(x).$$

$$C_m(B_m(f^i_m(x)), B_m(f^{i-1}_m(x)), \ldots, B_m(f_m(x))) = B_m(x).$$

$$C_m(b^G_{m,0}(f^j_m(x)), b^G_{m,1}(f^j_m(x)), \ldots, b^G_{m,i-1}(f^j_m(x))) = b^G_{m,i}(f^j_m(x)).$$

$$C_m(b^G_{m,0}(x'), b^G_{m,1}(x'), \ldots, b^G_{m,i-1}(x')) = b^G_{m,i}(x').$$

However, the mapping $x \longrightarrow x'$ is a permutation of X_m. Hence, using inequality (2) one obtains that

$$Pr\left[x' \in X_m : C_m(b^G_{m,0}(x'), \ldots, b^G_{m,i-1}(x')) = b^G_{m,i}(x')\right] \geq \frac{1}{2} + \frac{1}{P(m)},$$

which completes the proof of the claim.

But, this is a contradiction since the predicate B is unapproximable. The proof of the theorem is now complete $\bullet$

Definition 6.7 A polynomial size statistical test, *abbreviated PSST, for the pseudorandom generator* $G = \{G_m : m \geq 0\}$, *where* $G_m : X_m \longrightarrow S_{Q(m)}$ *for some polynomial* Q, *is a polynomial size* $0,1$-*valued circuit* $C = \{C_m : m \geq 0\}$, *which has* $Q(m)$ *input gates, for each* $m \geq 0$.

Definition 6.8 *Let* C *be a PSST for the generator* G. *For each* $m \geq 0$, *consider the probabilities:*

$$p_m^{C,G} = Pr[x \in X_m : C_m(G_m(x)) = 1],$$

$$p_m^{C,R} = Pr[u \in S_{Q(m)} : C_m(u) = 1].$$

Definition 6.9 *The pseudorandom generator* G **passes the PSST** C, *if for all polynomials* P, *and for all but a finite number of integers* m,

$$\left| p_m^{C,G} - p_m^{C,R} \right| < \frac{1}{P(m)}.$$

Definition 6.10 *The pseudorandom generator* G *passes* **Yao's** *(statistical) test, abbreviated YST, if for any PSST* C *for* G, *G passes C.*

Theorem 6.2 *(Yao's PSST Theorem, A. Yao) For any pseudorandom generator* $G = \{G_m : m \geq 0\}$, *the following statements are equivalent:*
(1) G passes the Blum-Micali Test.
(2) G passes the Yao Statistical Test.

Proof: Assume that for each $m \geq 0$, $G_m : X_m \longrightarrow S_{Q(m)}$, where Q is a polynomial.
$(2) \Rightarrow (1)$
Assume, by way of contradiction, that (2) is true, but (1) fails. Let P be a polynomial, $C = \{C_m : m \geq 0\}$ a polynomial size circuit, and M the infinite set of integers m such that there exists an $i < Q(m)$ so that the following holds:

$$Pr\left[x \in X_m : C_m(b_{m,0}^G(x), \ldots, b_{m,i-1}^G(x)) = b_{m,i}^G(x)\right] \geq \frac{1}{2} + \frac{1}{P(m)}. \quad (3)$$

For each $m \in M$ let i_m be an integer $i < Q(m)$ that satisfies inequality (3). Define a new polynomial size circuit $C' = \{C'_m : m \geq 0\}$, which for any given $u = < u_0, \ldots, u_{Q(m)-1} > \in S_{Q(m)}$ is given by the formula:

$$C'_m(u) = C_m(u_0, \ldots, u_{i_m-1}) \oplus u_{i_m} \oplus 1.$$

It is then clear that for all $u \in S_{Q(m)}$,

$$C'_m(u) = 1 \Leftrightarrow C_m(u_0, \ldots, u_{i_m-1}) = u_{i_m}.$$

It is an immediate consequence of definition 6.8 that for all $m \in M$,

$$p_m^{C',G} = Pr[C_m(b_{m,0}^G(x), \ldots, b_{m,i_m-1}^G(x)) = b_{m,i_m}^G(x)] \geq \frac{1}{2} + \frac{1}{P(m)}. \quad (4)$$

Now it can be proved that:

Claim 1: $(\forall m \in M) \left[p_m^{C',G} \geq 1/2 + 1/(2P(m)) \right]$

Proof of Claim 1: Sinse G passes YST it must also pass the test C'. Thus, the following inequality holds for all but a finite number of m:

$$\left| p_m^{C',G} - p_m^{C',R} \right| < \frac{1}{2P(m)}.$$

It follows from (4) that for all but a finite number of $m \in M$,

$$p_m^{C',R} > p_m^{C',G} - \frac{1}{2P(m)} \geq \frac{1}{2} + \frac{1}{P(m)} - \frac{1}{2P(m)} = \frac{1}{2} + \frac{1}{2P(m)},$$

which completes the proof of claim 1. However, this is a contradiction since

$$p_m^{C',R} = Pr[u \in S_{Q(m)} : C_m(u_0, \ldots, u_{i_m-1}) = u_{i_m}] =$$

$$Pr[C_m(u_0, \ldots, u_{i_m-1}) = 0 | u_{i_m} = 0] \cdot Pr[u_{i_m} = 0] +$$

$$Pr[C_m(u_0, \ldots, u_{i_m-1}) = 1 | u_{i_m} = 1] \cdot Pr[u_{i_m} = 1] =$$

$$\frac{1}{2}(Pr[C_m(u_0, \ldots, u_{i_m-1}) = 0 | u_{i_m} = 0] +$$

$$Pr[C_m(u_0, \ldots, u_{i_m-1}) = 1 | u_{i_m} = 1]) =$$

$$\frac{1}{2}\left(Pr[C_m(u_0, \ldots, u_{i_m-1}) = 0] + Pr[C_m(u_0, \ldots, u_{i_m-1}) = 1]\right) = \frac{1}{2}.$$

$(1) \Rightarrow (2)$

Given two sequences of bits $u = <u_1, \ldots, u_m>$, $v = <v_1, \ldots, v_n>$, where $m, n \geq 0$, let the **concatenation**, of u, v, abbreviated $u \frown v$, denote the sequence $<u_1, \ldots, u_m, v_1, \ldots, v_n>$. The number m is called the **length** of u, and is abbreviated $\ell(u)$. Assume by way of contradiction, that G does not pass the YST. Let $C = \{C_m : m \geq 0\}$ be a polynomial size circuit and

P a polynomial such that the following inequality holds for infinitely many m,

$$\left| p_m^{C,G} - p_m^{C,R} \right| \geq \frac{1}{P(m)}. \tag{5}$$

Let M be the set of integers that satisfy (5). For each $i \leq Q(m)$, define: p_m^i = probability the circuit C_m will output 1 if given as input the sequence

$$t \frown < b_{m,i-1}^G(x), \ldots, b_{m,0}^G(x) >,$$

where t is a random sequence of bits of length $\ell(t) = Q(m) - i$ and $x \in X_m$ is a random seed.

It is then clear from definition 6.8 that

$$p_m^0 = p_m^{C,R} \text{ and } p_m^{Q(m)} = p_m^{C,G}.$$

Moreover, using (5), for all $m \in M$ one has the following inequalities:

$$\frac{1}{P(m)} \leq p_m^{C,R} - p_m^{C,G} = p_m^{Q(m)} - p_m^0 \leq \sum_{i=0}^{Q(m)-1} \left(p_m^{i+1} - p_m^i \right).$$

Hence, for each $m \in M$ there exists an $i < Q(m)$, call it i_m, such that

$$\left| p_m^{i_m+1} - p_m^{i_m} \right| \geq \frac{1}{Q'(m)}, \tag{6}$$

where $Q'(m) = P(m) \cdot Q(m)$.

The polynomial size circuit $C' = \{C_m' : m \geq 0\}$ which predicts the generator G is defined as follows:

Input: $u_0, \ldots, u_{i_m-1}$

Step 1: Choose a random $v = < v_{Q(m)-i_m-1}, \ldots, v_0 >$ of length $\ell(v) = Q(m) - i_m$.

Output:

$$C_m'(u_0, \ldots, u_{i_m-1}) = \begin{cases} v_0 & \text{if } C_m(v \frown < u_0, \ldots, u_{i_m-1} >) = 1 \\ 1 \oplus v_0 & \text{if } C_m(v \frown < u_0, \ldots, u_{i_m-1} >) = 0. \end{cases} \tag{7}$$

It is not hard to see that

$$Pr[C_m'(b_{m,i_m-1}^G(x), \ldots, b_{m,0}^G(x)) = b_{m,i_m}^G(x)] \geq \frac{1}{2} + \frac{1}{2Q'(m)}. \tag{8}$$

This completes the proof of the theorem ●

EXERCISES

1: Show that the circuit defined in (7) satisfies inequality (8). **Hint:** Show that the left hand side of (8) is $\geq 1/2 + (p_m^{i_m+1} - p_m^{i_m})/2$.

2: Assume that the family $X = \{X_m : m \geq 0\}$ satisfies the following property: there is a polynomial time algorithm, which on input m will output a random element of X_m. Use a Monte Carlo computation to compute the index i_m in inequality (6).

6.3　Pseudorandom Functions

Recall that $S_m = \{0,1\}^m$. Let $R = \{R_m : m \geq 0\}$, where R_m is the set of all functions $f : S_m \longrightarrow S_m$. A *PSST* **for functions** is a probabilistic $0,1$ - valued polynomial time algorithm T, which has a separate **query tape** and a separate **answer tape**. When T is given an input m, and access to a function $f : S_m \longrightarrow S_m$, it can write some $y \in S_m$ on the query tape; it then reads the answer $f(y)$ (which is printed in one step) in the answer tape.

Let $F = \{F_m : m \geq 0\}$, where $F_m \subseteq R_m$, for all $m \geq 0$. By analogy to definitions 6.8, 6.9, and 6.10, let $P_m^{T,F}$ (respectively $P_m^{T,R}$) be the probability that T outputs 1 on input m and access to a random $f \in F_m$ (respectively $f \in R_m$). F **passes the test** T if and only if for any polynomial Q, and all but a finite number of m,

$$|P_m^{T,F} - P_m^{T,R}| < \frac{1}{Q(m)}.$$

The **family** F **is pseudorandom** if and only if for any *PSST* T for functions, F passes the test T.

The construction of a family $F = \{F_m : m \geq 0\}$, which passes all polynomial size statistical tests for functions is based on the following theorem.

Theorem 6.3 *(Goldreich-Goldwasser-Micali) If there exists a pseudorandom generator $G = \{G_m : m \geq 0\}$, which passes Yao's test and such that each G_m stretches m-bit seeds into 2m-bit sequences, then there exists a pseudorandom family $F = \{F_m : m \geq 0\}$.*

Proof: Let G be as in the hypothesis of the theorem. For each r-bit sequence $s = < s_1, \ldots, s_r >$ define a family $G^s = \{G_m^s : m \geq 0\}$ of functions, where for each $x \in S_m$, $G_m^s(x)$ is defined as follows by induction on the length of s:

$$G_m^\emptyset(x) = x, \quad G_m^{s^\frown <b>}(x) = G_m^{<b>}(G_m^s(x)),$$

$$G_m^{<0>}(x) = \text{ the first } m \text{ bits of } G_m(x),$$

$$G_m^{<1>}(x) = \text{ the last } m \text{ bits of } G_m(x).$$

Finally, for each $m \geq 0$ define $F_m = \{f_x : x \in S_m\}$, where

$$f_x : S_m \longrightarrow S_m : y \longrightarrow f_x(y) = G_m^y(x).$$

It will be shown that the family $F = \{F_m : m \geq 0\}$, passes all *PSST* for functions. Indeed, assume on the contrary that F fails the test T. Let Q be a polynomial such that for infinitely many m:

$$|P_m^{T,F} - P_m^{T,R}| \geq \frac{1}{Q(m)}. \tag{9}$$

Let M be the infinite set of indices m such inequality (9) is true.

For each m and each $0 \leq i \leq m-1$ define a polynomial size family C_m^i of circuits. Given $u, v \in S_m$, $C_m^i(u \frown v)$ is the output of the following computation:

> Start executing the algorithm T on input m. If y is the first query with prefix $y_1, \ldots, y_i$, which is stored in the query tape of T, then store the pairs $< y_1 \ldots y_i 0, u >$, $< y_1 \ldots y_i 1, v >$, and write in the answer tape of T the value t given by:
>
> $$t = \begin{cases} G_m^{<y_{i+2}, \ldots, y_m>}(u) & \text{if } y_{i+1} = 0 \\ G_m^{<y_{i+2}, \ldots, y_m>}(v) & \text{if } y_{i+1} = 1. \end{cases}$$
>
> **Else:** retrieve the pair $< y_1 \ldots y_i y_{i+1}, w >$, and write in the answer tape of T the value $G_m^{<y_{i+2}, \ldots, y_m>}(w)$. Continue the execution of T. Repeat the above procedure any time a new query appears in the query tape.

It is now easy to check that for all $m \in M$ and all $0 \leq i < m$,

$$P_m^{T,F} = p_m^{C^0,G}, \ P_m^{T,R} = p_m^{C^{m-1},G}, p_m^{C^{i-1},R} = p_m^{C^i,G}. \tag{10}$$

Using inequality (9) and equations (10) it follows that for each $m \in M$ there exists an $0 \leq i < m-1$, say i_m, such that

$$|p_m^{C^{i_m},G} - p_m^{C^{i_m},R}| = |p_m^{C^{i_m},G} - p_m^{C^{i_m+1},G}| \geq \frac{1}{(m-1)Q(m)}. \tag{11}$$

Hence, the pseudorandom generator G fails the polynomial size statistical test $C = \{C_m^{i_m} : m \geq 0\}$, which is a contradiction •

EXERCISES

1: Prove equations (10).

2: Assume that the family $X = \{X_m : m \geq 0\}$ satisfies the following property: there is a polynomial time algorithm, which on input m will output a random element of X_m. Use a Monte Carlo computation to compute the index i_m in inequality (10).

6.4   Xoring

The notion of xor, to be studied below, enables one to construct predicates, pseudorandom generators, and public key cryptosystems with improved security properties.

Definition 6.11 *Given the functions $B_m^1, \ldots, B_m^k$, where for each index $i = 1, \ldots, k$, $B_m^i : X_m^i \longrightarrow \{0,1\}$, the* **xor** *$B_m = B_m^1 \oplus \cdots \oplus B_m^k$ of the predicates $B_m^1, \ldots, B_m^k$, is defined for each $< x_1, \ldots, x_m >\in X_m^1 \times \cdots \times X_m^k$ by:*

$$B_m(x_1, \ldots, x_k) = B_m^1(x_1) \oplus \cdots \oplus B_m^k(x_k).$$

Definition 6.12 *Given the families of predicates $B^i = \{B_m^i : m \geq 0\}$, where $i = 1, \ldots, k$, the* **xor** *family of $B^1, \ldots, B^k$, abbreviated $B = B^1 \oplus \cdots \oplus B^k$, is the following family of predicates $B = \{B_m : m \geq 0\}$, defined for each $m \geq 0$ by*

$$B_m = B_m^1 \oplus \cdots \oplus B_m^k.$$

Definition 6.13 *Given an infinite sequence $B^i = \{B_m^i : m \geq 0\}$, where $i = 1, 2, \ldots$, of families of predicates, and a function g with domain the set of positive integers and range a subset of the set of positive integers, the* **g-xor** *family of $B^1, B^2, \ldots$, abbreviated $B^{(g)} = \{B_m^{(g)} : m \geq 0\}$, is defined by*

$$B_m^{(g)} = B_m^1 \oplus \cdots \oplus B_m^{g(m)}.$$

If in the definition above, the function g is costant, i.e. $g(m) = k$, for all m, then the g-xor $B^{(g)}$ will also be denoted by $B^{(k)}$.

This and the next subsection will be concerned with answering the following:

Question: Let $B^i = \{B^i_m : m \geq 0\}$, where $i = 1, 2, \ldots$, be an infinite sequence of families of predicates and let g be a polynomial time computable function whose domain is the set of positive integers and whose range is a subset of the set of positive integers. If a polynomial size circuit approximates the g-xor family $B^{(g)} = \{B^{(g)}_m : m \geq 0\}$ with a certain advantage, do there exist polynomial size circuits approximating each of the predicates $B^1, B^2, \ldots$? Do the advantages of the approximations of the predicates $B^1, B^2, \ldots$ obtained via the approximation for $B^{(g)}$, amplify the original advantage of $B^{(g)}$?

Theorem 6.4 *(The Projection Theorem)* *Let $B^{(g)}$ be the g-xor of the predicates $B^1, B^2, \ldots$, where g is a function with domain the set of positive integers and range a subset of the set of positive integers. Let $C = \{C_m : m \geq 0\}$ be a polynomial size circuit and let $\{\epsilon_m : m \geq 0\}$ be a family of positive real numbers such that $\epsilon_m < 1/2$. If*

$$\Pr[x \in X^1_m \times \cdots \times X^{g(m)}_m : C_m(x) = B^{(g)}_m(x)] \geq \frac{1}{2} + \epsilon_m,$$

then for all $1 \leq i \leq g(m)$,

$$Pr[x_i \in X^i_m : C^i_m(x_i) = B^i_m(x_i)] \geq \frac{1}{2} + \epsilon_m.$$

Proof: It will be assumed, without loss of generality, that for all m, $g(m) = 2$. The following picture will be helpful in understanding the proof that follows.

Fix $m \geq 0$. The assumption of the theorem asserts that at least for a ratio $(1/2) + \epsilon_m$ of the points in the $< x_1, x_2 >$-plane, the circuit C_m correctly predicts the value of the xor $B = B^1 \oplus B^2$. Let

$$p(x_1) = Pr[x_2 \in X^2_m : C_m(x_1, x_2) = B^1_m(x_1) \oplus B^2_m(x_2)],$$

and

$$p(x_2) = Pr[x_1 \in X^1_m : C_m(x_1, x_2) = B^1_m(x_1) \oplus B^2_m(x_2)].$$

However, it is true that

$$Pr[< x_1, x_2 > \in X^1_m \times X^2_m : C_m(x_1, x_2) = B_m(x_1, x_2)] =$$

$$\frac{1}{|X^1_m|} \cdot \sum_{x_1 \in X^1_m} p(x_1) = \frac{1}{|X^2_m|} \cdot \sum_{x_2 \in X^2_m} p(x_2) \geq \frac{1}{2} + \epsilon_m.$$

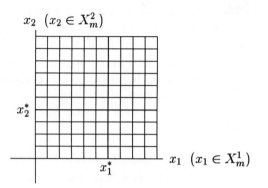

Figure 1: The XOR-predicate

It follows that there exist points $x_1^* \in X_m^1, x_2^* \in X_m^2$, such that

$$p(x_1^*) \geq \frac{1}{2} + \epsilon_m, p(x_2^*) \geq \frac{1}{2} + \epsilon_m.$$

Now, it is easy to see that the following two polynomial size circuits satisfy the requirements of the theorem:

$$C_m^1(x_1) = C_m(x_1, x_2^*) \oplus B_m^2(x_2^*), C_m^2(x_2) = C_m(x_1^*, x_2) \oplus B_m^1(x_1^*) \bullet \quad (12)$$

Theorem 6.4 will be very useful in the sequel, but what makes an XOR result interesting is some amplification of advantage in the passage from an approximation of the xor of two predicates to an approximation of each of the predicates which form the xor (see also exercise 5).

To give the proofs of the XOR theorems stated below a further property of the predicates $B = \{B_m : m \geq 0\}$ will be needed, called the **Random Generation Hypothesis**, abbreviated RGH. A predicate $B = \{B_m : m \geq 0\}$, where $B_m : X_m \longrightarrow \{0, 1\}$, satisfies the RGH if there exists an algorithm running in polynomial time in m which on input m will output a random pair $< x, y >$, where $x \in X_m$ and $y \in \{0, 1\}$ such that $B_m(x) = y$.

Example 6.3 *The predicates in examples 6.1 and 6.2 satisfy RGH.*

From now on and for the rest of this section, whenever Yao's XOR theorem is applied to a predicate B it will be assumed that

B satisfies RGH. **The necessity of this assumption will become apparent in the course of the formal proof of the XOR lemma.** In particular, there exists an algorithm running in polynomial time in m which on input m will output a random $x \in X_m$. **In addition, the set M of indices appearing in the statements of Yao's XOR theorems must be such that there is a sufficiently large positive constant C so that for all $m \in M$, $m > C$; the size of the constant C can be easily determined from the formal proof of the XOR lemma.**

The most interesting result on xoring is the following:

Theorem 6.5 *(XOR Theorem, A. Yao) Let M be an infinite set of integers, let g, h be polynomial time computable functions such that $g(m) \geq 2^{h(m)}$. Let $B = \{B_m : m \geq 0\}$, $B_m : X_m \longrightarrow \{0, 1\}$ be a family of predicates on the family $X = \{X_m : m \geq 0\}$. Further, assume that there exists a polynomial Q and a polynomial size circuit $C = \{C_m : m \geq 0\}$ such that for all $m \in M$,*

$$Pr\left[x \in (X_m)^{g(m)} : B_m^{(g)}(x) = C_m(x)\right] \geq \frac{1}{2} + \frac{1}{Q(m)}.$$

Then for any function k such that $2^{h(m)} \geq (\log_2 m)k(m)(1 + \deg(Q)) > 0$ for all $m \in M$, there exists a polynomial size circuit $C' = \{C'_m : m \geq 0\}$ such that for all but a finite number of $m \in M$, the following inequality holds:

$$Pr\left[x \in X_m : B_m(x) = C'_m(x)\right] \geq 1 - \frac{1}{k(m)} \bullet$$

The above theorem is in fact an immediate consequence of the following

Theorem 6.6 *(XOR Lemma, A. Yao) Let M be an infinite set of integers, and let $0 < 2\epsilon_m, \delta_m < 1$, for each $m \in M$. Let $B = \{B_m : m \geq 0\}$, $B_m : X_m \longrightarrow \{0, 1\}$ be a family of predicates on the family $X = \{X_m : m \geq 0\}$. If there exists a polynomial size circuit $C = \{C_m : m \geq 0\}$ such that for all $m \in M$,*

$$Pr\left[< x, x' > \in X_m \times X_m : B_m^{(2)}(x, x') = C_m(x, x')\right] \geq \frac{1}{2} + \epsilon_m,$$

then there exists a polynomial size circuit $C' = \{C'_m : m \geq 0\}$ such that for all $m \in M$,

$$Pr\left[x \in X_m : B_m(x) = C'_m(x)\right] \geq \frac{1}{2} + (1 - \delta_m) \cdot \sqrt{\frac{\epsilon_m}{2}} \bullet$$

Proof of the XOR theorem from the XOR lemma: Let B, C, g, Q satisfy the hypothesis of the XOR theorem. Let P be an arbitrary polynomial. Put $\delta_m = 1/(2k(m))$. Using the projection theorem, it can be assumed without loss of generality that for all m, $g(m) = 2^{h(m)}$. The idea is for each m to apply the XOR lemma a sufficient number of times, namely $h(m)$ times, to the predicate $B_m^{(g)}$. Indeed, fix $m \in M$; define by induction on $i = 1, \ldots, h(m)$, $\epsilon_{i,m} > 0$ and circuits $C^i = \{C_m^i : m \geq 0\}$ as follows:

$$\epsilon_{1,m} = \frac{1}{Q(m)}, \quad \epsilon_{i+1,m} = (1 - \delta_m) \cdot 2^{-\frac{1}{2}} \cdot \sqrt{\epsilon_{i,m}}.$$

Assume that the circuits $C^1 = C, C^2, \ldots, C^i$ have already been defined. For each $i \geq 1$ apply the XOR lemma to the circuit C^i and the xor

$$\left(B_m^{(2^{h(m)-i})} \right)^{(2)},$$

to find a polynomial size circuit C^{i+1} such that

$$Pr\left[B_m^{(2^{h(m)-i})}(x) = C_m^{i+1}(x) \right] \geq \frac{1}{2} + (1 - \delta_m) \cdot 2^{-\frac{1}{2}} \cdot \sqrt{\epsilon_{i,m}} = \frac{1}{2} + \epsilon_{i+1,m}.$$

It will be shown that the circuit $C' = C^{h(m)+1}$ satisfies the conclusion of the XOR theorem. It is clear that

$$Pr[x \in X_m : B_m(x) = C_m^{h(m)+1}(x)] \geq \frac{1}{2} + \epsilon_{h(m)+1,m}.$$

Moreover,

$$\epsilon_{h(m)+1,m} = \gamma_m \cdot \beta_m \cdot \alpha_m,$$

where

$$\gamma_m = 2^{-1/2 - 1/2^2 - \cdots - 1/2^{h(m)}},$$

$$\beta_m = (1 - \delta_m)^{1 + 1/2 + 1/2^2 + \cdots + 1/2^{h(m)-1}} = (1 - \delta_m)^{2(1 - 2^{-h(m)})},$$

$$\alpha_m = \left(\frac{1}{Q(m)} \right)^{1/2^{h(m)}}. \tag{13}$$

It is now easy to show that $\gamma_m > 1/2$. Next put $c = 1 + \deg(Q)$. It follows from equation (13) that

$$\alpha_m = 2^{-\log_2 Q(m)/2^{h(m)}} \geq 2^{-c \log_2 m/2^{h(m)}} \geq 1 - \frac{c \log_2 m}{2^{h(m)}}. \tag{14}$$

Since by assumption $2^{h(m)} \geq (\log_2 m)k(m)c$, inequality (14) implies that

$$\alpha_m \geq 1 - \frac{1}{k(m)}. \tag{15}$$

In addition it is true that

$$\beta_m = (1 - \delta_m)^{2(1 - 2^{-h(m)})} > 1 - 2(1 - 2^{-h(m)})\delta_m > 1 - 2\delta_m. \tag{16}$$

Taking into account inequalities (15), (16) one finally obtains that

$$\epsilon_{h(m)+1,m} \geq \frac{1}{2}\left(1 - \frac{1}{k(m)}\right)^2 \geq \frac{1}{2} - \frac{1}{k(m)},$$

which completes the proof of the reduction of the XOR theorem to the XOR lemma •

An immediate corollary of the XOR theorem and the projection theorem is the following:

Theorem 6.7 *(Multiple XOR Theorem) Let M be an infinite set of integers and suppose that f, g, h are polynomial time computable functions such that $g(m) \geq 2^{h(m)}$ for all $m \in M$. For each i, let $B^i = \{B^i_m : m \geq 0\}$, be a family of predicates on $X^i = \{X^i_m : m \geq 0\}$ and put $L = B^{(f)}$. Further assume that there exists a polynomial Q and a polynomial size circuit $C = \{C_m : m \geq 0\}$ such that for all $m \in M$,*

$$Pr\left[L_m^{(g)}(x) = C_m(x)\right] \geq \frac{1}{2} + \frac{1}{Q(m)}.$$

Then for any function k such that $2^{h(m)} \geq (\log_2 m)k(m)(1 + \deg(Q)) > 0$ for all $m \in M$, there exists polynomial size circuits $C^i = \{C^i_m : m \geq 0\}$ such that for all but a finite number of $m \in M$ the following inequality holds for all indices $i \leq f(m)$,

$$Pr\left[x_i \in X^i_m : B^i_m(x_i) = C^i_m(x_i)\right] \geq 1 - \frac{1}{k(m)} \bullet$$

EXERCISES

1: Show that the circuits defined via (12) satisfy the conclusion of the projection theorem.

2: Show that the general case in the statement of the projection theorem follows from the special case: for all m, $g(m) = 2$.

3: RGH for a predicate B should not be confused with predicting B. Show that the predicates defined in examples 6.1, 6.2 satisfy RGH.

4: Prove in detail theorem 6.7.

5: Let B be an unapproximable predicate with a friendship function f, on the family $X = \{X_m : m \geq 0\}$, and g a polynomial time computable function from positive integers to positive integers such that for all $m, g(m) \geq 2$. For each polynomial size circuit C and each $u \in X_m$, let

$$p_u^1[C] = Pr\left[x \in (X_m)^{g(m)} : B_m^{(g)}(x) = C_m(x)|u = 1 - \text{st component of } x\right].$$

Show that if there exist polynomials P, P' and a polynomial size circuit C such that for infinitely many m,

$$\frac{1}{|X_m|}\left|\left\{u \in X_m : p_u^1[C] \geq \frac{1}{2} + \frac{1}{P(m)}\right\}\right| \geq \frac{1}{P'(m)},$$

then for any polynomial Q there exists a polynomial size circuit $C' = \{C'_m : m \geq 0\}$ such that for infinitely many m,

$$Pr\left[u \in X_m : B_m(u) = C'_m(u)\right] \geq 1 - \frac{1}{Q(m)}.$$

Hint: Use the weak law of large numbers.

6.5   Proof of the XOR Lemma

This subsection will be divided into two parts. The first part will be concerned with an intuitive, geometric discussion of the proof of the XOR lemma. The formal aspects of the proof will be discussed in part two.

PART 1: INTUITIVE PROOF OF THE XOR LEMMA

Assume that the hypothesis of the XOR lemma is true. i.e. M is an infinite set of integers such that $0 < 2\epsilon_m, \delta_m < 1$, for each $m \in M$, and $B = \{B_m : m \geq 0\}$, $B_m : X_m \longrightarrow \{0,1\}$ is a family of predicates on the family $X = \{X_m : m \geq 0\}$. Assume there exists a polynomial size circuit $C = \{C_m : m \geq 0\}$ such that for all $m \in M$,

$$Pr\left[< x, x' >\in X_m \times X_m : B_m^{(2)}(x, x') = C_m(x, x')\right] \geq \frac{1}{2} + \epsilon_m.$$

Put:

$$\eta_m = \left(1 - \frac{\delta_m}{2}\right) \cdot \sqrt{\frac{\epsilon_m}{2}}.$$

It is required to find a polynomial size circuit $C' = \{C'_m : m \geq 0\}$ such that for all $m \in M$,

$$Pr\left[x \in X_m : B_m(x) = C'_m(x)\right] \geq \frac{1}{2} + \eta_m. \tag{17}$$

For each $x \in X_m$ put:

$$k(x) = |\{x' \in X_m : B_m^{(2)}(x, x') = C_m(x, x')\}|, p(x) = \frac{k(x)}{|X_m|}.$$

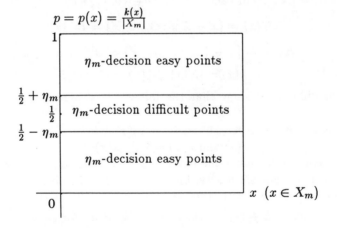

Figure 2: Distribution of the η_m-decision points

Figure 2 pictures the difficulty involved in deciding the values of the predicate $B = \{B_m : m \geq 0\}$. One can distinguish the following two cases.

Case 1: $(\exists x \in X_m)(|p(x) - 1/2| \geq \eta_m)$.

In other words, in this case there is an η_m-decision easy point. Call such a point x_0. Define a polynomial size circuit C' as follows:

$$C'_m(x') = \begin{cases} C_m(x_0, x') \oplus B_m(x_0) & \text{if } p(x_0) \geq 1/2 + \eta_m \\ C_m(x_0, x') \oplus B_m(x_0) \oplus 1 & \text{if } p(x_0) \leq 1/2 - \eta_m. \end{cases}$$

It is easy to see that C' satisfies the requirements of inequality (17). Indeed, on the one hand if $p(x_0) \geq 1/2 + \eta_m$ then

$$p(x_0) = Pr\left[x' \in X_m : B_m(x') = C'_m(x')\right] \geq \frac{1}{2} + \eta_m,$$

while on the other hand if $p(x_0) \leq 1/2 - \eta_m$, then

$$1 - p(x_0) = Pr\left[x' \in X_m : B_m(x') = C'_m(x')\right] \geq \frac{1}{2} + \eta_m.$$

Case 2: $(\forall x)(|p(x) - 1/2| < \eta_m).$

Put $t_m = |X_m|$. For each $x \in X_m$, $b \in \{0, 1\}$, let

$$K(x) = \{x' \in X_m : C_m(x, x') = B_m(x')\},$$

$$K_b(x) = \{x' \in X_m : C_m(x, x') = B_m^{(2)}(x, x') \oplus b\},$$

$$k(x) = |K(x)|, k_b(x) = |K_b(x)|.$$

It is not difficult to show that the following properties must hold for all $x \in X_m$:

(1) $X_m = K_0(x) \cup K_1(x)$ and $t_m = k_0(x) + k_1(x)$.

(2) $K(x) = K_{B_m(x)}(x)$ and $k(x) = k_{B_m(x)}(x)$.

For each $k \leq t_m$ define the **bucket** $\Sigma(k) = \{x \in X_m : k(x) = k\}$ and put $\sigma(k) = |\Sigma(k)|$. For simplicity, figure 3 pictures the situation in which the function $k(x)$ assumes only the values $k_1 < \cdots < k_n$, in increasing order.

Notice that if $k \notin \{k_1, \ldots, k_n\}$ then $\sigma(k) = 0$. For each $k \leq t_m$, let

$$a(k) = Pr[x \in X_m : k(x) = k] = \frac{\sigma(k)}{t_m},$$

i.e. $a(k)$ is the ratio of points $x \in X_m$ which lie in the bucket $\Sigma(k)$. Put $a_r = a(k_r)$, $\sigma_r = \sigma(k_r)$. The r-th rectangle pictured, has a base of length a_r, and height equal to $p(x) = k_r/t_m$, for each $x \in \Sigma(k_r)$. It is clear that

$$\sum_{k=0}^{t_m} a(k) = \sum_{k=0}^{t_m} Pr[x \in X_m : k(x) = k] = 1. \tag{18}$$

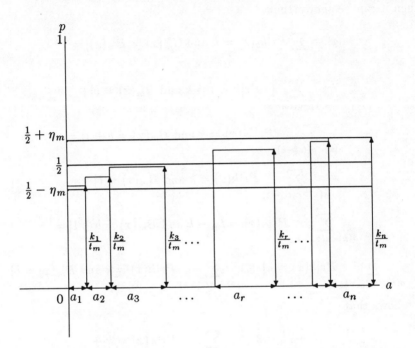

Figure 3: Graph of $p = \frac{k(x)}{t_m}, a = Pr[x \in X_m : k(x) = k]$

The circuit C' which predicts the predicate B, is based on a comparison of sizes of buckets. To be more specific one defines C_m^b as follows:

Input: x.

Step 1: Compute $k = k_b(x)$.

Output:

$$C_m^b(x) = \begin{cases} b & \text{if } \sigma(k) \geq \sigma(t_m - k) \\ b \oplus 1 & \text{if } \sigma(k) < \sigma(t_m - k). \end{cases}$$

It will now be shown that one of the circuits C_m^0, C_m^1 satisfies the requirements of the XOR lemma. Indeed, for each $b \in \{0,1\}$ let

$$p^b = Pr[x \in X_m : C_m^b(x) = B_m(x)].$$

Then it can be shown that

$$p^b = \sum_k Pr[k_b(x) = k \text{ and } C_m^b(x) = B_m(x)] =$$

$$\sum_{a(k) \geq a(t_m - k)} Pr[k_b(x) = k \text{ and } B_m(x) = b] +$$

$$\sum_{a(k) < a(t_m - k)} Pr[k_b(x) = k \text{ and } B_m(x) = b \oplus 1] =$$

$$\sum_{a(k) \geq a(t_m - k)} Pr[k(x) = k \text{ and } B_m(x) = b] +$$

$$\sum_{a(k) < a(t_m - k)} Pr[k(x) = t_m - k \text{ and } B_m(x) = b \oplus 1] =$$

$$\sum_{a(k) > a(t_m - k)} Pr[k(x) = k] + \sum_{a(k) = a(t_m - k)} Pr[k(x) = k \text{ and } B_m(x) = b].$$

It follows that

$$p^0 + p^1 = 2 \cdot \sum_{a(k) > a(t_m - k)} Pr[k(x) = k] +$$

$$\sum_{a(k) = a(t_m - k)} Pr[k(x) = k \text{ and } B_m(x) = 0] +$$

$$\sum_{a(k) = a(t_m - k)} Pr[k(x) = k \text{ and } B_m(x) = 1] =$$

$$2 \cdot \sum_{a(k) > a(t_m - k)} Pr[k(x) = k] + \sum_{a(k) = a(t_m - k)} a(k) =$$

$$\sum_{a(k) > a(t_m - k)} a(k) + \sum_{a(k) < a(t_m - k)} a(t_m - k) + \sum_{a(k) = a(t_m - k)} a(k) =$$

$$\sum_k \max\{a(k), a(t_m - k)\}.$$

However, using equation 18, as well as

$$\max\{a(k), a(t_m - k)\} = \frac{1}{2}(a(k) + a(t_m - k) + |a(k) - a(t_m - k)|),$$

it can be shown that

$$p^0 + p^1 = 1 + \frac{1}{2} \cdot \sum_k |a(k) - a(t_m - k)| = 1 + \sum_{k > t_m/2} |a(k) - a(t_m - k)|.$$

Hence, for some $b \in \{0, 1\}$:

$$p^b \geq \frac{1}{2} + \frac{1}{2} \cdot \sum_{k > t_m/2} |a(k) - a(t_m - k)|.$$

Let $C'_m = C^b_m$, where b satisfies the inequality above. It is then immediate that

$$Pr[x \in X_m : C'_m(x) = B_m(x)] \geq \frac{1}{2} + \sum_{k > t_m/2} |a(k) - a(t_m - k)|. \quad (19)$$

Let Ω denote the area under the pictured graph. The area of the r-th rectangle is equal to $a_r \cdot (k_r/t_m)$. Hence, Ω is equal to the sum of the areas of the n regtangles. It follows that on the one hand

$$\Omega = \sum_{r=1}^n \frac{k_r}{t_m} \cdot a_r = \sum_{k=0}^{t_m} \frac{k}{t_m} \cdot a(k), \quad (20)$$

and on the other hand

$$\Omega = Pr\left[< x, x' > \in X_m \times X_m : B_m^{(2)}(x, x') = C_m(x, x') \right] \geq \frac{1}{2} + \epsilon_m. \quad (21)$$

Let $d(k) = k/t_m - 1/2$, i.e. if the r-th rectangle lies above (respectively below) the horizontal line of height $1/2$, then $d(k_r)$ is the positive (respectively negative) distance of the highest point of the rectangle from the horizontal line drawn at height $1/2$. It follows from (20), (18), and the assumption in case 2 that

$$\Omega = \frac{1}{2} + \sum_{k=0}^{t_m} d(k) \cdot a(k) =$$

$$\frac{1}{2} + \sum_{k > t_m/2} d(k) \cdot a(k) + \sum_{k < t_m/2} d(k) \cdot a(k) =$$

$$\frac{1}{2} + \sum_{k > t_m/2} d(k) \cdot a(k) + \sum_{k > t_m/2} -d(k) \cdot a(t_m - k) =$$

$$\frac{1}{2} + \sum_{1/2+\eta_m > k/t_m > 1/2} d(k) \cdot (a(k) - a(t_m - k)) \le$$

$$\frac{1}{2} + \eta_m \cdot \sum_{1/2+\eta_m > k/t_m > 1/2} |a(k) - a(t_m - k)|. \qquad (22)$$

It follows from (21), (22) that

$$\sum_{k/t_m > 1/2} |a(k) - a(t_m - k)| \ge$$

$$\sum_{1/2+\eta_m > k/t_m > 1/2} |a(k) - a(t_m - k)| \ge \frac{\epsilon_m}{\eta_m} = \frac{\sqrt{2\epsilon_m}}{1 - \delta_m/2}. \qquad (23)$$

Using this, as well as inequalities (19), (23) one obtains that

$$Pr[x \in X_m : C'_m(x) = B_m(x)] \ge \frac{1}{2} + \frac{1}{2} \cdot \frac{\sqrt{2\epsilon_m}}{1 - \delta_m/2} \ge \frac{1}{2} + \eta_m.$$

PART 2: FORMAL PROOF OF THE XOR LEMMA

At this point the reader may find it useful to review the intuitive proof of the XOR lemma given in part 1 of this subsection. The main idea of the formal proof is to replace computations in the intuitive proof requiring the whole space X_m, by computations involving only a sufficiently large, but polynomial size, sample of X_m. This makes it possible to apply laws of large numbers to show that the resulting polynomial size circuit satisfies the conclusion of the XOR lemma. Of course, these random samples can be generated by using RGH.

Assume that the hypothesis of the XOR lemma is true, i.e. M is an infinite set of integers, $0 < \epsilon_m, \delta_m < 1$, for each $m \in M$, and $B = \{B_m : m \ge 0\}$, $B_m : X_m \longrightarrow \{0,1\}$ is a family of predicates on the family $X = \{X_m : m \ge 0\}$. Assume there exists a polynomial size circuit $C = \{C_m : m \ge 0\}$ such that for all $m \in M$,

$$\beta = Pr\left[< x, x' >\in X_m \times X_m : B_m^{(2)}(x, x') = C_m(x, x')\right] \ge \frac{1}{2} + \epsilon_m. \qquad (24)$$

Fix $m \in M$, and put $\epsilon_m = \epsilon, \delta_m = \delta, \eta_m = \eta = (1 - \delta)\sqrt{\epsilon/2}$. Also define

$$s = 2 \cdot \left(\left\lceil \frac{\log_2 m}{\epsilon \cdot \delta^2} \right\rceil\right)^5 + 1, \ell = s^9,$$

and notice that s is odd. **Throughout the proof below x (respectively y) with subscripts or superscripts will range over elements of X_m (respectively of $\{0,1\}$).** On the basis of the previous geometric discussion, one defines the circuit C'_m which predicts the predicate B_m with an η advantage as follows:

Input: x.

Step 1: Let $< x_1, y_1 >, \ldots, < x_\ell, y_\ell >$ be a random sample such that $B_m(x_i) = y_i$, for all $i = 1, \ldots, \ell$.

Step 2: Let $< x'_1, y'_1 >, \ldots, < x'_s, y'_s >$ be a random sample such that $B_m(x'_j) = y'_j$, for all $j = 1, \ldots, s$.

Step 3: Compute the following quantities:

$$K'(x_i, y_i) = \{j \le s : C_m(x_i, x'_j) = y_i \oplus y'_j\}, k'(x_i, y_i) = |K'(x_i, y_i)|,$$

$$\Sigma'(k) = \{i \le \ell : k'(x_i, y_i) = k\}, \sigma'(k) = |\Sigma'(k)|.$$

Step 4:

$$\text{Case 1}: \ (\exists i \le \ell) \left| \frac{k'(x_i, y_i)}{s} - \frac{1}{2} \right| \ge \left(1 - \frac{\delta}{2} \right) \cdot \sqrt{\frac{\epsilon}{2}}.$$

In this case compute :

$$k'_0 = \min\{k'(x_i, y_i) \text{ as in case 1} : i = 1, \ldots, \ell\},$$

$$i_0 = \min\{i \le \ell : i \in \Sigma'(k'_0)\}, \text{ and}$$

$$a = \begin{cases} C_m(x_{i_0}, x) \oplus y_{i_0} & \text{if } k'_0/s > 1/2 \\ C_m(x_{i_0}, x) \oplus y_{i_0} \oplus 1 & \text{if } k'_0/s < 1/2. \end{cases}$$

$$\text{Case 2}: \ (\forall i \le \ell) \left| \frac{k'(x_i, y_i)}{s} - \frac{1}{2} \right| < \left(1 - \frac{\delta}{2} \right) \cdot \sqrt{\frac{\epsilon}{2}}.$$

In this case compute:

$$k' = |\{j \le s : C_m(x, x'_j) = y'_j\}|, \text{ and}$$

$$a = \begin{cases} 0 & \text{if } \sigma'(k') \ge \sigma'(s - k') \\ 1 & \text{if } \sigma'(k') < \sigma'(s - k'). \end{cases}$$

Output: $C_m(x) = a$.

The rest of this section will be devoted to a proof of

$$\gamma = Pr\left[B_m(x) = C'_m(x) \right] \ge \frac{1}{2} + \eta. \tag{25}$$

Let G denote the event: $C'_m(x) = B_m(x)$; let A the event: after execution of step 3, case 1 occurs in step 4; and let $\overline{A}$ be the event: after execution of step 3, case 2 occurs in step 4. It is then clear that

$$\gamma = \alpha \cdot Pr[A] + \overline{\alpha} \cdot Pr[\overline{A}],$$

where $\alpha = Pr[G|A], \overline{\alpha} = Pr[G|\overline{A}]$.

The proof of the theorem will be divided into two claims. In Claim 1, a lower bound on $\alpha Pr[A]$ will be determined and in Claim 2, a lower bound on $\overline{\alpha} Pr[\overline{A}]$ will be determined.

Claim 1: $\alpha Pr[A] \geq (1/2 + (1 - \frac{3}{4}\delta)\sqrt{\epsilon/2})Pr[A] - \exp[-\sqrt{s}]$.

The proof is in several steps. For each x, y such that $B_m(x) = y$ put:

$$g(x, y) = Pr\left[C_m(x, x') = y \oplus y' | B_m(x') = y'\right],$$

$$k'(x, y) = |\{j \leq s : C_m(x, x'_j) = y \oplus y'_j\}|,$$

and consider the events F_1 and F_2 respectively defined by:

$$\left(\frac{k'(x, y)}{s} - \frac{1}{2}\right) \geq \left(1 - \frac{\delta}{2}\right) \cdot \sqrt{\frac{\epsilon}{2}} \text{ and } g(x, y) < \frac{1}{2} + \left(1 - \frac{3\delta}{4}\right) \cdot \sqrt{\frac{\epsilon}{2}},$$

$$\left(\frac{k'(x, y)}{s} - \frac{1}{2}\right) \leq -\left(1 - \frac{\delta}{2}\right) \cdot \sqrt{\frac{\epsilon}{2}} \text{ and } g(x, y) > \frac{1}{2} - \left(1 - \frac{3\delta}{4}\right) \cdot \sqrt{\frac{\epsilon}{2}}.$$

It will be shown that

Subclaim 1: $Pr[F_1 \cup F_2] \leq \exp(-s^{2/3})$.

Since, $k'(x, y \oplus 1) = s - k'(x, y), g(x, y \oplus 1) = 1 - g(x, y)$ it is clear that for all x, y such that $B_m(x) = y$,

$$< x, y > \in F_1 \Leftrightarrow < x, y \oplus 1 > \in F_2,$$

and hence,

$$Pr[F_1] = Pr[F_2].$$

Consequently, it is enough to find an upper bound for $Pr[F_1]$. The idea is to think of $k'(x, y)$ as a Monte Carlo computation of $g(x, y)$. Let $\theta = (\delta/4) \cdot \sqrt{\epsilon/2}$. Apply Bernshtein's law of large numbers (see exercise 1) to obtain

$$Pr\left[\left|\frac{k'(x, y)}{s} - g(x, y)\right| > \theta\right] \leq 2\exp(-s\theta^2).$$

Put:

$$F_1^0 = \{< x, y >\in F_1 : g(x, y) > 1/4\}, F_1^1 = \{< x, y >\in F_1 : g(x, y) \leq 1/4\},$$

and notice that $Pr[F_1] = Pr[F_1^0] + Pr[F_1^1]$. Then, using the definition of s,

$$Pr[F_1^0] \leq Pr\left[\frac{k'(x, y)}{s} - g(x, y) > \theta\right] \leq \tag{26}$$

$$2 \exp(-s\theta^2) \leq 2 \exp\left(-\frac{s\delta^2\epsilon}{32}\right) \leq 2 \exp(-s^{3/4}).$$

In addition, it is true that

$$Pr[F_1^1] \leq Pr\left[\frac{k'(x, y)}{s} - \frac{1}{4} \geq \theta\right].$$

Thus, applying the previous argument to the right side of the above inequality, with $g(x, y) = 1/4$, it will follow that

$$Pr[F_1^1] \leq 2 \exp(-s^{3/4}). \tag{27}$$

Subclaim 1 now follows from inequalities (26), (27).
   Consider the events A_1, A_2 respectively defined by:

$$\frac{k_0'}{s} > \frac{1}{2} \text{ and } (\forall i \in \Sigma(k_0')) \left[g(x_i, y_i) \geq \frac{1}{2} + \left(1 - \frac{3\delta}{4}\right)\sqrt{\frac{\epsilon}{2}}\right],$$

$$\frac{k_0'}{s} < \frac{1}{2} \text{ and } (\forall i \in \Sigma(k_0')) \left[g(x_i, y_i) \leq \frac{1}{2} - \left(1 - \frac{3\delta}{4}\right)\sqrt{\frac{\epsilon}{2}}\right],$$

and let

$$L = A \cap (A_1 \cup A_2), \overline{L} = \text{ the complement of } L.$$

Now it will be shown that:
   Subclaim 2: $Pr[A \cap \overline{L}] \leq \exp(-\sqrt{s})$.
   Indeed, $Pr[A \cap \overline{L}] = Pr[A \cap \overline{A_1} \cap \overline{A_2}] \leq$

$$Pr\left[\frac{k_0'}{s} > \frac{1}{2} \text{ and } (\exists i \leq \ell) \left(g(x_i, y_i) < \frac{1}{2} + \left(1 - \frac{3\delta}{4}\right)\sqrt{\frac{\epsilon}{2}}\right)\right] +$$

$$Pr\left[\frac{k_0'}{s} < \frac{1}{2} \text{ and } (\exists i \leq \ell) \left(g(x_i, y_i) > \frac{1}{2} - \left(1 - \frac{3\delta}{4}\right)\sqrt{\frac{\epsilon}{2}}\right)\right] \leq$$

$$\ell Pr[F_1] + \ell Pr[F_2] \leq$$

$$2 \cdot s^9 \cdot \exp\left(-s^{2/3}\right) \leq \exp(-\sqrt{s}),$$

which completes the proof of subclaim 2. Consequently,

$$Pr[G|L] \cdot Pr[A \cap \overline{L}] \leq \exp(-\sqrt{s}). \tag{28}$$

To finish the proof of claim 1, notice that the definition of g implies that for all $i = 1, \ldots, s$,

$$g(x_i, y_i) = Pr[B_m(x') = C_m(x_i, x') \oplus B_m(x_i)].$$

Moreover, the definition of C'_m implies that

$$Pr[G|L, A_1] \geq E[g(x_i, y_i)|L, A_1] \geq \frac{1}{2} + \left(1 - \frac{3\delta}{4}\right)\sqrt{\frac{\epsilon}{2}},$$

$$Pr[G|L, A_2] \geq E[1 - g(x_i, y_i)|L, A_2] \geq \frac{1}{2} + \left(1 - \frac{3\delta}{4}\right)\sqrt{\frac{\epsilon}{2}}.$$

Thus, using the identity:

$$Pr[G|L] = Pr[G|L, A_1] \cdot Pr[A_1|L] + Pr[G|L, A_2] \cdot Pr[A_2|L], \tag{29}$$

(see exercise 2), it follows that

$$Pr[G|L] \geq \frac{1}{2} + \left(1 - \frac{3\delta}{4}\right)\sqrt{\frac{\epsilon}{2}}. \tag{30}$$

However, it is clear that

$$\alpha Pr[A] = Pr[G|A]Pr[A] \geq Pr[G|L]Pr[L] =$$

$$Pr[G|L](Pr[A] - Pr[A \cap \overline{L}]) = Pr[G|L]Pr[A] - Pr[G|L]Pr[A \cap \overline{L}]). \tag{31}$$

Claim 1 is now a consequence of (28), (30) and (31).

Claim 2: $\overline{\alpha} Pr[\overline{A}] \geq (1/2 + (1 - \frac{3}{4}\delta)\sqrt{\epsilon/2})Pr[\overline{A}] - 1/(4s^2).$

For each i, j, $i = 1, \ldots, s, j = 1, \ldots, \ell$ consider the $\ell \cdot s$ independent random variables $X_{i,j}$ defined by:

$$X_{i,j}(x, x') = \begin{cases} 1 & \text{if } C_m(x, x') = B_m^{(2)}(x, x') \\ 0 & \text{if } C_m(x, x') \neq B_m^{(2)}(x, x'), \end{cases}$$

and let

$$\xi(x, x') = \frac{1}{\ell \cdot s} \cdot \sum_{i,j} X_{i,j}(x, x'),$$

$$q_k(x, x') = \frac{1}{\ell} \cdot \left| \left\{ 1 \leq j \leq \ell : \sum_{i=1}^{s} X_{i,j}(x, x') = k \right\} \right|.$$

It is clear that q_k is the random variable corresponding to the quantity $\sigma'(k)$. Setting $d_k = k/s - 1/2$, and using the fact that s is odd, it is easy to see (exercise 4) that

$$\xi(x, x') = \frac{1}{2} + \sum_{k > s/2} d_k \cdot (q_k(x, x') - q_{s-k}(x, x')). \tag{32}$$

Let a'_k be the expectation of the random variable q_k i.e. $a'_k = E[q_k]$. q_k can be regarded as a Monte-Carlo computation of a'_k. It is clear from (24) that for all i, j, $\beta = E[X_{i,j}]$. Hence $\beta = E[\xi]$, using the expectation theorem. It follows that

$$\beta = E[\xi] = \frac{1}{2} + \sum_{k > s/2} d_k \cdot (a'_k - a'_{s-k}) \leq \frac{1}{2} + \sum_{k > s/2} d_k \cdot |a'_k - a'_{s-k}|. \tag{33}$$

Next, it will be necessary to consider two subcases.
Subcase 1: There exists $k \leq s$ such that

$$a'_k \geq \frac{1}{s^3} \text{ and } \left| \frac{k}{s} - \frac{1}{2} \right| \geq \eta.$$

Let k be as in subcase 1. Using the weak law of large numbers one obtains that

$$Pr\left[|a'_k - q_k| > \frac{s-1}{s^4} \right] \leq \frac{s^8}{4\ell(s-1)^2} \leq \frac{1}{2s^3}.$$

Consequently, since $a'_k \geq 1/s^3$,

$$Pr\left[q_k < \frac{1}{s^4} \right] = Pr\left[q_k < \frac{1}{s^4} \text{ and } |a'_k - q_k| > \frac{s-1}{s^4} \right] \leq \frac{1}{2s^3}.$$

It follows that

$$Pr[A] \geq Pr\left[q_k \geq \frac{1}{s^4} \right] \geq 1 - \frac{1}{2s^3}.$$

Hence, the desired inequality (25) follows easily using the result of Claim 1.

Subcase 2: For all $k \leq s$,

$$\left| \frac{k}{s} - \frac{1}{2} \right| \geq \eta \Rightarrow a'_k \leq \frac{1}{s^3}.$$

Consider the event J defined by:

$$(\forall k)\left(|a'_k - a'_{s-k}| \geq \frac{1}{s^2} \Rightarrow a'_k - a'_{s-k}, q_k - q_{s-k} \text{ have the same sign} \right).$$

It is an immediate application of the weak law of large numbers that

$$Pr[J] \geq 1 - \frac{1}{4s^2}, \tag{34}$$

(see exercise 5). Thus,

$$\overline{\alpha} Pr[\overline{A}] = Pr[G|\overline{A}]Pr[\overline{A}] = Pr[J]Pr[G|\overline{A}, J]Pr[\overline{A}] \geq$$

$$Pr[G|\overline{A}, J]Pr[\overline{A}] - \frac{1}{4s^2}.$$

However, (24), (33) and the assumption in Case 2 imply that

$$\frac{1}{2} + \epsilon \leq \beta \leq \frac{1}{2} + \sum_{1/2 < k/s < 1/2 + \eta} d_k \cdot |a'_k - a'_{s-k}| + \frac{s}{s^3}. \tag{35}$$

It follows from (35) that

$$\sum_{1/2 < k/s < 1/2 + \eta} |a'_k - a'_{s-k}| \geq \frac{\epsilon - 1/s^2}{\eta}. \tag{36}$$

Using the definition of J it follows that

$$Pr[G|\overline{A}, J] \geq \tag{37}$$

$$\sum_{1/2 < k/s, |a'_k - a'_{s-k}| \geq 1/s^2} \max\{a'_k, a'_{s-k}\} +$$

$$\sum_{1/2 < k/s, |a'_k - a'_{s-k}| < 1/s^2} \min\{a'_k, a'_{s-k}\} \geq$$

$$\sum_{1/2 < k/s, |a'_k - a'_{s-k}| \geq 1/s^2} \max\{a'_k, a'_{s-k}\} +$$

$$\sum_{1/2 < k/s, |a'_k - a'_{s-k}| < 1/s^2} \left\{ \max\{a'_k, a'_{s-k}\} - \frac{1}{s^2} \right\} \geq$$

$$\sum_{1/2 < k/s} \max\{a'_k, a'_{s-k}\} - \frac{1}{2s} =$$

$$\frac{1}{2} + \frac{1}{2} \sum_{1/2 < k/s} |a'_k - a'_{s-k}| - \frac{1}{2s}.$$

Together, this last inequality and (36) imply the result in Claim 2.

Now the XOR lemma follows easily from Claim 1, Claim 2 •

EXERCISES

1: Show that in subclaim 1, $\theta \leq g(x,y)(1 - g(x,y))$ and, hence, one can apply Bernshtein's law of large numbers.

2: Prove identity (29).

3: If $b_{i,j} \in \{0, 1\}$ for all $i = 1, \ldots, s, j = 1, \ldots, \ell$ then show that

$$\sum_{j=1}^{\ell} \sum_{i=1}^{s} b_{i,j} = \sum_{k=1}^{s} k \cdot |\{1 \leq j \leq \ell : \sum_{i=1}^{s} b_{i,j} = k\}|.$$

4: Use exercise 2 to prove equation (32). **Hint:** Notice that

$$\sum_{k=0}^{s} q_k(x, x') = 1.$$

5: Prove inequality (34).

6.6   Two Applications of the XOR Lemma

There are three main applications of the XOR theorem. The first two concern unapproximable predicates and pseudorandom generators, and will be presented in the present subsection. The third application is the notion of strong (respectively weak) one way functions and will be presented in the next subsection 6.7.

APPLICATION 1: UNAPPROXIMABLE PREDICATES.

Definition 6.14 *(Blum-Micali-Goldwasser) A predicate $B = \{B_m : m \geq 0\}$ defined on the family $X = \{X_m : m \geq 0\}$ is $1/P$ unapproximable, and this will be abbreviated $UPR(B, 1/P)$, if there is no polynomial size circuit $C = \{C_m : m \geq 0\}$ such that for infinitely many m,*

$$Pr\left[x \in X_m : B_m(x) = C_m(x)\right] \geq \frac{1}{2} + \frac{1}{P(m)}.$$

Definition 6.15 *Let P be any polynomial. A predicate $B = \{B_m : m \geq 0\}$ defined on the family $X = \{X_m : m \geq 0\}$ is $(1/2 - 1/P)$-unapproximable, and this will be abbreviated $UPR(B, 1/2 - 1/P)$, if there is no polynomial size circuit $C = \{C_m : m \geq 0\}$ such that for infinitely many m,*

$$Pr\left[x \in X_m : B_m(x) = C_m(x)\right] \geq 1 - \frac{1}{P(m)}.$$

Remark: Notice that the preceding definition of B as $1/P$ unapproximable is equivalent to $(\forall C)(C$ does not P-predict $B)$ in definition 6.2.

An immediate application of the XOR theorem is the following:

Theorem 6.8 *Let g, h be polynomial time computable functions such that $g(m) \geq 2^{h(m)} \geq (\log_2 m) m P(m)$. Then for all predicates B the following holds:*

$$UPR(B, 1/2 - 1/P) \Rightarrow (\forall Q) UPR(B^{(g)}, 1/Q) \bullet$$

APPLICATION 2: PSEUDORANDOM GENERATORS.

Recall the definition of pseudorandom generator on the family $X = \{X_m : m \geq 0\}$ given in definition 6.4. To any such pseudorandom generator G associate the sequence of bitts $b^G_{m,0}(x), \ldots, b^G_{m,Q(m)-1}(x)$ generated by G, where for each m, $b^G_{m,i}(x)$ is the i−th bit generated by G_m on input $x \in X_m$.

Definition 6.16 *Let P be a polynomial and $G = \{G_m : m \geq 0\}$ a pseudorandom generator on the family $X = \{X_m : m \geq 0\}$. The generator G, passes the $1/P$ Blum-Micali Test (and this will be abbreviated by $BMT(X, G, 1/P)$), if, for all polynomial size circuits $C = \{C_m : m \geq 0\}$, the following cannot hold for infinitely many m: there exists an $i < Q(m)$ such that*

$$Pr\left[x \in X_m : C_m(b^G_{m,0}(x), \ldots, b^G_{m,i-1}(x)) = b_{m,i}(x)\right] \geq \frac{1}{2} + \frac{1}{P(m)}.$$

The Blum-Micali generator theorem (theorem 6.1) shows how to construct from an unapproximable predicate and its friendship function, a psuedorandom generator that passes the Blum-Micali test. The same result can now be obtained from a slightly weaker hypothesis. Call a predicate $B = \{B_m : m \geq 0\}$ on the family $X = \{X_m : m \geq 0\}$ **weakly unapproximable** if and only if for any polynomial P, B is $(1/2 - 1/P)$ unapproximable. It is then clear that for all predicates B,

Theorem 6.9 $(\exists Q)UPR(B, 1/Q) \Rightarrow (\forall P)UPR(B, 1/2 - 1/P)$ •

Now the following improvement of theorem 6.1 can be proved.

Theorem 6.10 *Assume that $B = \{B_m : m \geq 0\}$ is a weakly unapproximable predicate on the family $X = \{X_m : m \geq 0\}$ and let $f = \{f_m : m \geq 0\}$ be its friendsip function. Then for any polynomial P there exists a pseudo randomgenerator G such that $BMT(X, G, 1/P)$* •

Proof: Consider polynomial time computable functions g, h such that $g(m) \geq 2^{h(m)} \geq (\log_2 m)m^2$. It is an immediate consequence of the XOR theorem that the predicate $B^{(g)}$ is $1/P$ unapproximable, for any polynomial P. Moreover, the permutation $f_m^{(g)}$ of $(X_m)^{g(m)}$ defined by:

$$f_m^{(g)}(x_1, \ldots, x_{g(m)}) = < f_m(x_1), \ldots, f_m(x_{g(m)}) >,$$

is a friendship function for $B_m^{(g)}$. Now the theorem follows by applying the Blum-Micali generator theorem to the pair $B^{(g)}, f^{(g)}$ •

EXERCISES

1: Complete the details of the proof of theorem 6.10.

6.7   (One to One) One Way Functions

The present subsection includes the third application of the XOR theorem. Let $f = \{f_m : m \geq 0\}$ be a family of functions such that each f_m is a permutation of X_m.

Definition 6.17 (A. Yao) *A polynomial size circuit $C = \{C_m : m \geq 0\}$ **weakly** (respectively **strongly**) P-inverts the family f if for infinitely many m,*

$$Pr\left[x \in X_m : C_m(f_m(x)) = x\right] \geq \frac{1}{P(m)}$$

202 6 TOWARDS A GENERAL THEORY

(respectively

$$Pr\left[x \in X_m : C_m(f_m(x)) = x\right] \geq 1 - \frac{1}{P(m)}).$$

Definition 6.18 $f = \{f_m : m \geq 0\}$ is **weak** *(respectively* **strong**) $1 - 1$, **one way** *(or simply* **one way**), *if the following holds:*

$(\forall P, C)(C$ does not strongly (respectively weakly) $P - $ invert f).

Theorem 6.11 *If the function $f = \{f_m : m \geq 0\}$ is a friendship function for the unapproximable predicate $B = \{B_m : m \geq 0\}$, then $f = \{f_m : m \geq 0\}$ is strong, one-way.*

Proof: Assume that the hypothesis of the theorem is true for the unapproximable predicate B and its friendship function f, defined on the family $X = \{X_m : m \geq 0\}$, but that the conclusion fails. Let $C = \{C_m : m \geq 0\}$ be a polynomial size circuit such that the following statement holds for infinitely many m,

$$Pr\left[x \in X_m : C_m(f_m(x)) = x\right] \geq \frac{1}{P(m)}.$$

Let M be the infinite set of integers m which satisfy the above inequality. For each bit $b \in \{0, 1\}$ let C_m^b be the following polynomial size circuit (due to Mike Fischer),
   Input: x.
   Step 1: Compute $y = C_m(x)$.
   Output:
$$C_m^b(x) = \begin{cases} B_m(x) & \text{if } f_m(y) = x \\ b & \text{if } f_m(y) \neq x. \end{cases}$$

Then the theorem will follow from the following:
Claim: For all $m \in M$ there exists $b \in \{0, 1\}$ such that

$$Pr\left[x \in X_m : B_m(x) = C_m^b(x)\right] \geq \frac{1}{2} + \frac{1}{2P(m)}.$$

Proof of the Claim: Let $m \in M$, and choose a $b \in \{0, 1\}$ such that

$$Pr[x \in X_m : B_m(x) = b | f_m(C_m(x)) \neq x] \geq \frac{1}{2}.$$

Put:

$$p = Pr[x \in X_m : f_m(C_m(x)) = x].$$

Then it can be shown, using basic properties of Pr that

$$Pr[x \in X_m : B_m(x) = C_m^b(x)] =$$

$$Pr[B_m(x) = C_m^b(x) \text{ and } f_m(C_m(x)) = x] +$$

$$Pr[B_m(x) = C_m^b(x) \text{ and } f_m(C_m(x)) \neq x] =$$

$$Pr[f_m(C_m(x)) = x] +$$

$$Pr[B_m(x) = C_m^b(x) | f_m(C_m(x)) \neq x] \cdot Pr[f_m(C_m(x)) \neq x] =$$

$$p + Pr[B_m(x) = C_m^b(x) | f_m(C_m(x)) \neq x] \cdot (1 - p) \geq$$

$$p + \frac{1}{2}(1 - p) = \frac{1}{2} + \frac{p}{2}.$$

Since, by assumption

$$p = Pr[f_m(C_m(x)) = x] \geq \frac{1}{P(m)},$$

it follows that

$$Pr\left[x \in X_m : B_m(x) = C_m^b(x)\right] \geq \frac{1}{2} + \frac{1}{2P(m)},$$

and the proof of the claim is complete.

Since the set M is infinite, it follows from the claim that there exists a $b \in \{0, 1\}$ and an infinite subset M' of M such that for each $m \in M'$,

$$Pr\left[x \in X_m : B_m(x) = C_m^b(x)\right] \geq \frac{1}{2} + \frac{1}{2P(m)}.$$

Then the circuit:

$$C' = \{C_m^b : m \geq 0\},$$

$(2 \cdot P)$-predicts the predicate B, which is a contradiction •

The following theorem is very important because it can be used in conjunction with theorem 6.1 to construct *secure* pseudorandom generators, assuming only the existence of weak one way functions.

Theorem 6.12 *(One Way Function Theorem, A. Yao) The following statements are equivalent:*

(1) There is a weak, one way function.

(2) There is a strong, one-way function.

(3) There is an unapproximable predicate $B = \{B_m : m \geq 0\}$ and its friendship function $f = \{f_m : m \geq 0\}$.

Proof: $(3) \Rightarrow (2)$

This was proved in detail in theorem 6.11.

$(2) \Rightarrow (1)$

This is immediate from definition 6.17.

$(1) \Rightarrow (3)$

Let $f = \{f_m : m \geq 0\}$ be a weak one way function such that $f_m : X_m \longrightarrow X_m$ is one to one, and onto. Let $B_{i,m} : X_m \longrightarrow \{0,1\}$ be the predicate defined by:

$$x \longrightarrow B_{i,m}(x) = \text{the } i - \text{th bit of } f_m^{-1}(x).$$

Further, let $L_m : (X_m)^m \longrightarrow \{0,1\}$ be the predicate defined by:

$$L_m(x_1, \ldots, x_m) = B_{1,m}(x_1) \oplus \cdots \oplus B_{m,m}(x_m).$$

Finally, consider the predicate $B = L^{(g)}$, where the function g is polynomial time computable and satisfies $g(m) \geq m^3$, for all $m \geq 0$. It will be shown that the predicate B is unapproximable with corresponding friendship function

$$f_m' : (X_m)^{mg(m)} \longrightarrow (X_m)^{mg(m)},$$

defined by:

$$f_m'(x_1, \ldots, x_{mg(m)}) =$$

$$< f_m(x_1), \ldots, f_m(x_m), \ldots, f_m(x_{m(g(m)-1)}), \ldots, f_m(x_{mg(m)}) > .$$

Using the identity

$$L_m(f_m(x_1), \ldots, f_m(x_m)) =$$

$$(1 - \text{st bit of } x_1) \oplus (2 - \text{nd bit of } x_2) \oplus \cdots \oplus (m - \text{th bit of } x_m),$$

it is not hard to show that $f' = \{f_m' : m \geq 0\}$ is a friendship function for the predicate B.

It remains to show that the predicate B is unapproximable. Assume on the contrary that there exists a polynomial size circuit $C' = \{C_m' : m \geq 0\}$

and a polynomial Q such that the following property holds for infinitely many m,

$$Pr\left[x \in (X_m)^{mg(m)} : B_m(x) = C'_m(x)\right] \geq \frac{1}{2} + \frac{1}{Q(m)}.$$

Let M be the infinite set of indices $m \geq 0$ that satisfy the inequality above. Since, $g(m) \geq (\log_2 m)m^2(1 + \deg(Q))$, the multiple XOR theorem implies that there exist polynomial size circuits $\{C_{i,m} : m \geq i \geq 1\}$ such that the following property holds for all but a finite number of $m \in M$:

$$(\forall i \leq m)\left(Pr\left[u \in X_m : B_{i,m}(u) = C_{i,m}(u)\right] \geq 1 - \frac{1}{m^2}\right).$$

Let M' be the infinite set of indices $m \in M$ such that the inequlity above holds. It will be shown that the circuit

$$C_m(u) = < C_{1,m}(u), \ldots, C_{m,m}(u) >,$$

strongly P-inverts the function f, where $P(m) = m$. Indeed, for each $m \in M'$ it can be shown that

$$Pr\left[u \in X_m : C_m(u) \neq f_m^{-1}(u)\right] \leq$$

$$\sum_{i=1}^{m} Pr\left[u \in X_m : C_{i,m}(u) \neq B_{i,m}(u)\right] \leq \sum_{i=1}^{m} \frac{1}{m^2} = \frac{1}{m}.$$

It follows that for all $m \in M'$,

$$Pr\left[u \in X_m : C_m(u) = f_m^{-1}(u)\right] \geq 1 - \frac{1}{m},$$

which is a contradiction. This completes the proof of the theorem •

Recall that in theorem 6.12, the passage from a strong one way function to a friendship function and its associated unapproximable predicate was accomplished by passing to a space of higher dimension, namely $(X_m)^m$. However, the answer to the following question seems to be open:

Question: Is every weak or strong one way function the friendship function of an unapproximable predicate?

EXERCISES

1: Show that the predicate B defined in the course of the proof of (1) $\Rightarrow$ (3) of theorem 6.12 satisfies RGH.

2: The circuit C' considered in the course of the proof of theorem 6.11 was defined nondeterministically. Show that if the function $f = \{f_m : m \geq 0\}$ is a friendship function for the unapproximable predicate $B = \{B_m : m \geq 0\}$ and satisfies $Pr[C_m(f_m(x)) = x] \geq 1/2 + 1/P(m)$ for infinitely many m, then the deterministic circuit pictured below satisfies the conclusion of the claim in theorem 6.11:

$$x \rightarrow \boxed{C_m} \rightarrow \boxed{B_m \circ f_m} \rightarrow B_m(f_m(C_m(x)))$$

3: Assuming the existence of a weak one way function, prove the existence of pseudorandom families of functions (see subsection 6.3).

6.8   Random Polynomial and Deterministic Time

For any integer x, let $|x|$ denote the binary length of x. Let A be any set of nonnegative integers; for any nonnegative integer n, let $A_n = \{x \in A : |x| \leq n\}$. Call A **computable in random polynomial time** if and only if there exists a polynomial P and a polynomial time computable predicate L such that for all x,

. (1) $x \notin A \Rightarrow \forall y < 2^{P(|x|)} L(x, y) = 0$, and
   (2) $x \in A \Rightarrow Pr[y < 2^{P(|x|)} : L(x, y) = 1] \geq 1/2$.

The following result clarifies the computational complexity of sets computable in random polynomial time.

Theorem 6.13 *(Adleman) If A is computable in random polynomial time, then A can be defined by a polynomial size family of deterministic circuits.*

Proof: Let P, L be as above. Fix n, and let $a_1, a_2, \ldots, a_t$ be an enumeration of the set A_n without repetitions. Consider the matrix $M = (m_{i,j})$, $i \leq t, j < P(n)$, where

$$m_{ij} = L\left(a_i, j \bmod \left(2^{P(|a_i|)}\right)\right).$$

Property (2) implies that at least half the entries of each row of M are ones. Therefore, there exists a column, say j_1, at least half of whose entries are ones. Consider the matrix M' obtained from M by deleting the j_1-th column, and for each i such that $m_{ij_1} = 1$, the i-th row. Every row of the resulting matrix has ones at least half of its entries. Hence, the procedure above can be repeated to find $j_1, \ldots, j_k$, with $k \leq n$, such that

$$\forall x < 2^{P(n)} [x \in A_n \Rightarrow (\exists r \leq k) L(x, j_r) = 1].$$

Using property (1), it follows that

$$\forall x < 2^{P(n)} [x \in A_n \Leftrightarrow (\exists r \leq k) L(x, j_r) = 1],$$

which completes the proof of the theorem •

Let **RP** be the class of sets computable in random polynomial time. For each positive integer valued function $g(n)$, let **DTIME**$(g(n))$ be the class of sets computable in deterministic time $g(n)$, for all but a finite number of n. Adleman's theorem can now be restated as follows:

Theorem 6.14

$$\mathbf{RP} \subseteq \bigcup_{\epsilon > 0} \mathbf{DTIME}\left(2^{n^\epsilon}\right) \bullet$$

Assuming the existence of weak one way functions, theorem 6.14 can be substantially improved. First, consider the class **BPP**, of sets computable in **bounded probabilistic polynomial time**. Define $A \in \mathbf{BPP}$ if and only if there exists a polynomial P and a polynomial time computable predicate L such that for all x,

(1) $x \notin A \Rightarrow Pr[y < 2^{P(|x|)} : L(x, y) = 1] \leq 1/4$, and
(2) $x \in A \Rightarrow Pr[y < 2^{P(|x|)} : L(x, y) = 1] \geq 3/4$.

It is well known that **RP** $\subseteq$ **BPP** (see exercise 1). The desired improvement of theorem 6.13 can be stated as follows:

Theorem 6.15 *(Hirshfeld-A. Yao) If there exists a weak one way function, then*

$$\mathbf{BPP} \subseteq \bigcap_{\epsilon > 0} \mathbf{DTIME}\left(2^{n^\epsilon}\right).$$

Proof: Suppose that $A \in \mathbf{BPP}$. Let P be a polynomial and L a polynomial time computable predicate which wittnesses that $A \in \mathbf{BPP}$. The one way function theorem shows that the existence of a weak one way function implies the existence of an unapproximable predicate B and its friendship function f. The Blum - Micali generator theorem, and Yao's $PSST$ theorem show that the generator $G = G^{B,f,P}$ passes Yao's test.

Fix $\epsilon > 0$. A new deterministic machine L' is defined as follows: $L'(x) = 1$ if and only if for at least half the seeds s of length n^ϵ, $L(x, G(s)) = 1$, otherwise $L'(x) = 0$. Clearly, the running time of L' is 2^{n^ϵ}. It remains to show that for all but a finite number of x,

$$x \in A \Leftrightarrow L'(x) = 1. \tag{38}$$

Assume on the contrary that equivalence (38) fails for infinitely many x, say $x_1, \ldots, x_m, \ldots$. Then for all m,

$$\text{either } (x_m \in A \text{ and } L'(x_m) = 0) \text{ or } (x_m \notin A \text{ and } L'(x_m) = 1). \tag{39}$$

Consider the circuit $C_m(y) = L(x_m, y)$. Then it is immediate from definition 6.8 that for all m,

$$|p_m^{C,G} - p_m^{C,R}| > \frac{1}{2}. \tag{40}$$

Hence, G fails the polynomial size statistical test $C = \{C_m : m \geq 0\}$ •

EXERCISES

1: Show that $\mathbf{RP} \subseteq \mathbf{BPP}$.

2: Derive inequality (40) from inequality (39).

3: $\mathbf{P} = \mathbf{NP} \Rightarrow$ there is no weak one way function. **Hint:** The existence of a weak one way function, implies the existence of a pseudorandom generator G, which passes all polynomial size statistical tests. Find a polynomial size statistical test that G fails.

4: The set of composite positive integers is computable in random polynomial time. **Hint:** Use any of the probabilistic primality tests of section 2.

6.9   Bibliographical Remarks

The first approach to the concept of *randomness for strings* to receive wide attention in the literature, was that of Kolmogorov complexity. Intuitively speaking, the **Kolmogorov complexity** of a string s, abbreviated $K(s)$, is the minimal length of a program (or algorithm) describing s. Then the string s is called **random** if

$$K(s) \geq |s|,$$

where s is the length of s. For more information see [K7], [M3], [Z2], [S4], and [M1]).

The second approach, which is the one studied in the present section, does not deal with the randomness of single strings, but rather with the *randomness of efficient pseudorandom generators*. The next bit (or Blum-Micali) test is derived from [B6] and Yao's statistical test from [Y1]. The construction of a family of pseudorandom functions is from [G7].

The importance of the notion of XOR for the construction of strong one way functions was first pointed out by A. Yao in [Y1]. The present proof of the XOR lemma is based on [K12]; the formal proof is based partly on [Y2]; Rackoff in [R3] gives a slightly different proof; in addition, a sketch of a proof is also given by Levin, who calls it the *Additive Isolation Lemma* (see [L15]).

A different notion of one way function and its relationship to the class **NP** is studied in [B7]. An immediate consequence of the results of this section is that the existence of weak one way functions implies the existence of pseudorandom generators that pass Yao's test. In an attempt to prove the converse of this last assertion, L. Levin has formulated an even weaker notion of weak one way function, whose existence is equivalent to the existence of pseudorandom generators that pass Yao's test (see [L15]).

The effect of the existence of weak one way functions on the class **RP** was first studied by A. Yao in [Y1], who proved that $\mathbf{RP} \subseteq \bigcap_{\epsilon>0} \mathbf{DTIME}(2^{n^{\epsilon}})$. The improvent of this result presented in subsection 6.8 is due to Hirshfeld (see [H6]).

The following abbreviations are used throughout the references below.

ACM	Association of Computing Machinery.
AMM	American Mathematical Monthly.
AMS	American Mathematical Society.
DCS	Department of Computer Science.
DVW	Deutcher Verlag der Wissenschaften.
FOCS	Symposium on Foundations of Computer Science.
IEEE	Institute of Electrical and Electronic Engineers.
MIT	Massachusets Institute of Technology.
SIAM	Society for Industrial and Applied Mathematics.
STOC	Symposium on Theory of Computing.
SV	Springer Verlag.
SVGTM	Springer Verlag Graduate Texts in Mathematics.
SVLNCS	Springer Verlag Lecture Notes in Computer Science.
SVLNM	Springer Verlag Lecture Notes in Mathematics.
TR	Technical Report.
VEB	Volkseigene Betrieb.

References

[A1]   Adleman, L., *A Subexponential Algorithm for the Discrete Logarithm Problem with Applications to Cryptography*, 20th IEEE FOCS, 1979, pp. 55 - 60.

[A2]   Adleman, L., *On Distinguishing Prime Numbers from Composite Numbers*, 21st IEEE FOCS, 1980, pp. 387-406.

[A3]   Adleman, L., *On Breaking the Iterated Merkle - Hellman Public Key Cryptosystem*, in: Advances in Cryptology, Proceedings of Crypto 82, D. Chaum et al., eds., Plenum 1983, pp. 303 - 308.

[A4]   Adleman, L., Manders, K. and Miller, G., *On Taking Roots in Finite Fields*, 20th IEEE FOCS, Vol. 20, 1977, pp. 175-178.

[A5] Adleman, L., Pomerance, C., Rumeley, R., *On Distinguishing Prime Numbers from Composite Numbers*, Annals of Mathematics, 117 (1983), pp. 173 - 206.

[A6] Ajtai, M., Ben - Or, M., *A Theorem on Probabilistic Constant Depth Computations*, 16th ACM STOC, pp. 471 - 474, 1984.

[A7] Alexi, W., Chor, B., Goldreich, O., and Schnorr, C., P., *RSA / RABIN bits are* $1/2 + 1/poly(\log N)$ *secure*, 25th IEEE FOCS, pp. 449 - 457, 1984.

[A8] Angluin, D., *Lecture Notes on the Complexity of Some Problems in Number Theory*, Yale University, DCS, August, 1982, TR 243.

[A9] Angluin, D., and Lichtenstein D., *Provable Security of Cryptosystems: a Survey*, Yale University, DCS, August, 1982, TR 288.

[B1] Bach, E., *Discrete Logarithm and Factoring*, 1985, to appear.

[B2] Bacon, F., *The Advancement of Learning*, Montague, Basil ed., Vol. II, London: William Pickering, 1825, page 200.

[B3] Berlekamp, E. R., *Factoring Polynomials over Large Finite Fields*, Mathematics of Computation, Vol. 24, 1970, pp. 713-735.

[B4] Beth, T., *Introduction to Cryptology*, in: Arbeitstagung über Kryptographie in Burg Feuerstein, T. Beth editor, pp. 1 - 28, SVLNCS, Vol. 149, 1983.

[B5] Blum, L., Blum, M., and Shub, M., *A Simple Secure Pseudo-Random Generator*, IEEE CRYPTO 82, 1982.

[B6] Blum, M., and Micali, S., *How to Generate Cryptographically Strong Sequences of Pseudo-Random Bits*, 23rd IEEE FOCS, pp. 112 - 117, 1982, also revised in SIAM J. Comp., Vol. 13, No. 4, pp. 850 - . 864, Nov. 1984.

[B7] Brassard, G., *Relativized Cryptography*, IEEE Transactions on Information Theory, Vol. IT - 29, No. 6, November 1983.

[B8]   Brillhart, J., Lehmer, D.H., Selfridge, J.L., Tuckerman, B., and
            Wagstaff Jr, S.S., *Factorizations of $b^n \pm 1$, $b = 2,3,5,6,7,10,$
            $11,12$ up to high powers*, pp. xxvii - lxi, Contemporary Math-
            ematics, Vol. 22, AMS, 1983, Providence, RI.

[B9]   Brown, G. W., *Monte Carlo Methods*, in: Modern Mathematics
            for the Engineer, Edwin F. Beckenbach editor, pp. 279 - 303,
            McGraw-Hill, 1956.

[C1]   Carmichael, R. D., *On Composite Numbers Which Satisfy the
            Fermat Congruence*, AMM, Vol. 19, 1912, pp. 22 - 27.

[C2]   Cohen, H., *Tests de Primalite d' après Adleman, Rumeley,
            Pomerance et Lenstra*, Séminaire de Theories des Nombres,
            Grenoble, June 1981.

[C3]   Cohn, H., *Advanced Number Theory*, Dover Publication, New
            York, 1962.

[C4]   Cooper, R. and Patterson, W., *A Generalization of the Knap-
            sack Algorithm Using Galois Fields*, Cryptologia, Vol. 8, Num-
            ber 4, 1984, pp. 343 - 347.

[D1]   Davenport, H., *Multiplicative Number Theory*, SVGTM, 2nd
            edition, Heidelberg 1980.

[D2]   DeLaurentis, J., M., *A Further Weakness in the Common Mod-
            ulus Protocol for the RSA Cryptoalgorithm*, Cryptologia, Vol.
            8, Number 3, 1984.

[D3]   Demillo, R., Davida, G., Dobking, D., Harrison, A., and Lip-
            ton, R., *Applied Cryptology, Cryptographic Protocols and Com-
            puter Security Models*, Proceedings of Symposia in Applied
            Mathematics, Vol. 29, AMS, 1983.

[D4]   Denning, D., *Cryptography and Data Security*, Addison Wesley
            1983.

[D5]   Dickson, L. E., *History of the Theory of Numbers*, Volume 1,
            Chelsea, New York, 1952.

[D6]   Diffie, W., and Hellman, M., *New Directions in Cryptography*,
            IEEE Transactions on Information Theory, IT 22, pp. 644 -
            654, 1976.

[E1]   Eier, R. and Lagger, H., *Trapdoors in Knapsack Cryptosystems*, in: Arbeitstagung über Kryptographie in Burg Feuerstein, T. Beth editor, pp. 316 - 322, SVLNCS, Vol. 149, 1983.

[E2]   Ellison, W. J., *Les Nombres Premiers*, Hermann, Paris, 1975.

[F1]   Feller, W., *An Introduction to Probability Theory and its Applications*, Wiley, 1966, New York.

[F2]   Floyd, D., *Annotated Bibliography in Conventional and Public Key Cryptography*, Cryptologia, Vol. 7, Number 1, 1983, pp. 12 - 24.

[F3]   Frieze, A. M., Kannan, R., and Lagarias, J. C., *Linear Congruencial Generators do not Produce Random Sequences*, in 25th IEEE FOCS, pp. 480 - 484, 1984.

[G1]   Gardner, M., *The Remarkable Lore of the Prime Numbers*, in: *Mathematics an Introduction to its Spirit and Use*, M. Kline editor, W. H. Freeman and Company, 1979, pp. 49 - 54, San Fransisco.

[G2]   Garey, M., and Johnson, D., *Computers and Intractability: A Guide to the Theory of NP - Completeness*, W. H. Freeman and Company, San Francisco, 1979.

[G3]   Gauss, C. F., *Untersuchungen über Höhere Arithmetik* (German translation of *Disquisitiones Arithmeticae*), Chelsea, 1965. Also English translation by Yale University Press, 1966.

[G4]   Gesternhaber, M., *The 152-nd Proof of the Law of Quadratic Reciprocity*, AMM, Vol. 70, 1963, pp. 397-398.

[G5]   Gnedenko, B. V., The *Theory of Probability*, Mir Publishers, 1976, Fifth Printing 1982, Moscow.

[G6]   Gnedenko, B. V., and Khinchin, A. Ya., *An Elementary Introduction to the Theory of Probability*, Dover Publications, 1962, New York.

[G7]   Goldreich, O., Goldwasser, S., and Micali, S., *How to Construct Random Functions*, 25th IEEE FOCS, 1984, pp. 464 - 479.

[G8]   Goldwasser, S., and Micali, S., *Probabilistic Encryption and
           How to Play Mental Poker Keeping Secret All Partial Infor-
           mation*, 14th ACM STOC, pp. 365 - 377, 1982, also revised
           in Journal of Computer and System Sciences, Vol. 28, No. 2,
           April 1984.

[G9]   Goldwasser, S., Micali, S., and Tong, P., *Why and How to
           Establish a Private Code on a Public Network*, In 23rd IEEE
           FOCS, pp. 134 - 144, 1982.

[G10]   Goldwasser, S., Micali, S., and Yao, A.,   *Strong Signature
           Schemes*, 15th ACM STOC, pp. 431 - 439, 1982.

[G11]   Grosswald, E., *Topics from the Theory of Numbers*, Birkäuser
           Verlag, 1984.

[H1]   Halton, J. H., *A Retrospective and Prospective Survey of the
           Monte Carlo Method*, SIAM Review, pp. 1 - 63, Vol. 12, No.
           1, January 1970.

[H2]   Hasse, H., *Vorlesungen über Zahlentheorie*, SV, 2nd edition,
           1964.

[H3]   Hawkins, D., *Mathematical Sieves*, in: *Mathematics an Intro-
           duction to its Spirit and Use*, M. Kline editor, W. H. Freeman
           and Company, 1979, pp. 55 - 62, San Fransisco.

[H4]   Heath, T. L., *Euclid's Elements*, translated with an introduc-
           tion by Heath, T. L., Vol. II, Books III - IX, Dover 1956.

[H5]   Hilbert, D., *Mathematical Problems*, Address presented at the
           1900 International Congress of Mathematics in Paris, Bulletin
           AMS, 8, 1901 - 2, pp. 437 - 479.

[H6]   Hirshfeld, R., Unpublished MIT Notes, May 1985.

[H7]   Hodges, A., *Alan Turing: The Enigma*, Simon and Schuster,
           New York 1983.

[H8]   Hooley, C., *On Artin's Conjecture*, Journal für die reine und
           angewandte Mathematik, pp. 208 - 220, Band 225, 1967.

[H9]   Householder, A. S., ed., *Monte Carlo Method*, U.S. Department of Commerce, National Bureau of Standards; Applied Mathematics Series, Volume 12, 1951, Washington D.C.

[K1]   Kahn, D., *The Codebreakers: The Story of Secret Writing*, Macmillan Publ. Co. Inc., New York 1967.

[K2]   Knuth, D. E., *The Art of Computer Programming: Seminumerical Algorithms*, Addison-Wesley, Vol. II, 1981, Reading Mass.

[K3]   Koblitz, N., *p-adic Numbers, p-adic Analysis and Zeta Functions*, SVGTM, 2nd edition, 1984.

[K4]   Koch, H. and Pieper, H., *Zahlentheorie*, VEB DVW, 1976, Berlin.

[K5]   Kolmogorov, A. N., *Grundbegriffe der Wahrscheinlichkeitsrechnung*, Erg. Math., SV 1933, English translation, Chelsea 1950.

[K6]   Kolmogorov, A. N., *The Theory of Probability*, in: *Mathematics: its content, methods and meaning*, Aleksandrov, Kolmogorov and Lavrent'ev eds., MIT press, 1963.

[K7]   Kolmogorov, A. N., *Three Aproaches to the Concept of the Amount of Information*, Problemy Peredachi Informatsii, 1: 1(1965), pp. 3 - 11.

[K8]   Konnheim, A., *Cryptography: A Primer*, John Wiley and Sons, 1981.

[K9]   Kraetzel, E., *Zahlentheorie*, VEB DVW, 1981, Berlin.

[K10]   Kranakis, E., *On the Efficiency of Probabilistic Primality Tests*, Yale University, DCS, April, 1984, TR 314.

[K11]   Kranakis, E., *A Class of Cryptosystems Equivalent to RSA*, Yale University, DCS, April, 1984, TR 316.

[K12]   Kranakis, E., *Theoretical Aspects of the Security of Public Key Cryptography*, Yale University, DCS, September, 1984, TR 331.

[K13]   Kurosh, A. G., *Theory of Groups*, Vol. 1, Chelsea Publishing Company, New York, 1960.

[L1]   Lamport, L., *The LATEX Document Preparation System*, 1983, LATEX *Update*, Version 2.08, March 27, 1985.

[L2]   Landau, Edmund, *Handbuch der Lehre von der Verteilung der Primzahlen*, Band 1, 1953, Chelsea, New York.

[L3]   Leclerc, G., *Essai d'Arithmetique Morale*, Oeuvres Complétes, Vol. 4, pp. 685 - 713, Dufour, Mulat et Boulanger, Libraires - Editeurs, 1858.

[L4]   Lehmer, D., *List of Prime Numbers from 1 to* 10,006,721, Carnegie Institution of Washington, 1914.

[L5]   Lehmer, D., *Guide to Tables in the Theory of Numbers*, Report 1, National Research Council, National Academy of Sciences, Washington D. C., 1941.

[L6]   Lehmer, D., *Computer Technology Applied to the Theory of Numbers*, in: Studies in Number Theory, W. J. LeVeque editor, MAA Studies in Mathematics, Vol. 6, 1969.

[L7]   Lehmer, D., Lehmer, E., and Schanks, D., *Integer Sequences Having Prescribed Quadratic Character*, Mathematics of Computation, 1970 (24), pp. 433 - 451.

[L8]   Lempel, A., *Cryptology in Transition*, Computing Surveys 11, 1979, pp. 285 - 303.

[L9]   Lenstra, H. W., *Miller's Primality Test*, Information Processing Letters, Vol. 8, (2), 1979.

[L10]   Lenstra, H. W., *Primality Testing Algorithms*, in: Séminaire Bourbaki, 33, (1980/81), no. 576, pp. 243 - 257, SVLNM, number 901.

[L11]   Lenstra, H. W., *Integer Programming with a Fixed Number of Variables*, University of Amsterdam, Department of Mathematics, TR 81-03, April, 1981.

[L12]   Lenstra, H. W., *Primality Testing*, in: *Computational Methods in Number Theory*, H. W. Lenstra and R. Tijdeman eds., Mathematical Centre Tracts, 154, Vol. 1, pp. 55 - 97, Mathematisch Centrum Amsterdam, 1982.

[L13]   LeVeque, W., *Topics in Number Theory*, Addison - Wesley, 1958, Reading Mass.

[L14]   LeVeque, W., *Fundamentals of Number Theory*, Addison - Wesley, 1977, Reading Mass.

[L15]   Levin, L. A., *One Way Functions and Pseudorandom Generators*, 17th ACM STOC, pp. 363 - 365, 1985.

[L16]   Lucas, E., *Theories des Nombres*, Tome 1, Librairie Blanchard, Paris 1961.

[M1]   Manin, Yu. I., *A Cource in Mathematical Logic* SVGTM 53, 1977, pp. 225 - 230.

[M2]   Mardzanisvili, K. K., and Postnikov, A. B., *Prime Numbers*, in: *Mathematics: its content, methods and meaning*, Aleksandrov, Kolmogorov and Lavrent'ev eds., MIT press, 1963.

[M3]   Martin Löf, P., *The Definition of Random Sequences*, Information and Control, Vol. 9, 1966, pp. 600 - 619.

[M4]   Mayer, C., and Matyas, S., *Cryptography*, John Wiley and Sons, 1982.

[M5]   Merkle, R., and Hellman M., *Hiding Information and Signatures in Trapdoor Knapsacks*, IEEE Transactions on Information Theory, IT 24-5, Sept. 1978.

[M6]   Metropolis, I., N. and Ulam, S., *The Monte Carlo Method*, Journal of the American Statistical Association, 1949.

[M7]   Mignotte, M., *Tests de Primalite*, Theor. Computer Science (12), 1980, pp. 109 - 117.

[M8]   Mignotte, M., *How to Share a Secret*, in: Arbeitstagung über Kryptographie in Burg Feuerstein, T. Beth editor, pp. 371 - 375, SVLNCS, Vol. 149, 1983.

[M9]   Miller, G. L., *Riemann's Hypothesis and Tests for Primality*, J. Comput. System Sci. 13 (1976), pp. 300 - 317.

[M10]   Monier, L., *Evaluation and Comparison of two Efficient Probabilistic Primality Testing Algorithms*, Theor. Computer Science (11) 1980, pp. 97 - 108.

[M11]   Montgomery, H. L., *Topics in Multiplicative Number Theory*, SVLNM, 227, Heidelberg 1971.

[N1]   Needham, J., Science and Civilization in China, Vol. 3, Cambridge University Press, 1959.

[N2]   Niederreiter, H., *Quasi - Monte Carlo Methods and Pseudo - Random Numbers*, Bulletin of AMS, pp. 957 - 1042, Vol. 84, 1978.

[N3]   Niven, I., and Zuckerman, H. S., *An Introduction to the Theory of Numbers*, John Wiley and Sons, 1960, New York.

[P1]   Pekelis, V., *Key to the Cipher*, in: *Cybernetics A to Z*, pp. 169-174, 1974, Mir Publishers, Moscow.

[P2]   Perron, O., *Die Lehre von den Kettenbrüchen*, Teubner, 3rd edition, 1954, Chelsea 1950.

[P3]   Pieper, H., *Variationen über ein zahlentheorisches Thema von C. F. Gauss*, VEB DVW, 1978, Berlin, and Birkhäuser Verlag, Basel.

[P4]   Plumstead, J., *Inferring a Sequence Generated by a Linear Congruence*, in 23rd IEEE FOCS, pp. 153 - 159, 1982.

[P5]   Pocklington, H. C., *The Determination of the Prime or Composite Nature of Large Numbers by Fermat's Theorem*, Proceedings of the Cambridge Philosophical Society, 18, 1914, pp. 29 - 30.

[P6]   Pohlig, S. C. and Hellman, M. E., *An Improved Algorithm for Computing Logarithms over $GF(p)$ and its Cryptographic Significance*, IEEE Transactions on Information Theory, Vol. IT-24, 1978, pp. 106 - 110.

[P7]   Pomerance, C., *Recent Developments in Primality Testing*, in: Mathematical Intelligencer, Vol. 3, number 3, pp. 97 - 105, 1980.

[P8]   Pomerance, C., *The Search for Prime Numbers*, in: Scientific American, Dec. 1982, pp. 136 - 147

[P9]   Pomerance, C.,*Analysis and Comparison of some Integer Factoring Algorithms*, in: *Computational Methods in Number Theory*, H. W. Lenstra and R. Tijdeman eds., Mathematical Centre Tracts, 154, Vol. 1, Mathematisch Centrum Amsterdam, 1982.

[P10]   Prachar, K., *Primzahlverteilung*, SV, Heidelberg, 1957.

[P11]   Pratt, V., *Every Prime has a succinct certificate*, SIAM Journal of Computing, pp. 214 - 220, 1975.

[P12]   Proth, E., Comptes Rendus, 87, Paris 1878, 926.

[R1]   Rabin, M. O., *Digitalized Signatures and Public Key Functions as Intractable as factorization*, MIT Laboratory for Computer Science, January, 1979, TR 212.

[R2]   Rabin, M. O., *Probabilistic Algorithm for Primality Testing*, Journal of Number Teory, 12 (1980), pp. 128 - 138.

[R3]   Rackoff, C., *Lecture Notes on Cryptographic Protocolls*, unpublished, Univ. of Toronto, 1984.

[R4]   Rackoff, C., *Lecture Notes on Cryptographic Protocolls*, unpublished, Univ. of Toronto, 1985.

[R5]   Rademacher, H., *Lectures on Elementary Number Theory*, R. E. Krieger Publishing Combany, Huntigton, New York, 1977.

[R6]   Reif, J. H. and Tygar, J. D., *Efficient Parallel Pseudo Random Number Generation*, presented in *Workshop on the Mathematical Theory of Security*, held at MIT in June 1985.

[R7]   Rényi, A., *Wahrscheinlichkeitsrechnung mit einem Anhang über die Informationstheorie*, VEB DVW, 1962, Berlin.

[R8]   Rényi, A., *Foundations of Probability Theory*, Holden Day, 1970, San Francisco.

[R9]   Rivest, R., Shamir, A., and Adleman, L., *A Method for Obtaining digital Signatures and Public Key Cryptosystems*, in: Comm. ACM, Vol. 21, pp. 120 - 126, 1978.

[R10]   Ross, S., *Introduction to Probability Models*, Academic Press, 1980, New York.

[R11]   Rosser, J., B. and Schoenfield, L., *Approximate Formulas for Some Functions of Prime Numbers*, Illinois J. Math. 6 (1962), pp. 64 - 94.

[R12]   Rozanov, Y., A., *Probability Theory: A Concise Course*, Dover Publications, New York 1969.

[S1]   Salomaa, A., *Cryptography*, in: *Computation and Automata*, Chapter 7, Vol. 25, pp. 186 - 230, *Encyclopedia of Mathematics and its Applications*, Cambridge University Press, 1985.

[S2]   Sattler, J., and Scnorr, C. P., *Ein Effizienzvergleich der Faktorisierungsverfahren von Morrison-Brillhart und Schroeppel*, in: Arbeitstagung über Kryptographie in Burg Feuerstein, T. Beth editor, pp. 331 - 351, SVLNCS, Vol. 149, 1983.

[S3]   Schanks, D., *Solved and Unsolved Problems in Number Theory*, Chelsea Publ. Co., Second Edition, 1978, New York.

[S4]   Schnorr, C., *Zufälligkeit und Wahrscheinlichkeit: Eine algorithmische Begründung der Wahrscheinlichkeitstheorie*, SVLNM, Vol. 218, 1971.

[S5]   Schnorr, C., *Is the RSA Scheme Safe?*, in : Arbeitstagung über Kryptographie in Burg Feuerstein, T. Beth editor, pp. 325 - 329, SVLNCS, Vol. 149, 1983.

[S6]   *Science and the Citizen*, Scientific American, July 1982, page 75.

[S7]   *Science and the Citizen*, Scientific American, January 1985, pp. 56 - 57.

[S8]   Selberg, A., *The General Sieve Method in Prime Number Theory*, Proceedings of the International Congress of Mathematics, Cambridge, Mass., 1, (1950), pp. 286 - 292.

[S9]   Shamir, A., *How to Share a Secret*, Comm. ACM, Vol 22, Number 11, pp. 612-613, Nov. 1979.

[S10]   Shamir, A., *A Polynomial Time Algorithm for Breaking the Basic Merkle-Hellman Cryptosystem*, 23rd IEEE FOCS, 1982, pp. 145 - 152.

[S11]   Shannon, C.E., *Communication Theory of Secrecy Systems*, Bell System Technical Journal, 1949, Vol. 28, pp. 656 - 715.

[S12]   Shreider, Yu. A., *The Monte Carlo Method*, Pergamom Press, 1966.

[S13]   Shulman, D., *An Annotated Bibliography of Cryptography*, Garland Publ., Inc., 1976.

[S14]   Sobol, I. M., *The Monte Carlo Method*, University of Chicago Press, 2nd edition, 1974.

[S15]   Solovay, R. and Strassen, V., *A Fast Monte Carlo Test for Primality*, SIAM J. Comp. 6 (1977), pp. 84 - 85, erratum 7 (1978), p. 118.

[T1]   Titchmarsh, E. C., *The Theory of the Riemann Zeta Function*, Oxford: Clarendon Press, 1951.

[V1]   Van der Waerden, *Algebra*, Vol. 1, Ungar, New York, 1970.

[V2]   Vinogradov, I. M., *Elements of Number Theory*, Dover Publications, Inc., 1954, New York.

[V3]   Voorhoeve, M., *Factorization Algorithms of Exponential Order* in: *Computational Methods in Number Theory*, H. W. Lenstra and R. Tijdeman eds., Mathematical Centre Tracts, 154, Vol. 1, Mathematisch Centrum Amsterdam, 1982.

[W1]   Weil, A., with the Collaboration of M. Rosenlicht, *Number Theory for Beginners*, SV, Heidelberg, 1979.

[W2]   Williams, H. C., *Primality Testing on a Computer*, Ars Combinatoria, 5, (1978), pp. 127 - 185.

[Y1]   Yao, A., C., *Theory and Applications of Trapdoors functions*, in 23rd IEEE FOCS, pp. 80 - 91, 1982.

[Y2]   Yao, A. C., *Lectures on the XOR Theorem*, Handwritten unpublished notes of four lectures delivered in Spring 83, Yale University.

[Z1]   Zagier, D., *Die ersten 50 Millionen Primzahlen*, in: *Lebendige Zahlen, Fünf Exkursionen, Mathematische Miniaturen*, by: Borho, W., Jantzen, J. C., Kraft H., Rohlfs, J. and Zagier, D., 1, pp. 39 - 73, Birkhäuser Verlag, 1981.

[Z2]   Zvonkin, A. K., and Levin, L. A., *The Complexity of Finite Objects and the Development of the concepts of Information and Randomness by Means of the Theory of Algorithms*, Russian Mathematical Surveys, Vol. 25, Number 6, Nov. - Dec. 1970, pp. 83 - 124.

FREQUENTLY USED NOTATION

Throughout the text the symbol • is used to indicate the end of the proof of a theorem, or lemma.

Mathematical Symbol	*Explanation*
$\exists$	There exists.
$\forall$	For all.
$\exists x \leq y$	There exists $x \leq y$.
$\forall x \leq y$	For all $x \leq y$.
$\exists x \geq y$	There exists $x \geq y$.
$\forall x \geq y$	For all $x \geq y$.
$\neg$	Not.
$\Rightarrow$	Implies.
$\Leftrightarrow$	If and only if.
$\emptyset$	Empty set.
$|A|$	Number of elements of set A.
$a \in A$	Element a belongs to set A.
$A \subseteq B$	A is a subset of B.
$A \cup B$	Union of sets A, B.
$A \cap B$	Intersection of sets A, B.
$A - B$	Difference of sets A, B.
$< x, y >$	Ordered pair.
$< x_1, \ldots, x_n >$	Ordered n tuple.
$A \times B$	Cartesian product of sets A, B.
A^n	Cartesian product of n copies of set A.
$f : A \longrightarrow B$	f is a mapping of set A into set B.
$x \longrightarrow y$	A mapping carries point x to point y.
f is $1 - 1$	$(\forall x, x')(f(x) = f(x') \Rightarrow x = x')$.
f is onto	$(\forall y)(\exists x)(f(x) = y)$.
$Im(f)$	Set of $f(x)$ with x in domain of f
$f^{-1}\{a\}$	Set of x such that $f(x) = a$.
$f \circ g(x) = f(g(x))$	Composition of f and g.

Mathematical Symbol	*Explanation*
$\oplus$	Addition modulo 2.
$\otimes$	Multiplication modulo 2.
$\mathbf{R}$	Set of real numbers.
$\leq$	Less than or equal.
$\geq$	Greater than or equal.
$<$	Less than.
$>$	Greater than.
$\lvert r \rvert$	Absolute value of r.
$\lvert r \rvert$	Length of binary representation of the positive integer r.
$[a, b]$	Closed interval of reals.
(a, b)	Open interval of reals.
$[a, b)$	Closed-open interval of reals.
$(a, b]$	Open-closed interval of reals.
$\log_b x$	Logarithm with base b of x.
$e = 2.718 \cdots$	Base of natural logarithms.
$g(x) = O(f(x))$	$(\exists M > 0)(\exists u)(\forall x \geq u)(\lvert g(x) \rvert \leq M \cdot \lvert f(x) \rvert)$.
$g(x) = \Omega(f(x))$	$(\exists M > 0)(\exists u)(\forall x \geq u)(\lvert g(x) \rvert \geq M \cdot \lvert f(x) \rvert)$.
$R = (1 + \sqrt{5})/2$	Golden mean, p. 3.
$x \vert y$	x divides y.
$\gcd(a, b)$	Greatest common divisor of a, b.
$\operatorname{lcm}(a, b)$	Least common multiple of a, b.
$x \equiv y \bmod n$	x congruent to y modulo n, p. 4.
$(x \vert y)$	Legendre-Jacobi symbol of integer x with respect to integer y, pp. 16, 17.
$Z_n = \{x : 0 \leq x < n\}$	Ring of integers modulo n, p. 4.
Z_n^*	Group of integers modulo n and relatively prime to n, p. 4.
$Z_n^*(+1)$	Set of $x \in Z_n^*$ with $(x \vert n) = +1$, p. 17.
$Z_n^*(-1)$	Set of $x \in Z_n^*$ with $(x \vert n) = -1$, p.17.
QR_n	Set of quadratic residues modulo n, p. 16.
QNR_n	Set of quadratic nonresidues modulo n, p. 16.
$\varphi(n) = \lvert Z_n^* \rvert$	Euler's function, p. 4.

Mathematical Symbol	*Explanation*
λ	Carmichael's function, p. 15.
$\pi(n)$	Number of primes $\leq n$, p. 28.
$\pi_{b,c}(n)$	Number of primes $\leq n$, which are of the form $b \cdot k + c$, for some k, p. 28.
$f(n) \sim g(n)$	$\lim_{n \to \infty}(f(n)/g(n)) = 1$.
$f(n) \approx g(n)$	$f(n)$ is approximately equal to $g(n)$.
$\delta_{n,m}$	Kronecker Delta, i.e 1, if $n = m$, and 0, if $n \neq m$.
$\mathrm{index}_{p,g}(x)$	Index of x with respect to the generator $g \in Z_p^*$, where $x \in Z_p^*$, p. 24.
$\lceil x \rceil$	Ceiling of x.
$\lfloor x \rfloor = [x]$	Floor or integral part of x.
$n! = 1 \cdot 2 \cdots n$	n factorial.
$\binom{n}{k} = n!/k!(n-k)!$	n choose k.
$F_n = 2^{2^n} + 1$	n-th Fermat number, p. 51.
$M_p = 2^p - 1$	Mersenne number corresponding to the prime number p, p. 52.
$\mathrm{order}_m(x)$	$=$ least $k \geq 0$ such that $x^k \equiv 1 \bmod m$, where $x \in Z_m^*$.
$\nu_m(t)$	$=$ largest k such that $m^k|t$.
$\Re(z)$	Real part of the complex number z.
$L_\chi(z) = \sum_{n=1}^{\infty} \frac{\chi(n)}{n^z}$	Dirichlet's L - function, p. 55.
ERH	Extended Riemann Hypothesis, p. 55.
$\overline{E}$	Complement of event E.
$E \cup F$	Sum of events E, F.
$E \cap F$	Product of events E, F.
$E - F$	Difference of events E, F.
$Pr[E]$	Probability of event E.
$Pr_A[E] = Pr[E|A]$	Conditional probability of event E with respect to event A.
$E[X]$	Expectation of random variable X, p. 83.

Mathematical Symbol	Explanation
$Var[X]$	variance of the random variable X, p. 83.
$D[X]$	divergence of the random variable X, p. 84.
$B_n(E)$	number of occurrences of the event E in n indepedent trials, p. 88.
$F_n(E)$	$= B_n(E)/n$; frequency of E in n independent trials, p. 88.
par (x)	Parity of the integer x, p. 117.
$LGEN$	Linear Generator, p. 100.
$PGEN$	$1/p$ Generator, p. 105.
$QRGEN$	Quadratic Residue Generator, p. 121.
$INDGEN$	Index Generator, p. 133.
APR	Advantage for Predicting a Generator, pp. 122, 133.
$APAR$	Advantage for Parity, p. 117.
AQR	Advantage for Quadratic Residuosity, pp. 117, 119.
$ALOC$	Advantage for Location, p.123.
$QRA(N)$	Quadratic Residuosity Assumption for the family N, p. 125.
QRA	Quadratic Residuosity Assumption, p. 126.
$AIND$	Advantage for Index, p. 128.
AB	Advantage for the Function $B_{p,g}$, p. 130.
$APQR$	Advantage for Principal Square Root, p. 130.
$DLA(N)$	Discrete Logarithm Assumption for the family N, p. 135.
DLA	Discrete Logarithm Assumption, p. 136.
PKC	Public Key Cryptosystem, p. 141.
$NPKC$	Nonpublic Key Cryptosystem, p. 139.
RSA	Rivest, Shamir, Adleman system, p.142.
QRS	Quadratic Residue System, p. 159.
AQR^+	Advantage for Quadratic Residuosity, assuming that a quadratic nonresidue is known, p. 161.

Mathematical Symbol	Explanation
RGH	Random Generation Hypothesis, p. 182.
BMT	Blum-Micali Test, p. 173.
$PSST$	Polynomial Size Statistical Test, p. 175.
YST	Yao's statistical test, p. 175.
$\deg(P)$	Degree of polynomial P.
$S_m = \{0,1\}^m$	Set of sequences of bits of length m.
$p_m^{C,G}$	Probability that C_m outputs 1 on input a random sequence generated by G_m, p. 175.
$p_m^{C,R}$	Probability that C_m outputs 1 on input a random sequence, p. 175.
RP	Class of sets computable in random polynomial time, p. 207.
BPP	Class of sets computable in bounded probabilistic polynomial time, p. 207.
DTIME$(g(n))$	Class of sets computable in deterministic time $g(n)$, for all but a finite number of n, p. 207.

INDEX

Additive isolation lemma, 209
Adjacent, 160
Adleman, 169, 206, 210, 211, 219
  algorithm of, for $index_{p,g}$, 38
  -Manders-Miller, theorem of,
  22, 110
  see Rivest
  see Rumeley
Ajtai, 211
Alexi, 211
Angluin, 211
Ankeny,
  -Mongomery, theorem of, 56,79
Artin,
  conjecture of, 14, 38
  constant of, 14
Assignment, 115
Advantage for
  index, 128
  parity, 117
  predicting, 122
  quadratic residuosity, 117
Approximation,
  see Diophantine
Assumption,
  discrete logarithm, 135, 137
  factoring, 137
  quadratic residuosity, 125, 137

Bach, 27, 211
  -Miller, 28
Bacon, viii, 210
Barinaga, theorem of, 42
Ben-Or, 211
Berlekamp, 211
Bernoulli,
  weak law of large numbers, of, 91

Bernshtein, 92, 94
  law of large numbers, of, 94, 97
Beth, 211
Bicycle-chain,
  see sieve
Binomial distribution, 88
  theorem of, 88
Bits,
  RSA, 145
  Rabin, 153
Blum, 211
  -Blum-Shub, 106, 111, 112, 114,
  126, 137
  -Goldwasser-Micali, 199
  -Micali, 129, 130, 132, 134
  generator theorem of, 173
  test of, *BMT*, 173
Bounded probabilistic
  polynomial time, **BPP**, 206
Brassard, 211
Breaks-up,
  a continued fraction, 32
Brickel, 169
Brillhart, 212
Brown, 211
Bucket, 188
Buffon, see Leclerc

Carmichael, 211
  function of, 1, 15
  theorem of, 15
Cataldi, 52
Character, 55
  of order p and conductor q, 73
Chinese remainder theorem, 7
Chebyshev, 29
  inequality of, 90

law of large numbers, of, 90
Chor, 210
Circuit, 114
  depth of, 115
  function, 115
  gates of 115
  size of, 115
Circuits,
  family of, 116
Cohen, H., 77, 212
Cohn, 211
Concatenation, 176
Conditional probability, 82
Congruence,
  solutions of, 6
  solvable
Congruent, 4
Continued fraction, 31
  expansion of α, 31
Cooper, 212
Convergent of α, 32
Coset, 2
Covariance, 84
Cryptosystem,
  Merkle-Hellman, 155
    iterated, 157
  nonpublic or private, 139
  public, 141
  Quadratic residue, 159
  Rabin, 150
  RSA, 142
  Vernam, 140
Cyclic group, 11

Davenport, 212
Davida, 211
De Bruijn sequence, 105
Deciphering
  algorithm, 139

function, 139
Decryption, see Deciphering
Decision function, 161
DeLaurentis, 211
De La Vallee Poussin, 28
Demillo, 212
Denning, 212
Detrministic polynomial
  time, **DTIME**, 206
Deviation, see Standard Deviation
Dickson, 212
Difference rule,
  of events, 82
Diffie, vii, viii, 168, 212
Diophantine approximation, 33
Diophantus, identity of, 45
Dirichlet, 28
  L - function, 55
Discrete logarithm, 24
  assumption, 135, 137
Disquisitiones Arithmeticae, 37
Distribution function, 83
Dobking, 212

Eier, 213
Ellison, 213
Enciphering or Encryption,
  algorithm, 139
  function, 139
Enigma machine, 168
Epimorphism, 2
Eratosthenes, sieve of, 40
Essentially
  identical, 45
  unique representation, 45
Euclid's Elements, 78
Euler, 52, 46
  criterion, of, 16
  sum of two squares test, of, 45

(totient) function, of, 4
  theorem of, 5
  -Fermat, theorem of, 4
Event,
  certain, 81
  impossible, 81
  observed, 81
Events,
  independent, 82
  difference of, 81
  product of, 81
  sum of, 81
Expectation, 83
  theorem of, 85
Exponentiation by repeated
squarings and multiplications, 10
Extended Riemann
  Hypothesis, ERH, 27, 55

Factoring Assumption, 137
Feller, 213
Fermat, 97
  numbers, 51
  pair, 46
  theorem of, 46
  see Euler
Fibonacci numbers, 3
File,
  private, 141
  public, 141
Floyd, 212
Friendship function, 172
Frieze, 213

Gardner, 213
Garey, 213
Gates, 115
  deterministic, 116
  random, 116

Gauss, 10, 37, 78, 80, 137, 213
  generalized sums of, 73
  lemma of, 19
  sums of, 73
  theorem of, 11
g-digit, 104
Generator, 172
  pseudorandom, 98, 172, 200
    index, 133
    linear congruence, 100
    middle square, 137
    $1/p$, 105
    quadratic residue, 121
Gesternhaber, 38, 213
Gillies, 52
Girard, 78
Gnedenko, 213
Golden ratio, 3
Goldreich, 210, 213
  -Goldwasser-Micali,
  theorem of, 178
Goldwasser, 119, 213, 214
  -Micali, lemma of, 161, 162
  -Micali, theorem of, 119, 165
  -Micali-Tong, theorem of, 146, 143
  see Blum
  see Goldreich
Graph, 114
  acyclic, 114
  directed or digraph, 114
  labeled, 114
Grosswald, 214

Hadamard, 28
Halton, 214
Hamming distance, 160
Harrison, 212
Hasse, 214
Hawkins, 214

Heath, 78, 214
Hellman, vii, viii, 168, 212, 217, 218
  see Merkle
  see Pohlig
Hensel, lemma of, 23
Hilbert, ix, 214
Hirshfeld, 214
  -Yao, theorem of, 207
Hodges, 168, 214
Hooley, 15, 214
Householder, 215
Hurwitz, 52

Ibn Albanna, 78
Incogruent, 4
Index,
  generator, 133
  of x with respect to g, 24
Interceptor, 140
Iyanaga, 98

Jacobi,
  see Legendre
Johnson, 213

Kahn, 168, 215
Kannan, 213
Kawada, 98
Kernel, 2
Key, 139
Keys, set of, 139
Khinchin, 213
Knuth, 215
Koblitz, 215
Koch, 215
Kolmogorov, 97, 215
  complexity, 208
  -Smirnov, test of, 98
Konnheim, 215
Kraetzel, 215

Kranakis, 215
Kurosh, 215

Lagarias, 169, 213
Lagger, 213
Lagrange, theorem of, 2
Lame, theorem of, 3, 21, 37
Lamport, xi, 216
Landau, E., 38, 113, 216
Last bit function, 146
Law of quadratic reciprocity, 19
Leclerc, 97
  known as Comte de Buffon
  Buffon needle
Legendre,
  symbol of, 16
  -Jacobi, symbol of, 17
Lehmer, 52, 136, 212, 216
  see Lucas
Lempel, 216
Length of sequence, 176
Lenstra, H. W., ix, 52, 53, 62, 63,
  79, 216, 219, 221
LeVeque, 217
Levin, 209, 217, 222
Lichtenstein, 211
Linear congruences,
  theorem on solving of, 6
Location function, 123
Lucas, 15, 52, 146, 217
  test of, 42
  -Lehmer, functions of, 54
  -Lehmer, test of, 53

Magic box, 170
Manders, 210
  see Adleman
Manin, 217
Mardzanisvili, 38, 217

Markov's inequality
Martin Löf, 217
Matyas, 217
Mayer, 217
Merkle, 217
  see cryptosystem
Mersenne integers, 51
Metropolis, 217
Micali, 211, 213, 214
  see Blum
  see Goldreich
  see Goldwasser
  see Tong
Mignotte, 8, 217
Modular
  exponentiation, 10
  multiplication, 10
Miller, 79, 210, 217
  deterministic test of, 59
  -Rabin-Monier, theorem of, 69
  see Adleman
  see Bach
Monier, 67, 218
  see Miller
Monte Carlo
  method, 94
  primality tests, 65
Montgomery, 79, 218
  see Ankeny
Multiple XOR theorem
  see XOR
Multiplier, 155

Needham, 37, 217
Nelson, 52
Nickel, 52
Node
  input, 114
  internal, 114

output, 115
Niederreiter, 218
Niven, 218
Noll, 52
Nonprincipal square root, 127

Odlyzko,
  -Pomerance, theorem of, 76
One
  way function, 141, 202
    theorem of, 204
    weak, 202
    strong, 202
  -time pad, 141
Order, 57

P
  -inverts, 201
  -predicts, 171, 173
Parity comparison function, 153
Pascal, 97
Patterson, 212
Pekelis, 218
Pepin
  test of, 51
Period, see quadratic residues
Perron, 218
Pervushin, 52
Pieper, 218
Pisano, 78
Plaintext message, 139
Plumstead, 217
  theorem of, 100, 103
Pocklington, 218
  lemma of, 50
Pohlig-Hellman, 136, 218
  theorem of, 25
Polynomial
  congruence, 5

size circuit, 116
size statistical test, *PSST*, 175
Pomerance, ix, 39, 210, 218, 219
see Odlyzko
Postnikov, 38
Prachar, 219
Powers, 52
Pratt, 219
sequence, 46
test of, 46
Predicate, 171
Primality,
sequence, 65
constant, 65
test, 30
Prime number theorem, 28
Primitive roots, 11
Principal square root, 127
Projection theorem, 181
Probabilistic circuit, 116
Probability,
conditional, 82
space, 80
mass or distribution function, 83
Product rule,
of events, 82
Proth, 219
test of, 49
Pseudorandom,
functions, 178
see generator

Quadratic
nonresidue, 16
residue, 16, 108
period of, 111
residuosity assumption, 125, 137
residuosity problem, 125
Quotient, 2

Rabin, 72, 137, 219
factorization theorem of, 110, 152
test of, 68
see Miller
see Monier
Rackoff, 209, 219
Rademacher, 219
Random
polynomial time, **RP**, 206
Generation Hypothesis, *RGH*, 182
sieve, 78
string, 208
variable, 82
Receiver, 139
Reif, 219
Relation, 4
equivalence, 4
reflexive, 4
symmetric, 4
transitive, 4
Relative frequency, 88
Renyi, 219
Representation, 146
Residue parity function, 153
Riemann
Hypothesis, 55
see extended
Riesel, 52
Rivest, 219
RSA system, 142
Robinson, 52
Ross, 220
Rosser, 220
Rozanov, 220
r - signature, 160
Rumeley, 211
-Adleman test, 73

Salomaa, 220

Sample space, 81
Sattler, 220
Schanks, 220
Schnorr, 211, 220
Schoenfield, 220
Security test, 171
Seed, 98, 172
Selberg, 220
Selfridge, 52, 212
  -Weinberger, test of, 63
Sender, 139
Shamir, 219, 220
  see Rivest
Shub, 211
  see Blum
Shannon, 221
Shreider, 221
Shulman, ix, 221
Sieve,
  bicycle-chain, 39
  method, limits of, 78
  see Eratosthenes
  see random
Signature, 160
  see r - signature
Significant position, 146
Slowinski, 52
Smirnov, see Kolmogorov
Sobol, 221
Solovay, 221
  -Strassen, test of, 66
  -Strassen, deterministic test of, 56
Special, 112, 126
Square
  -free, 57
  root, 21, 108
Standard deviation, 84
Strassen, 221
  see Solovay

Sum of two squares test, 45
Sum rule,
  of events, 82
Sun Tzu, 37
Superincreasing, 155

Threshold,
  scheme, 8
  sequence, 8, 37
Tijdeman, ix, 216, 219, 221
Titchmarsh, 221
Tong, 214
  see Goldwasser
Trapdoor function 141, 157
Tuckerman, 52, 211
Tygar, 219

Ulam, 217
Unapproximable, 126, 136, 172
  predicate, 200
  weakly, 201

Van der Waerden, 221
Variance, 83
  theorem of, 87
Vector random variable, 82
Vernam, see cryptosystem
Vinogradov, 221
Von Neumann, 137
Voorhoeve, 221

Wagstaff, 212
Weak law of large numbers, 91
Weakly unapproximable
  see unapproximable
Weinberger,
  see Selfridge
Williams, 221
Wilson,
  test of, 41

XOR, 180
  family, 180
  lemma, 183
   intuitive proof of, 186
   formal proof of, 192
   two applications of, 199
  predicate
  theorem, 183
  g - xor, 180
  multiple XOR theorem, 185
  see Yao
Xoring, 180

Yao, 201, 209, 214, 221
  One way function theorem of, 204
  PSST theorem of, 175
  test of, 175
  XOR lemma of, 183
  XOR theorem of, 183
  see Hirshfeld

Zagier, 29, 38, 222
Zuckerman, 218
Zvonkin, 222